HOLINESS IS ALWAYS IN SEASON

BENEDICT XVI

HOLINESS IS ALWAYS IN SEASON

Edited by Leonardo Sapienza

IGNATIUS PRESS   SAN FRANCISCO

Original Italian edition: *La Santità non passa mai di moda*
© 2009 by Libreria Editrice Vaticana, Vatican City
Reprinted by permission of Libreria Editrice Vaticana

Cover art:
The Forerunners of Christ with Saints and Martyrs (detail)
Fra Angelico
National Gallery, London, Great Britain
© National Gallery, London/Art Resource, New York

Cover design by Roxanne Mei Lum

Published in 2010 by Ignatius Press, San Francisco
ISBN 978-1-58617-444-6
Library of Congress Control Number 2010931417
Printed in the United States of America ♾

CONTENTS

INTRODUCTION

If you ask a child what he would like to be or do in life, the child will answer naively but candidly, proposing what he considers a model of human excellence. He will say he wants to be a hero, an astronaut, a sports star, a rich man, a scientist, somebody great, a "superman". The ideal of a superman is deeply rooted in the imagination of a child.

For a Christian, what is true perfection?

Christ's words are clear, sublime, and disconcerting: "Be perfect, as your heavenly Father is perfect" (Mt 5:48).

To have God as your model of perfection! Now there is a dizzying thought! Yet the Second Vatican Council has already reminded us: "All the faithful, whatever their condition or state, are called by the Lord, each in his own way, to that perfect holiness whereby the Father himself is perfect" (*Lumen Gentium*, 11).

The Church reminds us that holiness is not the concern of a privileged few, nor does it pertain only to Christians of the past. Holiness is always in season; it is and always will be a call to every Christian of every age, a challenge that remains current for anyone who desires to follow in the footsteps of Christ.

Pope Benedict XVI says: "Holiness ... never goes out of fashion; on the contrary, with the passage of time it shines out ever more brightly, expressing man's perennial effort to reach God."

9

And Mother Teresa of Calcutta wrote: "Holiness is not something extraordinary; it is not the luxury of the few. Holiness is the simple duty for each one of us."

It is not true that holiness is impossible. Just read the lives of the saints and see how they, above all, experienced the very same difficulties and weaknesses that we do. Nevertheless, they succeeded in meriting the name of saints.

The world of the saints is a world of wonders, and Pope Benedict XVI helps us to enter into this world.

It seemed valuable, therefore, to gather together into a single volume the numerous reflections on the saints that the Holy Father has offered in his Wednesday catechetical addresses, homilies, messages, and other occasional discourses.

Arranged according to the calendar year, these reflections are a resource that can complement the readings of the Liturgy of the Hours, enrich personal and communal meditation, and aid in preparation for catechesis or homilies.

They are starting points for getting to know the saints better. If we were more familiar with the saints, we too might become more faithful, more loving, more Christian.

The saints, the heroes, the perfect—like mirrors they are held up before us today so that we may come to know ourselves. The saints also are able to obtain for us those gifts that we admire in them: their faith, their courage, their love of Christ.

The world waits for saints to step forward, for as Pope John Paul II said, "where the saints walk, God walks together with them."

And all of us need to be saints, because the world is in need of saints.

The world needs the testimony of saints. Only new saints are capable of renewing the world.

After the Great Jubilee of 2000, the "high standard" of ordinary Christian living was proposed with vigor once again (cf. *Novo Millenio Ineunte* 31). This reminds us that if mediocrity is inexcusable in anyone, it is least of all in a Christian. "No Christian can prefer the easy path of mediocrity over the difficult road of perfection" (Pope Paul VI).

"It is easier to be a saint than to be mediocre", says Cardinal Carlo Maria Martini. A comfortable and easy Christianity does not exist. What does exist is a strong and joyful Christianity: one that is uncomfortable with mediocrity, that is not content to be lived in whatever way one pleases. Either you live Christianity to thc full, or you betray it!

The exhortation to holiness that shines through in these pages is both the simplest and highest synthesis of Pope Benedict XVI's teaching.

That is why the Pope, in company with every spiritual master, repeats: "Be holy! Be saints!"

Leonardo Sapienza

THE GARDEN OF THE SAINTS

Visiting a botanical nursery garden,
one is amazed
by the variety of plants and flowers,
and often one is drawn to think
of the imagination of the Creator
who has given the earth a wonderful garden.
A similar feeling of wonder strikes us
when we consider the spectacle of sainthood:
the world appears to us as a "garden",
where the Spirit of God has given life
with admirable imagination
to a multitude of men and women saints,
of every age and social condition,
of every language, people, and culture.
Every one is different from the other,
each unique in his own personality
and spiritual charism.
All of them, however,
were impressed with the "seal" of Jesus (cf. Rv 7:3)
or the imprint of his love
witnessed through the Cross.
They are all in joy,
in a festival without end,
but, like Jesus, they achieved this goal
passing through difficulties and trials (cf. Rv 7:14),
each of them shouldering his own share of sacrifice

in order to participate in the glory of the Resurrection.
... This spiritual destination,
toward which all the baptized strive,
is reached by following the way of the Gospel "beatitudes"....
It is the same path Jesus indicated
that men and women saints
have striven to follow,
while at the same time being aware of their human
    limitations.
In their earthly lives, in fact,
they were poor in spirit,
suffering for sins, meek,
hungering and thirsting for justice,
merciful, pure of heart,
peacemakers, persecuted for the sake of justice.

And God let them partake in his very own happiness:
they tasted it already in this world, and in the next,
they enjoy it in its fullness.
They are now consoled, inheritors of the earth,
satisfied, forgiven, seeing God whose children they are....
We feel revive[d] within us
our attraction to Heaven,
which impels us to quicken the steps
of our earthly pilgrimage.
We feel enkindled in our hearts
the desire to unite ourselves forever
to the family of saints,
in which already now we have the grace to partake.
As a famous spiritual song says:
"Oh, when the saints go marching in,
Lord, how I want to be
in that number!"
May this beautiful aspiration burn within all Christians

and help them to overcome every difficulty, every fear,
  every tribulation!
Let us place, dear friends, our hand
in Mary's maternal hand,
may the Queen of All Saints
lead us toward our heavenly homeland,
in the company of the blessed spirits
"from every nation, people and language" (cf. Rv 7:9).

(BENEDICT XVI, *1 November 2008*)

Saint Basil

One of the great Fathers of the Church, Saint Basil, [was] described by Byzantine liturgical texts as "a luminary of the Church". He was an important Bishop in the fourth century to whom the entire Church of the East, and likewise the Church of the West, looks with admiration because of the holiness of his life, the excellence of his teaching, and the harmonious synthesis of his speculative and practical gifts. He was born in about 330 A.D. into a family of saints, "a true domestic Church", immersed in an atmosphere of deep faith. He studied with the best teachers in Athens and Constantinople. Unsatisfied with his worldly success and realizing that he had frivolously wasted much time on vanities, he himself confessed: "One day, like a man roused from deep sleep, I turned my eyes to the marvelous light of the truth of the Gospel..., and I wept many tears over my miserable life" (cf. *Letter* 223: *PG* 32, 824a). Attracted by Christ, Basil began to look and listen to him alone (cf. *Moralia* 80, 1: *PG* 31, 860bc). He devoted himself with determination to the monastic life through prayer, meditation on the Sacred Scriptures and the writings of the Fathers of the Church, and the practice of charity (cf. *Letters* 2, 22), also following the example of his sister, Saint Macrina, who was already living the ascetic life of a nun. He was then ordained a priest and finally, in the year 370, Bishop of Caesarea in Cappadocia in present-day Turkey.

Through his preaching and writings, he carried out immensely busy pastoral, theological, and literary activities. With a wise balance, he was able to combine service to souls with dedication to prayer and meditation in solitude. Availing himself of his personal experience, he encouraged the foundation of numerous "fraternities", in other words, communities of Christians consecrated to God, which he visited frequently (cf. Gregory Nazianzen, *Oratio* 43, 29, *in laudem Basilii: PG* 36, 536b). He urged them with his words and his writings, many of which have come down to us (cf. *Regulae brevius tractatae*, Proemio: *PG* 31, 1080ab), to live and to advance in perfection. Various legislators of ancient monasticism drew on his works, including Saint Benedict, who considered Basil his teacher (cf. *Rule* 73, 5). Indeed, Basil created a very special monasticism: it was not closed to the community of the local Church but instead was open to it. His monks belonged to the particular Church; they were her life-giving nucleus and, going before the other faithful in the following of Christ and not only in faith, showed a strong attachment to him—love for him—especially through charitable acts. These monks, who ran schools and hospitals, were at the service of the poor and thus demonstrated the integrity of Christian life. In speaking of monasticism, the Servant of God John Paul II wrote: "For this reason many people think that the essential structure of the life of the Church, monasticism, was established, for all time, mainly by Saint Basil; or that, at least, it was not defined in its more specific nature without his decisive contribution" (Apostolic Letter *Patres Ecclesiae*, no. 2, January 1980; *L'Osservatore Romano* English edition, 25 February, p. 6).

As the Bishop and Pastor of his vast Diocese, Basil was constantly concerned with the difficult material conditions in which his faithful lived; he firmly denounced the evils; he did all he could on behalf of the poorest and most marginalized people; he also intervened with rulers to alleviate the sufferings of the population, especially in times of disaster; he watched over the Church's freedom, opposing even the powerful in order to defend the right to profess the true faith (cf. Gregory Nazianzen, *Oratio* 43, 48–51 *in laudem Basilii: PG* 36, 557c–561c). Basil bore an effective witness to God, who is love and charity, by building for the needy various institutions (cf. Basil, *Letter* 94: *PG* 32, 488bc), virtually a "city" of mercy, called *"Basiliade"* after him (cf. Sozomeno, *Historia Eccl.* 6, 34: *PG* 67, 1397a). This was the origin of the modern hospital structures where the sick are admitted for treatment.

Aware that "the liturgy is the summit toward which the activity of the Church is directed", and "also the fount from which all her power flows" (*Sacrosanctum Concilium*, no. 10), and in spite of his constant concern to do charitable acts, which is the hallmark of faith, Basil was also a wise "liturgical reformer" (cf. Gregory Nazianzen, *Oratio* 43, 34 *in laudem Basilii: PG* 36, 541c). Indeed, he has bequeathed to us a great Eucharistic Prayer [or *anaphora*] which takes its name from him and has given a fundamental order to prayer and psalmody: at his prompting, the people learned to know and love the Psalms and even went to pray them during the night (cf. Basil, *In Psalmum* 1, 1–2: *PG* 29, 212a–213c). And we thus see how liturgy, worship, prayer with the Church, and charity go hand in hand and condition one another.

With zeal and courage, Basil opposed the heretics who denied that Jesus Christ, like the Father, was God (cf. Basil, *Letter* 9, 3: *PG* 32, 272a; *Letter* 52, 1–3: *PG* 32, 392b–396a; *Adv. Eunomium* 1, 20: *PG* 29, 556c). Likewise, against those who would not accept the divinity of the Holy Spirit, he maintained that the Spirit is also God and "must be equated and glorified with the Father and with the Son" (cf. *De Spiritu Sancto: SC* 17ff., 348). For this reason Basil was one of the great Fathers who formulated the doctrine on the Trinity: the one God, precisely because he is love, is a God in three Persons who form the most profound unity that exists: divine unity.

In his love for Christ and for his Gospel, the great Cappadocian also strove to mend divisions within the Church (cf. *Letters* 70, 243), doing his utmost to bring all to convert to Christ and to his Word (cf. *De Iudicio* 4: PG 31, 660b–661a), a unifying force which all believers were bound to obey (cf. *ibid.*, 1–3: PG 31, 653a–656c).

To conclude, Basil spent himself without reserve in faithful service to the Church and in the multiform exercise of the episcopal ministry. In accordance with the program that he himself drafted, he became an "apostle and minister of Christ, steward of God's mysteries, herald of the Kingdom, a model and rule of piety, an eye of the Body of the Church, a Pastor of Christ's sheep, a loving doctor, father, and nurse, a cooperator of God, a farmer of God, a builder of God's temple" (cf. *Moralia* 80, 11–20: PG 31, 864b–868b).

This is the program which the holy Bishop consigns to preachers of the Word—in the past as in the present—a program which he himself was generously committed to putting into practice. In 379 A.D. Basil, who was not yet fifty, returned to God "in the hope of eternal life, through Jesus Christ Our Lord" (*De Baptismo* 1, 2, 9). He was a man who truly lived with his gaze fixed on Christ. He was a man of love for his neighbor. Full of the hope and joy of faith, Basil shows us how to be true Christians.

(4 July 2007)

Saint Gregory Nazianzen

Like Basil, [Gregory Nazianzen] too was a native of Cappadocia. As a distinguished theologian, orator, and champion of the Christian faith in the fourth century, he was famous for his eloquence, and as a poet, he also had a refined and sensitive soul.

Gregory was born into a noble family in about A.D. 330, and his mother consecrated him to God at birth. After his education at home, he attended the most famous schools of his time: he first went to Caesarea in Cappadocia, where he made friends with Basil, the future Bishop of that city, and went on to stay in other capitals of the ancient world, such as Alexandria, Egypt, and in particular Athens, where once again he met Basil (cf. *Orationes* 43:14–24: *SC* 384, 146–80). Remembering this friendship, Gregory was later to write: "Then not only did I feel full of veneration for my great Basil because of the seriousness of his morals and the maturity and wisdom of his speeches, but he induced others who did not yet know him to be like him.... The same eagerness for knowledge motivated us.... This was our competition: not who was first, but who allowed the other to be first. It seemed as if we had one soul in two bodies" (*Orationes* 43:16, 20: *SC* 384, 154–56, 164]. These words more or less paint the self-portrait of this noble soul. Yet, one can also imagine how this man, who was powerfully cast beyond earthly values, must have suffered deeply for the things of this world.

On his return home, Gregory received Baptism and developed an inclination for monastic life: solitude as well as philosophical and spiritual meditation fascinated him. He himself wrote:

> Nothing seems to me greater than this: to silence one's senses, to emerge from the flesh of the world, to withdraw into oneself, no longer to be concerned with human things other than what is strictly necessary; to converse with oneself and with God, to lead a life that transcends the visible; to bear in one's soul divine images, ever pure, not mingled with earthly or erroneous forms; truly to be a perfect mirror of God and of divine things, and to become so more and more, taking light from light ...; to enjoy, in the present hope, the future good, and to converse with angels; to have already left the earth even while continuing to dwell on it, borne aloft by the spirit. (*Orationes* 2:7: *SC* 247, 96)

As he confides in his autobiography (cf. *Carmina [historica]* 2:1, *De Vita Sua* 340–49: *PG* 37, 1053), he received priestly ordination with a certain reluctance, for he knew that he would later have to be a Bishop, to look after others and their affairs, hence, could no longer be absorbed in pure meditation. However, he subsequently accepted this vocation and took on the pastoral ministry in full obedience, accepting, as often happened to him in his life, to be carried by Providence where he did not wish to go (cf. Jn 21:18). In 371, his friend Basil, Bishop of Caesarea, against Gregory's own wishes, desired to ordain him Bishop of Sasima, a strategically important locality in Cappadocia. Because of various problems, however, he never took possession of it and instead stayed on in the city of Nazianzus.

In about 379, Gregory was called to Constantinople, the capital, to head the small Catholic community faithful to the Council of Nicaea and to belief in the Trinity. The majority adhered instead to Arianism, which was "politically correct" and viewed by emperors as politically useful. Thus, he found himself in a condition of minority, surrounded by hostility. He delivered five *Theological Orations* (*Orationes* 27–31: SC 250, 70–343) in the little Church of the Anastasis precisely in order to defend the Trinitarian faith and to make it intelligible. These discourses became famous because of the soundness of his doctrine and his ability to reason, which truly made clear that this was the divine logic. And the splendor of their form also makes them fascinating today. It was because of these orations that Gregory acquired the nickname: "The Theologian". This is what he is called in the Orthodox Church: the "Theologian". And this is because to his way of thinking theology was not merely human reflection or, even less, only a fruit of complicated speculation, but rather sprang from a life of prayer and holiness, from a persevering dialogue with God. And in this very way he causes the reality of God, the mystery of the Trinity, to appear to our reason. In the silence of contemplation, interspersed with wonder at the marvels of the mystery revealed, his soul was engrossed in beauty and divine glory.

While Gregory was taking part in the Second Ecumenical Council in 381, he was elected Bishop of Constantinople and presided over the Council; but he was challenged straightaway by strong opposition, to the point that the situation became untenable. These hostilities must have been unbearable to such a sensitive soul. What Gregory had previously lamented with heartfelt words was repeated: "We have divided Christ, we who so loved God and Christ! We have lied to one another because of the Truth, we have harbored sentiments of hatred because of Love, we are separated from one another" (*Orationes* 6:3: SC 405, 128). Thus, in a tense atmosphere, the time came for him to resign. In the packed cathedral, Gregory delivered a farewell discourse of great effectiveness and dignity (cf. *Orationes* 42: *SC* 384, 48–114). He ended his heartrending speech with these words: "Farewell, great city, beloved by Christ.... My children, I beg you, jealously guard the deposit [of faith] that has been entrusted to you (cf. 1 Tm 6:20); remember my suffering (cf. Col 4:18). May the grace of Our Lord Jesus Christ be with you all" (cf. *Orationes* 42:27: *SC* 384, 112–14).

Gregory returned to Nazianzus and for about two years devoted himself to the pastoral care of this Christian community. He then withdrew definitively to solitude in nearby Arianzo, his birthplace, and dedicated himself to studies and the ascetic life. It was in this period that he wrote the majority of his poetic works and especially his autobiography: the *De Vita Sua*, a reinterpretation in verse of his own human and spiritual journey, an exemplary journey of a suffering Christian, of a man of profound interiority in a world full of conflicts. He is a man who makes us aware of God's primacy and, hence, also speaks to us, to this world of ours: without God, man loses his grandeur; without God, there is no true humanism. Consequently, let us, too, listen to this voice and seek to know God's Face. In one of his poems he wrote, addressing himself to God: "May you be benevolent, you, the hereafter of all things" (*Carmina [dogmatica]* 1:1, 29: *PG* 37, 508). And in 390, God welcomed into his arms this faithful servant who had defended him in his writings with keen intelligence and had praised him in his poetry with such great love.

(*8 August 2007*)

Charles of Saint Andrew Houben

"The love of God has been poured into our hearts by the Holy Spirit which has been given us." Truly, in the case of the Passionist priest Charles of Saint Andrew Houben, we see how that love overflowed in a life totally dedicated to the care of souls. During his many years of priestly ministry in England and Ireland, the people flocked to him to seek out his wise counsel, his compassionate care, and his healing touch. In the sick and the suffering he recognized the face of the Crucified Christ, to whom he had a lifelong devotion. He drank deeply from the rivers of living water that poured forth from the side of the Pierced One, and in the power of the Spirit he bore witness before the world to the Father's love. At the funeral of this much-loved priest, affectionately known as Father Charles of Mount Argus, his superior was moved to observe: "The people have already declared him a saint."

(3 June 2007)

Saint Gregory of Nyssa

Saint Gregory of Nyssa...showed himself to be a man disposed to meditation with a great capacity for reflection and a lively intelligence open to the culture of his time. He has thus proved to be an original and profound thinker in the history of Christianity.

He was born in about 335 A.D. His Christian education was supervised with special care by his brother Basil—whom he called "father and teacher" (*Ep.* 13, 4: *SC* 363, 198)—and by his sister Macrina. He completed his studies, appreciating in particular philosophy and rhetoric. Initially, he devoted himself to teaching and was married. Later, like his brother and sister, he too dedicated himself entirely to the ascetic life. He was subsequently elected Bishop of Nyssa and showed himself to be a zealous Pastor, thereby earning the community's esteem. When he was accused of embezzlement by heretical adversaries, he was obliged for a brief period to abandon his episcopal See but later returned to it triumphant (cf. *Ep.* 6: *SC* 363, 164–170) and continued to be involved in the fight to defend the true faith.

Especially after Basil's death, by more or less gathering his spiritual legacy, Gregory cooperated in the triumph of orthodoxy. He took part in various Synods; he attempted to settle disputes between Churches; he had an active part in the reorganization of the Church, and, as a "pillar of orthodoxy", played a leading role at the Council of Constantinople in 381, which defined the divinity of the Holy Spirit. Various difficult official tasks were entrusted to him by the Emperor Theodosius, he delivered important homilies and funeral discourses, and he devoted himself to writing various theological works. In addition, in 394, he took part in another Synod, held in Constantinople. The date of his death is unknown.

Gregory expressed clearly the purpose of his studies, the supreme goal to which all his work as a theologian was directed: not to engage his life in vain things but to find the light that would enable him to discern what is truly worthwhile (cf. *In Ecclesiasten hom.* 1: *SC* 416, 106–46). He found this supreme good in Christianity, thanks to which "the imitation of the divine nature" is possible (*De Professione Christiana*: *PG* 46, 244c). With his acute intelligence and vast philosophical and theological knowledge, he defended the Christian faith against heretics who denied the divinity of the Son and of the Holy Spirit (such as Eunomius and the Macedonians) or compromised the perfect humanity of Christ (such as Apollinaris). He commented on Sacred Scripture, reflecting on the creation of man. This was one of his central topics: creation. He saw in the creature the reflection of the Creator and found here the way that leads to God. But he also wrote an important book on the life of Moses, whom he presents as a man journeying toward God: this climb to Mount Sinai became for him an image of our ascent in human life toward true life, toward the encounter with God. He also interpreted the Lord's Prayer, the Our Father, as well as the Beatitudes. In his "Great Catechetical Discourse" (*Oratio Catechetica Magna*), he developed theology's fundamental directions, not for an academic theology closed in on itself, but in order to offer catechists a reference system to keep before them in their instructions, almost as a framework for a pedagogical interpretation of the faith.

Furthermore, Gregory is distinguished for his spiritual doctrine. None of his theology was academic reflection; rather, it was an expression of the spiritual life, of a life of faith lived. As a great "father of mysticism", he pointed out in various treatises—such as his *De Professione Christiana* and *De Perfectione Christiana*—the path Christians must take if they are to reach true life, perfection. He exalted consecrated virginity (*De Virginitate*) and proposed the life of his sister Macrina, who was always a guide and example for him (cf. *Vita Macrinae*), as an outstanding model of it. Gregory gave various discourses and homilies and wrote numerous letters. In commenting on man's creation, he highlighted the fact that God, "the best artist, forges our nature so as to make it suitable for the exercise of royalty. Through the superiority given by the soul and through the very make-up of the body, he arranges things in such a way that man is truly fit for regal power" (*De Hominis Opificio* 4: *PG* 44, 136b). Yet, we see that man, caught in the net of sin, often abuses creation and does not exercise true kingship. For this reason, in fact, that is, to act with true responsibility for creatures, he must be penetrated by God and live in his light. Indeed, man is a reflection of that original beauty which is God: "Everything God created was very good", the holy Bishop wrote. And he added: "The story of creation (cf. Gn 1:31) witnesses to it. Man was also listed among those very good things, adorned with a beauty far superior to all of the good things. What else, in fact, could be good, on par with one who was similar to pure and incorruptible beauty?... The reflection and image of eternal life, he was truly good; no, he was very good, with the radiant sign of life on his face" (*Homilia in Canticum* 12: *PG* 44, 1020c).

Man was honored by God and placed above every other creature: The sky was not made in God's image, not the moon, not the sun, not the beauty of the stars, no other things which appear in creation. Only you (*human soul*) were made to be the image of nature that surpasses every intellect, likeness of incorruptible beauty, mark of true divinity, vessel of blessed life, image of true light, that when you look upon it you become what he is, because through the reflected ray coming from your purity you imitate him who shines within you. Nothing that exists can measure up to your greatness. (*Homilia in Canticum* 2: PG 44, 805d)

Let us meditate on this praise of man. Let us also see how man was degraded by sin. And let us try to return to that original greatness: only if God is present does man attain his true greatness.

Man therefore recognizes in himself the reflection of the divine light: by purifying his heart he is once more, as he was in the beginning, a clear image of God, exemplary Beauty (cf. *Oratio Catechetica* 6: SC 453, 174). Thus, by purifying himself, man can see God, as do the pure of heart (cf. Mt 5:8): "If, with a diligent and attentive way of life, you wash away the bad things that have been deposited upon your heart, the divine beauty will shine in you.... Contemplating yourself, you will see within you him who is the desire of your heart, and you will be blessed" (*De Beatitudinibus* 6: PG 44, 1272ab). We should therefore wash away the ugliness stored within our hearts and rediscover God's light within us.

Man's goal is therefore the contemplation of God. In him alone can he find his fulfillment. To anticipate this goal somehow in this life, he must work ceaselessly toward a spiritual life, a life in dialogue with God. In other words—and this is the most important lesson that Saint Gregory of Nyssa has bequeathed to us—total human fulfillment consists in holiness, in a life lived in the encounter with God, which thus becomes luminous also to others and to the world.

(29 August 2007)

Saint Hilary of Poitiers

Saint Hilary of Poitiers [was] one of the important episcopal figures of the fourth century. In the controversy with the Arians, who considered Jesus the Son of God to be an excellent human creature but only human, Hilary devoted his whole life to defending faith in the divinity of Jesus Christ, Son of God, and God as the Father who generated him from eternity.

We have no reliable information on most of Hilary's life. Ancient sources say that he was born in Poitiers, probably in about the year 310 A.D. From a wealthy family, he received a solid literary education, which is clearly recognizable in his writings. It does not seem that he grew up in a Christian environment. He himself tells us of a quest for the truth which led him little by little to recognize God the Creator and the incarnate God who died to give us eternal life. Baptized in about 345, he was elected Bishop of his native city around 353–354. In the years that followed, Hilary wrote his first work, the *Commentary on Saint Matthew's Gospel*. It is the oldest extant commentary in Latin on this Gospel. In 356, Hilary took part as a Bishop in the Synod of Béziers in the South of France, the "synod of false apostles", as he himself called it, since the assembly was in the control of philo-Arian Bishops who denied the divinity of Jesus Christ. "These false apostles" asked the Emperor Constantius to have the Bishop of Poitiers sentenced to exile. Thus, in the summer of 356, Hilary was forced to leave Gaul.

Banished to Phrygia in present-day Turkey, Hilary found himself in contact with a religious context totally dominated by Arianism. Here too, his concern as a Pastor impelled him to work strenuously to re-establish the unity of the Church on the basis of right faith as formulated by the Council of Nicaea. To this end he began to draft his own best-known and most important dogmatic work: *De Trinitate* (*On the Trinity*). Hilary explained in it his personal journey toward knowledge of God and took pains to show that not only in the New Testament but also in many Old Testament passages, in which Christ's mystery already appears, Scripture clearly testifies to the divinity of the Son and his equality with the Father. To the Arians he insisted on the truth of the names of Father and Son and developed his entire Trinitarian theology based on the formula of Baptism given to us by the Lord himself: "In the name of the Father and of the Son and of the Holy Spirit".

The Father and the Son are of the same nature. And although several passages in the New Testament might make one think that the Son was inferior to the Father, Hilary offers precise rules to avoid misleading interpretations: some scriptural texts speak of Jesus as God; others highlight instead his humanity. Some refer to him in his pre-existence with the Father; others take into consideration his state of emptying of self (*kenosis*), his descent to death; others, finally, contemplate him in the glory of the Resurrection. In the years of his exile, Hilary also wrote the *Book of Synods*, in which, for his brother Bishops of Gaul, he reproduced confessions of faith and commented on them and on other documents of Synods which met in the East in about the middle of the fourth century. Ever adamant in opposing the radical Arians, Saint Hilary showed a conciliatory spirit to those who agreed to confess that the Son was essentially *similar* to the Father, seeking of course to lead them to the true faith, according to which there is not only a likeness but a true equality of the Father and of the Son in divinity. This too seems to me to be characteristic: the spirit of reconciliation that seeks to understand those who have not yet arrived and helps them with great theological intelligence to reach full faith in the true divinity of the Lord Jesus Christ.

In 360 or 361, Hilary was finally able to return home from exile and immediately resumed pastoral activity in his Church, but the influence of his magisterium extended in fact far beyond its boundaries. A Synod celebrated in Paris in 360 or 361 borrows the language of the Council of Nicaea. Several ancient authors believe that this anti-Arian turning point of the Gaul episcopate was largely due to the fortitude and docility of the Bishop of Poitiers. This was precisely his gift: to combine strength in the faith and docility in interpersonal relations. In the last years of his life, he also composed the *Treatises on the Psalms*, a commentary on fifty-eight Psalms interpreted according to the principle highlighted in the introduction to the work: "There is no doubt that all the things that are said in the Psalms should be understood in accordance with Gospel proclamation, so that, whatever the voice with which the prophetic spirit has spoken, all may be referred nevertheless to the knowledge of the coming of Our Lord Jesus Christ, the Incarnation, Passion, and Kingdom, and to the power and glory of our resurrection" (*Instructio Psalmorum* 5). He saw in all the Psalms this transparency of the mystery of Christ and of his Body which is the Church. Hilary met Saint Martin on various occasions: the future Bishop of Tours founded a monastery right by Poitiers, which still exists today. Hilary died in 367. His liturgical Memorial is celebrated on 13 January. In 1851 Blessed Pius IX proclaimed him a Doctor of the universal Church.

To sum up the essentials of his doctrine, I would like to say that Hilary found the starting point for his theological reflection in baptismal faith. In *De Trinitate*, Hilary writes:

> Jesus has commanded us to baptize *in the name of the Father and of the Son and of the Holy Spirit* (cf. Mt 28:19), that is, in the confession of the Author, of the Only-Begotten One, and of the Gift. The Author of all things is one alone, for *one alone is God the Father, from whom all things proceed.* And *one alone is Our Lord Jesus Christ, through whom all things exist* (cf. I Cor 8:6), *and one alone is the Spirit* (cf. Eph 4:4), a gift in all.... In nothing can be found to be lacking so great a fullness, in which the immensity in the Eternal One, the revelation in the Image, joy in the Gift, converge in the Father, in the Son, and in the Holy Spirit. (*De Trinitate* 2, 1)

God the Father, being wholly love, is able to communicate his divinity to his Son in its fullness. I find particularly beautiful the following formula of Saint Hilary: "God knows not how to be anything other than love; he knows not how to be anyone other than the Father. Those who love are not envious, and the one who is the Father is so in his totality. This name admits no compromise, as if God were father in some aspects and not in others" (*ibid.*, 9, 61).

For this reason the Son is fully God without any gaps or diminishment. "The One who comes from the perfect is perfect because he has all, he has given all" (*ibid.*, 2, 8). Humanity finds salvation in Christ alone, Son of God and Son of man. In assuming our human nature, he has united himself with every man, "he has become the flesh of us all" (*Tractatus super Psalmos* 54, 9); "he took on himself the nature of all flesh and through it became true life; he has in himself the root of every vine shoot" (*ibid.*, 51, 16). For this very reason the way to Christ is open to all—because he has drawn all into his being as a man—even if personal conversion is always required: "Through the relationship with his flesh, access to Christ is open to all, on condition that they divest themselves of their former self (cf. Eph 4:22), nailing it to the Cross (cf. Col 2:14); provided we give up our former way of life and convert in order to be buried with him in his baptism, in view of life (cf. Col 1:12; Rom 6:4)" (*ibid.*, 91, 9).

Fidelity to God is a gift of his grace. Therefore, Saint Hilary asks, at the end of his Treatise on the Trinity, to be able to remain ever faithful to the baptismal faith. It is a feature of this book: reflection is transformed into prayer, and prayer returns to reflection. The whole book is a dialogue with God. I would like to end today's Catechesis with one of these prayers, which thus becomes our prayer: "Obtain, O Lord", Saint Hilary recites with inspiration, "that I may keep ever faithful to what I have professed in the symbol of my regeneration, when I was baptized in the Father, in the Son, and in the Holy Spirit. That I may worship you, our Father, and with you, your Son; that I may deserve your Holy Spirit, who proceeds from you through your Only-Begotten Son.... Amen" (*De Trinitate* 12, 57).

(10 October 2007)

Saint Anthony, Abbot

While still a young man, but mature in the faith, Anthony distributed all his possessions to the poor. He dedicated himself entirely to a life of penance and ascetical practice. People called him the friend of God. Saint Augustine admired his faith. Moved by his example, let us give aid to those who are poor and in need!...

May the example of Saint Anthony Abbot, the distinguished Father of monasticism who worked hard for the Church by supporting martyrs during the persecution, encourage you, dear *young people*, to seek Christ constantly and follow him faithfully; may it comfort you, dear *sick* people, in bearing your suffering patiently and in offering it up so that the Kingdom of God may be spread throughout the world; and may it help you, dear *newly-weds*, to be witnesses of Christ's love in your family life.

(16 January 2008)

Translated in part by Andrew Matt.

Saints Timothy and Titus, Bishops

Timothy is a Greek name which means "one who honors God". Whereas Luke mentions him six times in the Acts, Paul in his Letters refers to him at least seventeen times (and his name occurs once in the Letter to the Hebrews). One may deduce from this that Paul held him in high esteem, even if Luke did not consider it worth telling us all about him. Indeed, the Apostle entrusted Timothy with important missions and saw him almost as an *alter ego*, as is evident from his great praise of him in his Letter to the Philippians. "I have no one like him (*isópsychon*) who will be genuinely anxious for your welfare" (2:20).

Timothy was born at Lystra (about two hundred kilometers northwest of Tarsus) of a Jewish mother and a Gentile father (cf. Acts 16:1). The fact that his mother had contracted a mixed-marriage and did not have her son circumcised suggests that Timothy grew up in a family that was not strictly observant, although it was said that he was acquainted with the Scriptures from childhood (cf. 2 Tm 3:15). The name of his mother, Eunice, has been handed down to us as well as that of his grandmother, Lois (cf. 2 Tm 1:5). When Paul was passing through Lystra at the beginning of his second missionary journey, he chose Timothy to be his companion because "he was well spoken of by the brethren at Lystra and Iconium" (Acts 16:2), but he had him circumcised "because of the Jews that were in those places" (Acts 16:3).

Together with Paul and Silas, Timothy crossed Asia Minor as far as Troy, from where he entered Macedonia. We are informed further that at Philippi, where Paul and Silas were falsely accused of disturbing public order and thrown into prison for having exposed the exploitation of a young girl who was a soothsayer by several unscrupulous individuals (cf. Acts 16:16–40), Timothy was spared. When Paul was then obliged to proceed to Athens, Timothy joined him in that city and from it was sent out to the young Church of Thessalonica to obtain news about her and to strengthen her in the faith (cf. 1 Thes 3:1–2). He then met up with the Apostle in Corinth, bringing him good news about the Thessalonians and working with him to evangelize that city (cf. 2 Cor 1:19).

We find Timothy at Ephesus during Paul's third missionary journey. It was probably from there that the Apostle wrote to Philemon and to the Philippians; he sent both Letters jointly with Timothy (cf. Phlm 1; Phil 1:1). From Ephesus, Paul sent Timothy to Macedonia, together with a certain Erastus (cf. Acts 19:22), and then also to Corinth with the mission of taking a letter to the Corinthians, in which he recommended that they welcome him warmly (cf. 1 Cor 4:17; 16:10–11). We encounter him again as the joint sender of the Second Letter to the Corinthians, and when Paul wrote the Letter to the Romans from Corinth he added Timothy's greetings as well as the greetings of the others (cf. Rom 16:21). From Corinth, the disciple left for Troy on the Asian coast of the Aegean See and there awaited the Apostle, who was bound for Jerusalem at the end of his third missionary journey (cf. Acts 20:4). From that moment in Timothy's biography, the ancient sources mention nothing further to us, except for a reference in the Letter to the Hebrews which says: "You should understand that our brother Timothy has been released, with whom I shall see you if he comes soon"

(13:23). To conclude, we can say that the figure of Timothy stands out as a very important pastor. According to the later *Ecclesiastical History* by Eusebius, Timothy was the first Bishop of Ephesus (cf. *Hist. eccles.*, III, 4). Some of his relics, brought from Constantinople, were found in Italy in 1239 in the Cathedral of Termoli in the Molise.

Then, as regards the figure of *Titus*, whose name is of Latin origin, we know that he was Greek by birth, that is, a pagan (cf. Gal 2:3). Paul took Titus with him to Jerusalem for the so-called Apostolic Council, where the preaching of the Gospel to the Gentiles that freed them from the constraints of Mosaic Law was solemnly accepted. In the Letter addressed to Titus, the Apostle praised him and described him as his "true child in a common faith" (Ti 1:4). After Timothy's departure from Corinth, Paul sent Titus there with the task of bringing that unmanageable community to obedience. Titus restored peace between the Church of Corinth and the Apostle, who wrote to this Church in these terms: "But God, who comforts the downcast, comforted us by the coming of Titus, and not only by his coming but also by the comfort with which he was comforted in you, as he told us of your longing, your mourning, your zeal for me.... And besides our own comfort we rejoiced still more at the joy of Titus, because his mind has been set at rest by you all" (2 Cor 7:6–7, 13). From Corinth, Titus was again sent out by Paul—who called him "my partner and fellow worker in your service" (2 Cor 8:23)—to organize the final collections for the Christians of Jerusalem (cf. 2 Cor 8:6). Further information from the Pastoral Letters describes him as Bishop of Crete (cf. Ti 1:5), from which, at Paul's invitation, he joined the Apostle at Nicopolis in Epirus (cf. Ti 3:12). Later, he also went to Dalmatia (cf. 2 Tm 4:10). We lack any further information on the subsequent movements of Titus or on his death.

To conclude, if we consider together the two figures of Timothy and Titus, we are aware of certain very significant facts. The most important one is that in carrying out his missions, Paul availed himself of collaborators. He certainly remains the Apostle par excellence, founder and pastor of many Churches. Yet it clearly appears that he did not do everything on his own but relied on trustworthy people who shared in his endeavors and responsibilities. Another observation concerns the willingness of these collaborators. The sources concerning Timothy and Titus highlight their readiness to take on various offices that also often consisted in representing Paul in circumstances far from easy. In a word, they teach us to serve the Gospel with generosity, realizing that this also entails a service to the Church herself. Lastly, let us follow the recommendation that the Apostle Paul makes to Titus in the Letter addressed to him: "I desire you to insist on these things, so that those who have believed in God may be careful to apply themselves to good deeds; these are excellent and profitable to men" (Ti 3:8). Through our commitment in practice we can and must discover the truth of these words, and precisely in this Season of Advent, we too can be rich in good deeds and thus open the doors of the world to Christ, our Savior.

(13 December 2006)

Saint Thomas Aquinas

Today the liturgical calendar commemorates Saint Thomas Aquinas, the great Doctor of the Church. With his charism as a philosopher and theologian, he offered an effective model of harmony between reason and faith, dimensions of the human spirit that are completely fulfilled in the encounter and dialogue with one another. According to Saint Thomas' thought, human reason, as it were, "breathes": it moves within a vast open horizon in which it can express the best of itself. When, instead, man reduces himself to thinking only of material objects or those that can be proven, he closes himself to the great questions about life, himself, and God and is impoverished. The relationship between faith and reason is a serious challenge to the currently dominant culture in the Western world, and for this very reason our beloved John Paul II decided to dedicate an Encyclical to it, entitled, precisely, *Fides et Ratio*—Faith and Reason. Recently, I too returned to this topic in my Discourse to the University of Regensburg.

In fact, the modern development of the sciences brings innumerable positive effects, as we all see, that should always be recognized. At the same time, however, it is necessary to admit that the tendency to consider true only what can be experienced constitutes a limitation of human reason and produces a terrible schizophrenia now clearly evident, which has led to the coexistence of rationalism and materialism, hyper-technology and unbridled instinct. It is urgent, therefore, to rediscover anew human rationality open to the light of the divine *Logos* and his perfect revelation which is Jesus Christ, Son of God made man. When Christian faith is authentic, it does not diminish freedom and human reason; so, why should faith and reason fear one another if the best way for them to express themselves is by meeting and entering into dialogue? Faith presupposes reason and perfects it, and reason, enlightened by faith, finds the strength to rise to knowledge of God and spiritual realities. Human reason loses nothing by opening itself to the content of faith, which, indeed, requires its free and conscious adherence.

Saint Thomas Aquinas, with farsighted wisdom, succeeded in establishing a fruitful confrontation with the Arab and Hebrew thought of his time, to the point that he is considered a timeless master of dialogue with other cultures and religions. He knew how to present that wonderful Christian synthesis of reason and faith which today too, for the Western civilization, is a precious patrimony from which to draw for an effective dialogue with the great cultural and religious traditions of the East and South of the world. Let us pray that Christians, especially those who work in an academic and cultural context, are able to express the reasonableness of their faith and witness to it in a dialogue inspired by love. Let us ask the Lord for this gift through the intercession of Saint Thomas Aquinas and above all, through Mary, Seat of Wisdom.

(28 January 2007)

Saint Aphraates

Aphraates, known also by the sobriquet "the Sage", ... was one of the most important and at the same time most enigmatic personages of fourth-century Syriac Christianity. A native of the Niniveh-Mossul region, today in Iraq, he lived during the first half of the fourth century. We have little information about his life; he maintained, however, close ties with the ascetic-monastic environment of the Syriac-speaking Church, of which he has given us some information in his work and to which he dedicates part of his reflection. Indeed, according to some sources he was the head of a monastery and later consecrated a Bishop. He wrote twenty-three homilies, known as *Expositions* or *Demonstrations*, on various aspects of Christian life, such as faith, love, fasting, humility, prayer, the ascetic life, and also the relationship between Judaism and Christianity, between the Old and New Testaments. He wrote in a simple style with short sentences and sometimes with contrasting parallelisms; nevertheless, he was able to weave consistent discourses with a well-articulated development of the various arguments he treated.

Aphraates was from an Ecclesial Community situated on the frontier between Judaism and Christianity. It was a community strongly-linked to the Mother Church of Jerusalem, and its Bishops were traditionally chosen from among the so-called "family" of James, the "brother of the Lord" (cf.

Mk 6:3). They were people linked by blood and by faith to the Church of Jerusalem. Aphraates' language was Syriac, therefore a Semitic language like the Hebrew of the Old Testament and like the Aramaic spoken by Jesus himself. Aphraates' Ecclesial Community was a community that sought to remain faithful to the Judeo-Christian tradition, of which it felt it was a daughter. It therefore maintained a close relationship with the Jewish world and its Sacred Books. Significantly, Aphraates defines himself as a "disciple of the Sacred Scripture" of the Old and New Testaments (*Expositions* 22, 26), which he considers as his only source of inspiration, having recourse to it in such abundance as to make it the center of his reflection.

Aphraates develops various arguments in his *Expositions*. Faithful to Syriac tradition, he often presents the salvation wrought by Christ as a healing and, thus, Christ himself as the physician. Sin, on the other hand, is seen as a wound that only penance can heal: "A man who has been wounded in battle", Aphraates said, "is not ashamed to place himself in the hands of a wise doctor ...; in the same way, the one who has been wounded by Satan must not be ashamed to recognize his fault and distance himself from it, asking for the medicine of penance" (*Expositions* 7, 3). Another important aspect in Aphraates' work is his teaching on prayer and, in a special way, on Christ as the teacher of prayer. The Christian prays following Jesus' teaching and example of oration: "Our Savior taught people to pray like this, saying: 'Pray in secret to the One who is hidden, but who sees all'; and again: 'Go into your room and shut the door and pray to your Father who is in secret; and your Father who sees in secret will reward you' (Mt 6:6).... Our Savior wants to show that God knows the desires and thoughts of the heart" (*Expositions* 4, 10).

For Aphraates, the Christian life is centered on the imitation of Christ, in taking up his yoke and following him on the way of the Gospel. One of the most useful virtues for Christ's disciple is humility. It is not a secondary aspect in the Christian's spiritual life: man's nature is humble, and it is God who exalts it to his own glory. Aphraates observed that humility is not a negative value: "If man's roots are planted in the earth, his fruits ascend before the Lord of majesty" (*Expositions* 9, 14). By remaining humble, even in the earthly reality in which one lives, the Christian can enter into relationship with the Lord: "The humble man is humble, but his heart rises to lofty heights. The eyes of his face observe the earth and the eyes of his mind the lofty heights" (*Expositions* 9, 2).

Aphraates' vision of man and his physical reality is very positive: the human body, in the example of the humble Christ, is called to beauty, joy, and light: "God draws near to the man who loves, and it is right to love humility and to remain in a humble state. The humble are simple, patient, loving, integral, upright, good, prudent, calm, wise, quiet, peaceful, merciful, ready to convert, benevolent, profound, thoughtful, beautiful, and attractive" (*Expositions* 9, 14). Aphraates often presented the Christian life in a clear ascetic and spiritual dimension: faith is the base, the foundation; it makes of man a temple where Christ himself dwells. Faith, therefore, makes sincere charity possible, which expresses itself in love for God and neighbor. Another important aspect in Aphraates' thought is fasting, which he understood in a broad sense. He spoke of fasting from food as a necessary practice to be charitable and pure, of fasting understood as continence with a view to holiness, of fasting from vain or detestable words, of fasting from anger, of fasting from the possession of goods with a view to ministry, of fasting from sleep to be watchful in prayer.

Dear brothers and sisters, to conclude, we return again to Aphraates' teaching on prayer. According to this ancient

"Sage", prayer is achieved when Christ dwells in the Christian's heart and invites him to a coherent commitment to charity toward one's neighbor. In fact, he wrote:

Give relief to those in distress, visit the ailing,
help the poor: this is prayer.
Prayer is good, and its works are beautiful.
Prayer is accepted when it gives relief to one's neighbor.
Prayer is heard when it includes forgiveness of affronts.
Prayer is strong
when it is full of God's strength. (*Expositions* 4, 14–16)

With these words Aphraates invites us to a prayer that becomes Christian life, a fulfilled life, a life penetrated by faith, by openness to God and therefore to love of neighbor.

(21 November 2007)

The Presentation of the Lord

Today's Feast of Jesus' Presentation at the Temple forty days after his birth places before our eyes a special moment in the life of the Holy Family: Mary and Joseph, in accordance with Mosaic Law, took the tiny Jesus to the Temple of Jerusalem to offer him to the Lord (cf. Lk 2:22). Simeon and Anna, inspired by God, recognized that Child as the long-awaited Messiah and prophesied about him. We are in the presence of a mystery, both simple and solemn, in which Holy Church celebrates Christ, the Anointed One of the Father, the firstborn of the new humanity.

The evocative candlelight procession at the beginning of our celebration has made us relive the majestic entrance, as we sang in the Responsorial Psalm, of the One who is "the King of glory", "the Lord, mighty in battle" (Ps 24[23]: 7, 8). But who is the powerful God who enters the Temple? It is a Child; it is the Infant Jesus in the arms of his Mother, the Virgin Mary. The Holy Family was complying with what the Law prescribed: the purification of the mother, the offering of the firstborn child to God, and his redemption through a sacrifice. In the First Reading the liturgy speaks of the oracle of the Prophet Malachi: "The Lord ... will suddenly come to his temple" (Mal 3:1). These words communicated the full intensity of the desire that had given life to the expectation of the Jewish people down the centuries. "The angel of the Covenant" at last entered his house and submitted to the Law: he came to Jerusalem to enter God's house in an attitude of obedience.

The meaning of this act acquires a broader perspective in the passage from the Letter to the Hebrews, proclaimed as the Second Reading today. Christ, the Mediator who unites God and man, abolishing distances, eliminating every division and tearing down every wall of separation, is presented to us here. Christ comes as a new "merciful and faithful high priest in the service of God, to make expiation for the sins of the people" (Heb 2:17). Thus, we note that mediation with God takes place, no longer in the holiness-separation of the ancient priesthood, but in liberating solidarity with human beings. While yet a Child, he sets out on the path of obedience that he was to follow to the very end. The Letter to the Hebrews highlights this clearly when it says: "In the days of his earthly life Jesus offered up prayers and supplications ... to him who was able to save him from death.... Although he was a Son, he learned obedience through what he suffered; and being made perfect he became the source of eternal salvation to all who obey him" (cf. Heb 5:7–9).

The first person to be associated with Christ on the path of obedience, proven faith, and shared suffering was his Mother, Mary. The Gospel text portrays her in the act of offering her Son: an unconditional offering that involves her in the first person. Mary is the Mother of the One who is "the glory of [his] people Israel" and a "light for revelation to the Gentiles", but also "a sign that is spoken against" (cf. Lk 2:32, 34). And in her immaculate soul, she herself was to be pierced by the sword of sorrow, thus showing that her role in the history of salvation did not end in the mystery of the Incarnation but was completed in loving and sorrowful participation in the death and Resurrection of her Son. Bringing her Son to Jerusalem, the Virgin Mother offered him to God as a true Lamb who takes away the sins of the world. She held him out to Simeon and Anna as the proclamation of redemption; she presented him to all as a light for a safe journey on the path of truth and love. The words that came to the lips of the elderly Simeon: "My eyes have seen your salvation" (Lk 2:30), are echoed in the heart of the Prophetess Anna. These good and devout people, enveloped in Christ's light, were able to see in the Child Jesus "the consolation of Israel" (Lk 2:25). So it was that their expectation was transformed into a light that illuminates history. Simeon was the bearer of an ancient hope, and the Spirit of the Lord spoke to his heart: for this reason he could contemplate the One whom numerous prophets and kings had desired to see: Christ, light of revelation for the Gentiles. He recognized that Child as the Savior, but he foresaw in the Spirit that the destinies of humanity would be played out around him and that he would have to suffer deeply from those who rejected him; he proclaimed the identity and mission of the Messiah with words that form one of the hymns of the newborn Church, radiant with the full communitarian and eschatological exultation of the fulfillment of the expectation of salvation. The enthusiasm was so great that to live and to die were one and the same, and the "light" and "glory" became a universal revelation. Anna is a "prophetess", a wise and pious woman who interpreted the deep meaning of historical events and of God's message concealed within them. Consequently, she could "give thanks to God" and "[speak of the Child] to all who were looking for the redemption of Jerusalem" (Lk 2:38). Her long widowhood devoted to worship in the Temple, fidelity to weekly fasting, and participation in the expectation of those who yearned for the redemption of Israel culminated in her meeting with the Child Jesus.

On this Feast of the Presentation of the Lord, the Church is celebrating the Day of Consecrated Life. This is an appropriate occasion to praise the Lord and thank him for the precious gift represented by the consecrated life in its different forms; at the same time it is an incentive to encourage in all the People of God knowledge and esteem for those who are totally consecrated to God. Indeed, just as Jesus' life in his obedience and dedication to the Father is a living parable of the "God-with-us", so the concrete dedication of consecrated persons to God and to their brethren becomes an eloquent sign for today's world of the presence of God's Kingdom. Your way of living and working can vividly express full belonging to the one Lord; placing yourselves without reserve in the hands of Christ and of the Church is a strong and clear proclamation of God's presence in a language understandable to our contemporaries. This is the first service that the consecrated life offers to the Church and to the world. *Consecrated persons are like watchmen among the People of God who perceive and proclaim the new life already present in our history....*

May the Lord renew in you and in all consecrated people each day the joyful response to his freely given and faithful love. Dear brothers and sisters, like lighted candles, always and everywhere shine with the love of Christ, Light of the world. May Mary Most Holy, the consecrated Woman, help you to live to the full your special vocation and mission in the Church for the world's salvation.

Amen!

(2 February 2006)

Saints Cyril and Methodius

Today the liturgy celebrates the memory of two holy brothers, Cyril the monk and Methodius the Bishop, Apostles to the Slavs and Patrons of Europe. Through their intercession we ask God that the European nations, ever more aware of their Christian roots, may remain united and open themselves to Christ and his Gospel.

(14 February 2007)

* * *

Saints Cyril and Methodius [were] brothers by blood and in the faith, the so-called "Apostles to the Slavs". Cyril was born in Thessalonica to Leo, an imperial magistrate, in 826 or 827. He was the youngest of seven. As a child he learned the Slavonic language. When he was fourteen years old, he was sent to Constantinople to be educated and was companion to the young Emperor, Michael III. In those years Cyril was introduced to the various university disciplines, including dialectics, and his teacher was Photius. After refusing a brilliant marriage, he decided to receive holy Orders and became "librarian" at the Patriarchate. Shortly afterward, wishing to retire in solitude, he went into hiding at a monastery but was soon discovered and entrusted with teaching

Translated in part by Andrew Matt.

the sacred and profane sciences. He carried out this office so well that he earned the title of "Philosopher". In the meantime, his brother Michael (born in about 815) left the world after an administrative career in Macedonia and withdrew to a monastic life on Mount Olympus in Bithynia, where he was given the name "Methodius" (a monk's monastic name had to begin with the same letter as his baptismal name) and became hegumen of the Monastery of Polychron.

Attracted by his brother's example, Cyril, too, decided to give up teaching and go to Mount Olympus to meditate and pray. A few years later (in about 861), the imperial government sent him on a mission to the Khazars on the Sea of Azov, who had asked for a scholar to be sent to them who could converse with both Jews and Saracens. Cyril, accompanied by his brother Methodius, stayed for a long time in Crimea, where he learned Hebrew and sought the body of Pope Clement I, who had been exiled there. Cyril found Pope Clement's tomb, and, when he made the return journey with his brother, he took Clement's precious relics with him. Having arrived in Constantinople, the two brothers were sent to Moravia by Emperor Michael III, who had received a specific request from Prince Ratislav of Moravia: "Since our people rejected paganism," Ratislav wrote to Michael, "they have embraced the Christian law; but we do not have a teacher who can explain the true faith to us in our own language." The mission was soon unusually successful. By translating the liturgy into the Slavonic language, the two brothers earned immense popularity.

However, this gave rise to hostility among the Frankish clergy who had arrived in Moravia before the brothers and considered the territory to be under their ecclesiastical jurisdiction. In order to justify themselves, in 867 the two brothers traveled to Rome. On the way they stopped in

Venice, where they had a heated discussion with the champions of the so-called "trilingual heresy", who claimed that there were only three languages in which it was lawful to praise God: Hebrew, Greek, and Latin. The two brothers obviously forcefully opposed this claim. In Rome Cyril and Methodius were received by Pope Adrian II, who led a procession to meet them in order to give a dignified welcome to Saint Clement's relics. The Pope had also realized the great importance of their exceptional mission. Since the middle of the first millennium, in fact, thousands of Slavs had settled in those territories located between the two parts of the Roman Empire, the East and the West, whose relations were fraught with tension. The Pope perceived that the Slav peoples would be able to serve as a bridge and thereby help to preserve the union between the Christians of both parts of the Empire. Thus he did not hesitate to approve the mission of the two brothers in Great Moravia, accepting and approving the use of the Slavonic language in the liturgy. The Slavonic Books were laid on the altar of Saint Mary of Phatmé (Saint Mary Major), and the liturgy in the Slavonic tongue was celebrated in the Basilicas of Saint Peter, Saint Andrew, and Saint Paul.

Unfortunately, Cyril fell seriously ill in Rome. Feeling that his death was at hand, he wanted to consecrate himself totally to God as a monk in one of the Greek monasteries of the City (probably Santa Prassede) and took the monastic name of Cyril (his baptismal name was Constantine). He then insistently begged his brother Methodius, who in the meantime had been ordained a Bishop, not to abandon their mission in Moravia and to return to the peoples there. He addressed this prayer to God: "Lord, my God,... hear my prayers and keep the flock you have entrusted to me faithful.... Free them from the heresy of the three languages, gather them all in unity, and make the people you have chosen agree in the true faith and confession." He died on 14 February 869.

Faithful to the pledge he had made with his brother, Methodius returned to Moravia and Pannonia (today, Hungary) the following year, 870, where once again he encountered the violent aversion of the Frankish missionaries, who took him prisoner. He did not lose heart, and when he was released in 873, he worked hard to organize the Church and train a group of disciples. It was to the merit of these disciples that it was possible to survive the crisis unleashed after the death of Methodius on 6 April 885: persecuted and imprisoned, some of them were sold as slaves and taken to Venice, where they were redeemed by a Constantinopolitan official, who allowed them to return to the countries of the Slavonic Balkans. Welcomed in Bulgaria, they were able to continue the mission that Methodius had begun and to disseminate the Gospel in the "Land of the Rus". God with his mysterious Providence thus availed himself of their persecution to save the work of the holy brothers. Literary documentation of their work is extant. It suffices to think of texts such as the *Evangeliarium* (liturgical passages of the New Testament), the *Psalter*, various *liturgical texts* in Slavonic, on which both the brothers had worked. Indeed, after Cyril's death, it is to Methodius and to his disciples that we owe the translation of the entire *Sacred Scriptures*, the *Nomocanone*, and the *Book of the Fathers*.

Wishing now to sum up concisely the profile of the two brothers, we should first recall the enthusiasm with which Cyril approached the writings of Saint Gregory Nazianzen, learning from him the value of language in the transmission of Revelation. Saint Gregory had expressed the wish that Christ would speak through him: "I am a servant of the Word, so I put myself at the service of the Word." Desirous of imitating Gregory in this service, Cyril asked Christ to deign to speak in Slavonic through him. He introduced his work of translation with the solemn invocation: "Listen, O all of you Slav Peoples, listen to the word that comes from God, the word that nourishes souls, the word that leads to the knowledge of God." In fact, a few years before the Prince of Moravia had asked Emperor Michael III to send missionaries to his country, it seems that Cyril and his brother Methodius, surrounded by a group of disciples, were already working on the project of collecting the Christian dogmas in books written in Slavonic. The need for new graphic characters closer to the language spoken was therefore clearly apparent: so it was that the Glagolitic alphabet came into being. Subsequently modified, it was later designated by the name "Cyrillic", in honor of the man who inspired it. It was a crucial event for the development of the Slav civilization in general. Cyril and Methodius were convinced that the individual peoples could not claim to have received Revelation fully unless they had heard it in their own language and read it in the characters proper to their own alphabet.

Methodius had the merit of ensuring that the work begun by his brother was not suddenly interrupted. While Cyril, the "Philosopher", was more inclined to contemplation, Methodius, on the other hand, had a leaning for the active life. Thanks to this he was able to lay the foundations of the successive affirmation of what we might call the "Cyrillian-Methodian idea": it accompanied the Slav peoples in the different periods of their history, encouraging their cultural, national, and religious development. This was already recognized by Pope Pius XI in his Apostolic Letter *Quod Sanctum Cyrillum*, in which he described the two brothers: "Sons of the East, Byzantines according to their homeland, Greeks by birth, Romans by their mission, Slavs by their apostolic fruit" (*AAS* 19 [1927] 93–96). The historic role they played was later officially proclaimed by Pope John Paul II, who, with his Apostolic Letter *Egregiae Virtutis*, declared them Co-Patrons of Europe, together with Saint Benedict (31 December 1980; *L'Osservatore Romano* English edition, 19 January 1981, p. 3). Cyril and Methodius are in fact a classic example of what today is meant by the term "inculturation": every people must integrate the message revealed into its own culture and express its saving truth in its own language. This implies a very demanding effort of "translation", because it requires the identification of the appropriate words to present anew, without distortion, the riches of the revealed Word. The two holy brothers have left us a most important testimony of this, to which the Church also looks today in order to draw from it inspiration and guidelines.

(17 June 2009)

Saint Peter Damian

In his life, Saint Peter Damian was proof of a successful synthesis of hermitic and pastoral activity. As a hermit, he embodied that Gospel radicalism and unreserved love for Christ so well expressed in the *Rule* of Saint Benedict: "Prefer nothing, absolutely nothing, to the love of Christ." As a man of the Church, he worked with farsighted wisdom and when necessary also made hard and courageous decisions. The whole of his human and spiritual life was played out in the tension between his life as a hermit and his ecclesiastical duty.

Saint Peter Damian was above all a hermit, indeed, the last theoretician of the hermitic life in the Latin Church exactly at the time of the East-West schism. In his interesting work entitled *The Life of Blessed Romuald*, he left us one of the most significant fruits of the monastic experience of the undivided Church. For him, the hermitic life was a strong call to rally all Christians to the primacy of Christ and his lordship. It is an invitation to discover Christ's love for the Church, starting from his relationship with the Father; a love that the hermit must in turn nourish *with, for,* and *in* Christ, in regard to the entire People of God. Saint Peter Damian felt the presence of the universal Church in the hermitic life so strongly that he wrote in his ecclesiological treatise entitled *Dominus vobiscum* that the Church is at the same time one in all and all in each one of her members.

This great holy hermit was also an eminent man of the Church who made himself available to move from the hermitage to go wherever his presence might be required in order to mediate between contending parties, were they Churchmen, monks, or simple faithful. Although he was radically focused on the *unum necessarium*, he did not shirk the practical demands that love for the Church imposed upon him. He was impelled by his desire that the Ecclesial Community always show itself as a holy and immaculate Bride ready for her heavenly Bridegroom and expressed with a lively *ars oratoria* his sincere and disinterested zeal for the Church's holiness. Yet, after each ecclesial mission he would return to the peace of the hermitage at Fonte Avellana and, free from all ambition, he even reached the point of definitively renouncing the dignity of Cardinal so as not to distance himself from his hermitic solitude, the cell of his hidden existence in Christ.

Lastly, Saint Peter Damian was the soul of the *"Riforma gregoriana"*, which marked the passage from the first to the second millennium and whose heart and driving force was Saint Gregory VII. It was, in fact, a matter of the application of institutional decisions of a theological, disciplinary, and spiritual character which permitted a greater *libertas Ecclesiae* in the second millennium. They restored the breath of great theology with reference to the Fathers of the Church and, in particular, to Saint Augustine, Saint Jerome, and Saint Gregory the Great. With his pen and his words he addressed all: he asked his brother hermits for the courage of a radical self-giving to the Lord which would as closely as possible resemble martyrdom; he demanded of the Pope, Bishops, and ecclesiastics a high level of evangelical detachment from honors and privileges in carrying out their ecclesial functions; he reminded priests of the highest ideal of their mission that they were to exercise by cultivating purity of morals and true personal poverty.

In an age marked by forms of particularism and uncertainties because it was bereft of a unifying principle, Peter Damian, aware of his own limitations—he liked to refer to himself as *peccator monachus*—passed on to his contemporaries the knowledge that only through a constant harmonious tension between the two fundamental poles of life—solitude and communion—can an effective Christian witness develop. Does not this teaching also apply to our times?

(20 February 2007)

* * *

One of the most significant figures of the eleventh century, Saint Peter Damian [was] a monk, a lover of solitude, and at the same time a fearless man of the Church, committed personally to the task of reform initiated by the Popes of the time. He was born in Ravenna in 1007, into a noble family but in straitened circumstances. He was left an orphan, and his childhood was not exempt from hardships and suffering, although his sister Roselinda tried to be a mother to him and his elder brother, Damian, adopted him as his son. For this very reason he was to be called Piero di Damiano, Pier Damiani [Peter of Damian, Peter Damian]. He was educated first at Faenza and then at Parma, where, already at the age of twenty-five, we find him involved in teaching. As well as a good grounding in the field of law, he acquired a refined expertise in the art of writing—the *ars scribendi*— and, thanks to his knowledge of the great Latin classics, became "one of the most accomplished Latinists of his time, one of the greatest writers of medieval Latin" (J. Leclercq, *Pierre Damien, ermite et homme d'Église*, Rome, 1960, p. 172).

He distinguished himself in the widest range of literary forms: from letters to sermons, from hagiographies to prayers, from poems to epigrams. His sensitivity to beauty led him to poetic contemplation of the world. Peter Damian conceived of the universe as a never-ending "parable" and a sequence of symbols on which to base the interpretation of inner life and divine and supra-natural reality. In this perspective, in about the year 1034, contemplation of the absolute of God impelled him gradually to detach himself from the world and from its transient realities and to withdraw to the Monastery of Fonte Avellana. It had been founded only a few decades earlier but was already celebrated for its austerity. For the monks' edification he wrote the *Life* of the Founder, Saint Romuald of Ravenna, and at the same time strove to deepen their spirituality, expounding on his ideal of eremitic monasticism.

One detail should be immediately emphasized: the Hermitage at Fonte Avellana was dedicated to the Holy Cross, and the Cross was the Christian mystery that was to fascinate Peter Damian more than all the others. "Those who do not love the Cross of Christ do not love Christ", he said (*Sermo XVIII*, 11, p. 117); and he described himself as "*Petrus crucis Christi servorum famulus*: Peter, servant of the servants of the Cross of Christ" (*Ep.* 9, 1). Peter Damian addressed the most beautiful prayers to the Cross, in which he reveals a vision of this mystery which has cosmic dimensions, for it embraces the entire history of salvation: "O Blessed Cross", he exclaimed, "You are venerated, preached, and honored by the faith of the Patriarchs, the predictions of the Prophets, the senate of Apostles that judges, the victorious army of Martyrs, and the throngs of all the Saints" (*Sermo XLVII*, 14, p. 304). Dear brothers and sisters, may the example of Saint Peter Damian spur us, too, always to look to the Cross as to the supreme act of love for mankind by God, who has given us salvation.

This great monk compiled a *Rule* for eremitical life in which he heavily stressed the "rigor of the hermit": in the silence of the cloister the monk is called to spend a life of prayer, by day and by night, with prolonged and strict fasting; he must put into practice generous brotherly charity in ever prompt and willing obedience to the Prior. In study and in the daily meditation of Sacred Scripture, Peter Damian discovered the mystical meaning of the Word of God, finding in it nourishment for his spiritual life. In this regard he described the hermit's cell as the "parlor in which God converses with men". For him, living as a hermit was the peak of Christian existence, "the loftiest of the states of life", because the monk, now free from the bonds of worldly life and of his own self, receives "a dowry from the Holy Spirit and his happy soul is united with its heavenly Spouse" (*Ep.* 18, 17; cf. *Ep.* 28, 43ff.). This is important for us today, too, even though we are not monks: to know how to make silence within us to listen to God's voice, to seek, as it were, a "parlor" in which God speaks with us: learning the Word of God in prayer and in meditation is the path to life.

Saint Peter Damian, who was essentially a man of prayer, meditation, and contemplation, was also a fine theologian: his reflection on various doctrinal themes led him to important conclusions for life. Thus, for example, he expresses with clarity and liveliness the Trinitarian doctrine, already using, under the guidance of biblical and patristic texts, the three fundamental terms which were subsequently to become crucial also for the philosophy of the West: *processio*, *relatio*, and *persona* (cf. *Opusc. XXXVIII: PL* 145, 633–642; and *Opusc.* II and III: *ibid.*, 41ff. and 58ff.). However, because theological analysis of the mystery led him to contemplate the intimate life of God and the dialogue of ineffable love between the three divine Persons, he drew ascetic conclusions from them for community life and even for relations between Latin and Greek Christians, divided on this topic. His meditation on the figure of Christ also had significant practical effects, since the whole of Scripture is centered on him. The "Jews", Saint Peter Damian notes, "through the pages of Sacred Scripture, bore Christ on their shoulders, as it were" (*Sermo XLVI*, 15). Therefore Christ, he adds, must be the center of the monk's life: "May Christ be heard in our language, may Christ be seen in our life, may he be perceived in our hearts" (*Sermo VIII*, 5). Intimate union with Christ engages not only monks but all the baptized. Here we find a strong appeal for us, too, not to let ourselves be totally absorbed by the activities, problems, and preoccupations of every day, forgetting that Jesus must truly be the center of our life.

Communion with Christ creates among Christians a unity of love. In Letter 28, which is a brilliant ecclesiological treatise, Peter Damian develops a profound theology of the Church as communion. "Christ's Church", he writes, is united by the bond of charity to the point that just as she has many members so is she, mystically, entirely contained in a single member; in such a way that the whole universal Church is rightly called the one Bride of Christ in the singular, and each chosen soul, through the sacramental mystery, is considered fully Church." This is important: not only that the whole universal Church should be united, but that the Church should be present in her totality in each one of us. Thus the service of the individual becomes "an expression of universality" (*Ep.* 28, 9–23). However, the ideal image of "Holy Church" illustrated by Peter Damian does not correspond—as he knew well—to the reality of his time. For this reason he did not fear to denounce the state of corruption that existed in the monasteries and among the clergy, because, above all, of the practice of the conferral by the lay authorities of ecclesiastical offices; various Bishops and

Abbots were behaving as the rulers of their subjects rather than as pastors of souls. Their moral life frequently left much to be desired. For this reason, in 1057 Peter Damian left his monastery with great reluctance and sorrow and accepted, if unwillingly, his appointment as Cardinal Bishop of Ostia. So it was that he entered fully into collaboration with the Popes in the difficult task of Church reform. He had seen that contemplation was not enough and had to forgo the beauty of contemplation in order to provide his own help in the work of the Church's renewal. He thus relinquished the beauty of the hermitage and courageously undertook numerous journeys and missions.

Because of his love for monastic life, ten years later, in 1067, he obtained permission to return to Fonte Avellana and resigned from the Diocese of Ostia. However, the tranquility he had longed for did not last long: two years later, he was sent to Frankfurt in an endeavor to prevent the divorce of Henry IV from his wife, Bertha. And again, two years later, in 1071, he went to Monte Cassino for the consecration of the abbey church and, at the beginning of 1072, to Ravenna, to re-establish peace with the local Archbishop, who had supported the antipope, bringing interdiction upon the city. On the journey home to his hermitage, an unexpected illness obliged him to stop at the Benedictine Monastery of Santa Maria Vecchia Fuori Porta in Faenza, where he died in the night between 22 and 23 February 1072.

Dear brothers and sisters, it is a great grace that the Lord should have raised up in the life of the Church a figure as exuberant, rich, and complex as Saint Peter Damian. Moreover, it is rare to find theological works and spirituality as keen and vibrant as those of the Hermitage at Fonte Avellana. Saint Peter Damian was a monk through and through, with forms of austerity which to us today might even seem excessive. Yet, in that way he made monastic life an eloquent testimony of God's primacy and an appeal to all to walk toward holiness, free from any compromise with evil. He spent himself, with lucid consistency and great severity, for the reform of the Church of his time. He gave all his spiritual and physical energies to Christ and to the Church, but always remained, as he liked to describe himself, *Petrus ultimus monachorum servus*, Peter, the lowliest servant of the monks.

(9 September 2009)

The Chair of Saint Peter

Today, the Latin-rite liturgy celebrates the Feast of the Chair of Saint Peter. This is a very ancient tradition, proven to have existed in Rome since the fourth century. On it we give thanks to God for the mission he entrusted to the Apostle Peter and his Successors. "Cathedra" literally means the established seat of the Bishop, placed in the mother church of a diocese, which for this reason is known as a "cathedral"; it is the symbol of the Bishop's authority and, in particular, of his "magisterium", that is, the evangelical teaching which, as a Successor of the Apostles, he is called to safeguard and to transmit to the Christian community. When a Bishop takes possession of the particular Church that has been entrusted to him, wearing his mitre and holding the pastoral staff, he sits on the *cathedra*. From this seat, as teacher and pastor, he will guide the journey of the faithful in faith, hope, and charity.

So what was the "Chair" of Saint Peter? Chosen by Christ as the "rock" on which to build the Church (cf. Mt 16:18), he began his ministry in Jerusalem, after the Ascension of the Lord and Pentecost. The Church's first "seat" was the Upper Room, and it is likely that a special place was reserved for Simon Peter in that room where Mary, Mother of Jesus, also prayed with the disciples. Subsequently, the See of Peter was Antioch, a city located on the Oronte River in Syria, today Turkey, which at the time was the third metropolis of the Roman Empire after Rome and Alexandria in Egypt. Peter was the first Bishop of that city, which was evangelized by Barnabas and Paul, where "the disciples were for the first time called Christians" (Acts 11:26) and, consequently, where our name "Christians" came into being. In fact, the Roman Martyrology, prior to the reform of the calendar, also established a specific celebration of the Chair of Peter in Antioch. From there, Providence led Peter to Rome. Therefore, we have the journey from Jerusalem, the newly born Church, to Antioch, the first center of the Church formed from pagans and also still united with the Church that came from the Jews. Then Peter went to Rome, the center of the Empire, the symbol of the "Orbis"—the "Urbs", which expresses "Orbis", the earth—where he ended his race at the service of the Gospel with martyrdom. So it is that the See of Rome, which had received the greatest of honors, also has the honor that Christ entrusted to Peter of being at the service of all the particular Churches for the edification and unity of the entire People of God.

The See of Rome, after Saint Peter's travels, thus came to be recognized as the See of the Successor of Peter, and its Bishop's "cathedra" represented the mission entrusted to him by Christ to tend his entire flock. This is testified by the most ancient Fathers of the Church, such as, for example, Saint Irenaeus, Bishop of Lyons, but who came from Asia Minor, who, in his treatise *Adversus Haereses*, describes the Church of Rome as the "greatest and most ancient, known by all ..., founded and established in Rome by the two most glorious Apostles, Peter and Paul"; and he added: "The universal Church, that is, the faithful everywhere, must be in agreement with this Church because of her outstanding superiority" (III, 3, 2–3). Tertullian, a little later, said for his part: "How blessed is the Church of Rome, on which the Apostles poured forth all their doctrine along with their blood!" (*De Praescriptione Hereticorum* 36). Consequently, the Chair of the Bishop of Rome represents not only his service to the Roman community but also his mission as guide of the entire People of God.

Celebrating the "Chair" of Peter, therefore, as we are doing today, means attributing a strong spiritual significance to it and recognizing it as a privileged sign of the love of God, the eternal Good Shepherd, who wanted to gather his whole Church and lead her on the path of salvation. Among the numerous testimonies of the Fathers, I would like to quote Saint Jerome's. It is an extract from one of his letters, addressed to the Bishop of Rome. It is especially interesting precisely because it makes an explicit reference to the "Chair" of Peter, presenting it as a safe harbor of truth and peace. This is what Jerome wrote: "I decided to consult the Chair of Peter, where that faith is found exalted by the lips of an Apostle; I now come to ask for nourishment for my soul there, where once I received the garment of Christ. I follow no leader save Christ, so I enter into communion with your beatitude, that is, with the Chair of Peter, for this I know is the rock upon which the Church is built" (cf. *Le lettere* I, 15, 1–2).

(22 February 2006)

10 March

Saint Marie Eugenie Milleret

Marie Eugenie Milleret reminds us first of all of the importance of the Eucharist in the Christian life and in spiritual growth. In fact, as she herself emphasizes, her First Holy Communion was an important moment, even if she was unaware of it at the time. Christ, present in the depths of her heart, was working within her, giving her time to follow her own pace and to pursue her inner quest, which was to lead her to the point of giving herself totally to the Lord in the religious life in response to the needs of her time. In particular, she realized how important it was to pass on to the young generations, especially young girls, an intellectual, moral, and spiritual training that would make them adults capable of taking charge of their family life and of making their contribution to the Church and society. Throughout her life she drew the strength for her mission from her life of prayer, ceaselessly combining contemplation and action. May the example of Saint Marie Eugenie invite men and women today to pass on to young people values that will help them to become strong adults and joyful witnesses of the Risen One! May young people never be afraid to welcome these moral and spiritual values, living them patiently and faithfully! In this way, they will build their personality and prepare for their future.

(3 June 2007)

18 March

Saint Cyril of Jerusalem

[Saint Cyril's] life is woven of two dimensions: on the one hand, pastoral care and, on the other, his involvement, in spite of himself, in the heated controversies that were then tormenting the Church of the East. Cyril was born at or near Jerusalem in 315 A.D. He received an excellent literary education which formed the basis of his ecclesiastical culture, centered on study of the Bible. He was ordained a priest by Bishop Maximus. When this Bishop died or was deposed in 348, Cyril was ordained a Bishop by Acacius, the influential Metropolitan of Caesarea in Palestine, a philo-Arian who must have been under the impression that in Cyril he had an ally; so as a result Cyril was suspected of having obtained his episcopal appointment by making concessions to Arianism.

Actually, Cyril very soon came into conflict with Acacius, not only in the field of doctrine but also in that of jurisdiction, because he claimed his own See to be autonomous from the Metropolitan See of Caesarea. Cyril was exiled three times within the course of approximately twenty years: the first time was in 357, after being deposed by a Synod of Jerusalem, followed by a second exile in 360, instigated by Acacius, and finally, in 367, by a third exile—his longest, which lasted eleven years—by the philo-Arian Emperor Valens. It was only in 378, after the Emperor's death, that Cyril could definitively resume possession of his See and restore unity and peace to his faithful.

Some sources of that time cast doubt on his orthodoxy, whereas other equally ancient sources come out strongly in his favor. The most authoritative of them is the Synodal Letter of 382 that followed the Second Ecumenical Council of Constantinople (381), in which Cyril had played an important part. In this Letter addressed to the Roman Pontiff, the Eastern Bishops officially recognized Cyril's flawless orthodoxy, the legitimacy of his episcopal ordination, and the merits of his pastoral service, which ended with his death in 387.

Of Cyril's writings, twenty-four famous catecheses have been preserved, which he delivered as Bishop in about 350. Introduced by a *Procatechesis* of welcome, the first eighteen of these are addressed to catechumens or candidates for illumination (*photizomenoi*) [candidates for Baptism]; they were delivered in the Basilica of the Holy Sepulcher. The first ones (nos. 1–5) treat, respectively, the prerequisites for Baptism, conversion from pagan morals, the Sacrament of Baptism, the ten dogmatic truths contained in the Creed or Symbol of the faith. The next catecheses (nos. 6–18) form an "ongoing catechesis" on the Jerusalem Creed in anti-Arian tones. Of the last five so-called "mystagogical catecheses", the first two develop a commentary on the rites of Baptism, and the last three focus on the Chrism, the Body and Blood of Christ, and the Eucharistic Liturgy. They include an explanation of the Our Father (*Oratio dominica*). This forms the basis of a process of initiation to prayer which develops on a par with the initiation to the three Sacraments of Baptism, Confirmation, and the Eucharist.

The basis of his instruction on the Christian faith also served to play a polemic role against pagans, Judeo-Christians, and Manichaeans. The argument was based on the fulfillment of the Old Testament promises, in a language rich in imagery. Catechesis marked an important moment in the broader context of the whole life—particularly liturgical—of the Christian community, in whose maternal womb the gestation of the future faithful took place, accompanied by prayer and the witness of the brethren. Taken as a whole, Cyril's homilies form a systematic catechesis on the Christian's rebirth through Baptism. He tells the catechumen: "You have been caught in the nets of the Church (cf. Mt 13:47). Be taken alive, therefore; do not escape, for it is Jesus who is fishing for you, not in order to kill you, but to resurrect you after death. Indeed, you must die and rise again (cf. Rom 6:11, 14).... Die to your sins and live to righteousness from this very day" (*Procatechesis* 5).

From the *doctrinal* viewpoint, Cyril commented on the Jerusalem Creed with recourse to the typology of the Scriptures in a "symphonic" relationship between the two Testaments, arriving at Christ, the center of the universe. The typology was to be described decisively by Augustine of Hippo: "In the Old Testament there is a veiling of the New, and in the New Testament there is a revealing of the Old" (*De catechizandis rudibus* 4, 8). As for the *moral* catechesis, it is anchored in deep unity to the doctrinal catechesis: the dogma progressively descends in souls, who are thus urged to transform their pagan behavior on the basis of new life in Christ, a gift of Baptism. The "mystagogical" catechesis, lastly, marked the summit of the instruction that Cyril imparted, no longer to catechumens, but to the newly baptized or neophytes during Easter week. He led them to discover the mysteries still hidden in the baptismal rites of the Easter Vigil. Enlightened by the light of a deeper faith by virtue of Baptism, the neophytes were at last able to understand these mysteries better, having celebrated their rites.

Especially with neophytes of Greek origin, Cyril made use of the faculty of sight, which they found congenial. It was the passage from the rite to the mystery that made the most of the psychological effect of amazement as well as the experience of Easter night. Here is a text that explains the mystery of Baptism:

> You descended three times into the water and ascended again, suggesting by a symbol the three days' burial of Christ, imitating Our Savior, who spent three days and three nights in the heart of the earth (cf. Mt 12:40). With the first emersion from the water, you celebrated the memory of the first day passed by Christ in the sepulcher; with the first immersion you confessed the first night passed in the sepulcher: for as he who is in the night no longer sees, but he who is in the day remains in the light, so in the descent, as in the night, you saw nothing, but in ascending again you were as in the day. And at the self-same moment you were both dying and being born; and that water of salvation was at once your grave and your mother.... For you ... the time to die goes hand in hand with the time to be born: one and the same time effected both of these events. (Cf. *Second Mystagogical Catechesis*, no. 4)

The mystery to be understood is God's plan, which is brought about through Christ's saving actions in the Church. In turn, the mystagogical dimension is accompanied by the dimension of symbols which express the spiritual experience they "explode". Thus, Cyril's catechesis, on the basis of the three elements described—doctrinal, moral, and lastly, mystagogical—proves to be a global catechesis in the Spirit. The mystagogical dimension brings about the synthesis of the two former dimensions, orienting them to the sacramental celebration in which the salvation of the whole man takes place.

In short, this is an integral catechesis which, involving body, soul, and spirit—remains emblematic for the catechetical formation of Christians today.

(27 June 2007)

19 March

Saint Joseph

Today, 19 March, is the Solemnity of Saint Joseph.... I like
to recall that beloved John Paul II was also very devoted
to Saint Joseph, to whom he dedicated the Apostolic Exhortation *Redemptoris Custos*, Guardian of the Redeemer,
and who surely experienced his assistance at the hour of
death.

The figure of this great saint, even though remaining
somewhat hidden, is of fundamental importance in the history of salvation. Above all, as part of the tribe of Judah,
he united Jesus to the Davidic lineage so that, fulfilling
the promises regarding the Messiah, the Son of the Virgin
Mary may truly be called the "son of David". The Gospel of Matthew highlights in a special way the Messianic
prophecies which reached fulfillment through the role that
Joseph played: the birth of Jesus in Bethlehem (2:1–6); his
journey through Egypt, where the Holy Family took refuge
(2:13–15); the title, the "Nazarene" (2:22–23). In all of this
he showed himself, like his spouse, Mary, an authentic heir
of Abraham's faith: faith in God, who guides the events of
history according to his mysterious salvific plan. His greatness, like Mary's, stands out even more because his mission
was carried out in the humility and hiddenness of the house
of Nazareth. Moreover, God himself, in the person of his
Incarnate Son, chose this way and style of life—humility
and hiddenness—in his earthly existence.

From the example of Saint Joseph we all receive a strong invitation to carry out with fidelity, simplicity, and modesty the task that Providence has entrusted to us. I think especially of fathers and mothers of families, and I pray that they will always be able to appreciate the beauty of a simple and industrious life, cultivating the conjugal relationship with care and fulfilling with enthusiasm the great and difficult educational mission.

To priests, who exercise a paternal role over Ecclesial Communities, may Saint Joseph help them love the Church with affection and complete dedication, and may he support consecrated persons in their joyous and faithful observance of the evangelical counsels of poverty, chastity, and obedience. May he protect workers throughout the world so that they contribute with their different professions to the progress of the whole of humanity, and may he help every Christian to fulfill God's will with confidence and love, thereby cooperating in the fulfillment of the work of salvation.

(19 March 2006)

23 March

Saint Turibius of Mongrovejo

Saint Turibius of Mongrovejo distinguished himself by working tirelessly and selflessly to build up and consolidate the Ecclesial Communities of his time. He did so in a great spirit of communion and collaboration, always seeking pathways to unity, as when he convoked the Third Provincial Council of Lima (1582–1583), which handed on a valuable patrimony of doctrine and pastoral norms. One of his most precious fruits was the so-called *Catechism of Saint Turibius*, which for centuries proved to be an extraordinarily effective instrument in providing thousands of persons with sound instruction in the faith in conformity with authentic Church doctrine. The lasting impact of Saint Turibius' work was that he was able to unite, at the deepest level and beyond any differences, all those who identify with one another because they have "one Lord, one faith, one baptism" (Eph 4:5).

(23 March 2006)

Translated by Andrew Matt.

25 March

The Annunciation of the Lord

In the Incarnation of the Son of God ... we recognize the origins of the Church. Everything began from there. Every historical realization of the Church and every one of her institutions must be shaped by that primordial wellspring. They must be shaped by Christ, the incarnate Word of God. It is he that we are constantly celebrating: Emmanuel, God-with-us, through whom the saving will of God the Father has been accomplished. And yet—today of all days we contemplate this aspect of the mystery—the divine wellspring flows through a privileged channel: the Virgin Mary. Saint Bernard speaks of this using the eloquent image of *aquaeductus* (cf. *Sermo in Nativitate B.V. Mariae: PL* 183, 437–448). In celebrating the Incarnation of the Son, therefore, we cannot fail to honor his Mother. The Angel's proclamation was addressed to her; she accepted it, and when she responded from the depths of her heart: "Here I am ... let it be done to me according to your word" (Lk 1:38), at that moment the eternal Word began to exist as a human being in time.

From generation to generation, the wonder evoked by this ineffable mystery never ceases. Saint Augustine imagines a dialogue between himself and the Angel of the Annunciation, in which he asks: "Tell me, O Angel, why did this happen in Mary?" The answer, says the Messenger, is contained in the very words of the greeting: "Hail, full of grace" (cf. *Sermo* 291:6). In fact, the Angel, "appearing to her", does not call her by her earthly name, Mary, but by her divine name, as she has always been seen and characterized by God: "Full of grace—*gratia plena*", . . . and the grace is none other than the love of God; thus, in the end, we can translate this word: "beloved" of God (cf. Lk 1:28). Origen observes that no such title had ever been given to a human being and that it is unparalleled in all of Sacred Scripture (cf. *In Lucam* 6:7). It is a title expressed in passive form, but this "passivity" of Mary, who has always been and is forever "loved" by the Lord, implies her free consent, her personal and original response: in *being loved*, in receiving the gift of God, Mary is fully *active*, because she accepts with personal generosity the wave of God's love poured out upon her. In this too, she is the perfect disciple of her Son, who realizes the fullness of his freedom and thus exercises the freedom through obedience to the Father. In the Second Reading, we heard the wonderful passage in which the author of the Letter to the Hebrews interprets Psalm 39 in the light of Christ's Incarnation: "When Christ came into the world, he said: . . . 'Here I am, I have come to do your will, O God'" (Heb 10:5–7). Before the mystery of these two "Here I am" statements, the "Here I am" of the Son and the "Here I am" of the Mother, each of which is reflected in the other, forming a single *Amen* to God's loving will, we are filled with wonder and thanksgiving, and we bow down in adoration. . . .

The icon of the Annunciation, more than any other, helps us to see clearly how everything in the Church goes back to that mystery of Mary's acceptance of the divine Word, by which, through the action of the Holy Spirit, the Covenant between God and humanity was perfectly sealed. Everything in the Church, every institution and ministry, including that of Peter and his Successors, is "included" under the Virgin's mantle, within the grace-filled horizon of her "yes" to God's will.

Everything in this world will pass away. In eternity only Love will remain. For this reason, my Brothers, ... let us commit ourselves to ensure that everything in our personal lives and in the ecclesial activity in which we are engaged is inspired by charity and leads to charity. In this respect too, we are enlightened by the mystery that we are celebrating today. Indeed, the first thing that Mary did after receiving the Angel's message was to go "in haste" to the house of her cousin Elizabeth in order to be of service to her (cf. Lk 1:39). The Virgin's initiative was one of genuine charity; it was humble and courageous, motivated by faith in God's Word and the inner promptings of the Holy Spirit. Those who love forget about themselves and place themselves at the service of their neighbor. Here we have the image and model of the Church! Every Ecclesial Community, like the Mother of Christ, is called to accept with total generosity the mystery of God who comes to dwell within her and guides her steps in the ways of love.

(25 March 2006)

* * *

The Annunciation, recounted at the beginning of Saint Luke's Gospel, is a humble, hidden event—no one saw it, no one except Mary knew of it—but at the same time it was crucial to the history of humanity. When the Virgin said her "yes" to the Angel's announcement, Jesus was conceived and with him began the new era of history that was to be ratified in Easter as the "new and eternal Covenant". In fact, Mary's "yes" perfectly mirrors that of Christ himself when he entered the world, as the Letter to the Hebrews says, interpreting Psalm 40[39]: "As is written of me in the book, I have come to do your will, O God" (Heb 10:7).

The Son's obedience was reflected in that of the Mother and thus, through the encounter of these two "yeses", God was able to take on a human face. This is why the Annunciation is a Christological feast as well, because it celebrates a central mystery of Christ: the Incarnation.

"Behold, I am the handmaid of the Lord, let it be done to me according to your Word." Mary's reply to the Angel is extended in the Church, which is called to make Christ present in history, offering her own availability so that God may continue to visit humanity with his mercy....

We often contemplate Our Lady, who on Calvary sealed the "yes" she pronounced at Nazareth. United to Christ, Witness of the Father's love, Mary lived martyrdom of the soul. Let us call on her intercession with confidence, so that the Church, faithful to her mission, may offer to the whole world a courageous witness of God's love.

(25 March 2007)

2 April

Saint Francis of Paola

Saint Francis of Paola, the renowned miracle worker from Calabria, was the Founder of the Order of Minims. His parents gave birth to him with much joy late in their lives through the intercession of Saint Francis of Assisi. Francis of Paola imitated that same spirit of humility and evangelical poverty and the special love of God, neighbor, and all creatures that belonged to his Patron Saint. He was also known for his spirit of penance, so much so that he and his companions lived out a perpetual vow of Lenten observance throughout the year. Everywhere he went, Francis of Paola promoted the reconciliation of kings and men with God and the Church. Diligent in his prayer life, he meditated constantly on the Passion of Christ crucified and cultivated a profound devotion to the Eucharist and to the Blessed Virgin Mary.

He was much loved and frequently called upon for help by the people. He resisted the abuse of power by kings and other leaders, denouncing without any hesitation the crimes and injustices they perpetrated. He distinguished himself by his obedience and love for the Supreme Pontiff, also offering him important advice on pressing issues of the day. This inspires me today, as it has many of my Predecessors, to call upon the heavenly aid of Saint Francis of Paola for myself

Translated by Andrew Matt.

and the whole Church and at the same time to propose him to the Church and the men and women of our time as a model of the spiritual life.

(2 April 2007)

4 April

Saint Isidore

Saint Isidore of Seville: He was a younger brother of Leander, Archbishop of Seville, and a great friend of Pope Gregory the Great. Pointing this out is important because it enables us to bear in mind a cultural and spiritual approach that is indispensable for understanding Isidore's personality. Indeed, he owed much to Leander, an exacting, studious, and austere person who created around his younger brother a family environment marked by the ascetic requirements proper to a monk and by a rhythm of work demanded by a serious dedication to study. Furthermore, Leander was concerned to prepare what was necessary to confront the political and social situation of that time: in those decades, in fact, the Visigoths, barbarians and Arians, had invaded the Iberian Peninsula and taken possession of territories that belonged to the Roman Empire. It was essential to regain them for the Roman world and for Catholicism. Leander and Isidore's home was furnished with a library richly endowed with classical pagan and Christian works. Isidore, who felt simultaneously attracted to both, was therefore taught under the stewardship of his elder brother to develop a very strong discipline, in devoting himself to study them with discretion and discernment.

Thus a calm and open atmosphere prevailed in the episcopal residence in Seville. We can deduce this from Isidore's cultural and spiritual interests, as they emerge from his works themselves, which include an encyclopedic knowledge of pagan classical culture and a thorough knowledge of Christian culture. This explains the eclecticism characteristic of Isidore's literary opus, which glided with the greatest of ease from Martial to Augustine or from Cicero to Gregory the Great. The inner strife that the young Isidore had to contend with, having succeeded his brother Leander on the episcopal throne of Seville in 599, was by no means unimportant. The impression of excessive voluntarism that strikes one on reading the works of this great author, considered to be the last of the Christian Fathers of antiquity, may, perhaps, actually be due to this constant struggle with himself. A few years after his death in 636, the Council of Toledo in 653 described him as "an illustrious teacher of our time and the glory of the Catholic Church".

Isidore was without a doubt a man of marked dialectic antitheses. Moreover, he experienced a permanent inner conflict in his personal life, similar to that which Gregory the Great and Saint Augustine had experienced earlier, between a desire for solitude to dedicate himself solely to meditation on the Word of God and the demands of charity to his brethren, for whose salvation, as Bishop, he felt responsible. He wrote, for example, with regard to Church leaders: "*The man responsible for a Church (vir ecclesiasticus)* must, on the one hand, allow himself to be crucified to the world with the mortification of his flesh and, on the other, accept the decision of the ecclesiastical order—when it comes from God's will—to devote himself humbly to government, even if he does not wish to" (*Sententiarum liber* III, 33, 1: *PL* 83, 705 B). Just a paragraph later he adds:

> Men of God (*sancti viri*) do not in fact desire to dedicate themselves to things of the world and groan when by some mysterious design of God they are charged with certain

responsibilities.... They do their utmost to avoid them but accept what they would like to shun and do what they would have preferred to avoid. Indeed, they enter into the secrecy of the heart and seek there to understand what God's mysterious will is asking of them. And when they realize that they must submit to God's plans, they bend their hearts to the yoke of the divine decision. (*Sententiarum liber* III, 33, 3: *PL* 83, 705–706)

To understand Isidore better it is first of all necessary to recall the complexity of the political situations in his time to which I have already referred: during the years of his boyhood he was obliged to experience the bitterness of exile. He was nevertheless pervaded with apostolic enthusiasm. He experienced the rapture of contributing to the formation of a people that was at last rediscovering its unity, both political and religious, with the providential conversion of Hermenegild, the heir to the Visigoth throne, from Arianism to the Catholic faith. Yet we must not underestimate the enormous difficulty of coming to grips with such very serious problems as the relations with heretics and with the Jews. There was a whole series of problems which appear very concrete to us today, too, especially if we consider what is happening in certain regions in which we seem almost to be witnessing the recurrence of situations very similar to those that existed on the Iberian Peninsula in that sixth century. The wealth of cultural knowledge that Isidore had assimilated enabled him constantly to compare the Christian newness with the Greco-Roman cultural heritage; however, rather than the precious gift of synthesis, it would seem that he possessed the gift of *collatio*, that is, of collecting, which he expressed in an extraordinary personal erudition, although it was not always ordered as might have been desired.

In any case, his deep concern not to overlook anything that human experience had produced in the history of his homeland and of the whole world is admirable. Isidore did not want to lose anything that man had acquired in the epochs of antiquity, regardless of whether they had been pagan, Jewish, or Christian. Hence, it should not come as a surprise if, in pursuing this goal, he did not always manage to filter the knowledge he possessed sufficiently through the purifying waters of the Christian faith as he would have wished. The point is, however, that in Isidore's intentions, the proposals he made were always in tune with the Catholic faith which he staunchly upheld. In the discussion of the various theological problems, he showed that he perceived their complexity and often astutely suggested solutions that summarize and express the complete Christian truth. This has enabled believers through the ages and to our times to profit with gratitude from his definitions. A significant example of this is offered by Isidore's teaching on the relations between active and contemplative life. He wrote: "Those who seek to attain repose in contemplation must first train in the stadium of active life; and then, free from the dross of sin, they will be able to display that pure heart which alone makes the vision of God possible" (*Differentiarum Lib. II*, 34, 133: *PL* 83, 91A). Nonetheless, the realism of a true pastor convinced him of the risk the faithful run of reducing themselves to one dimension. He therefore added: "The middle way, consisting of both of these forms of life, normally turns out to be more useful in resolving those tensions which are often aggravated by the choice of a single way of life and are instead better tempered by an alternation of the two forms" (*op. cit.*, 134; *ibid.*, col. 91B).

Isidore sought in Christ's example the definitive confirmation of a just orientation of life and said: "The Savior Jesus offers us the example of active life when during the day he devoted himself to working signs and miracles in the town, but he showed the contemplative life when he withdrew to the mountain and spent the night in prayer" (*op. cit.*, 134: *ibid.*). In the light of this example of the divine Teacher, Isidore can conclude with this precise moral teaching: "Therefore let the servant of God, imitating Christ, dedicate himself to contemplation without denying himself active life. Behaving otherwise would not be right. Indeed, just as we must love God in contemplation, so we must love our neighbor with action. It is therefore impossible to live without the presence of both the one and the other form of life, nor can we live without experiencing both the one and the other" (*op. cit.*, 135; *ibid.*, 91C). I consider that this is the synthesis of a life that seeks contemplation of God, dialogue with God in prayer and in the reading of Sacred Scripture, as well as action at the service of the human community and of our neighbor. This synthesis is the lesson that the great Bishop of Seville has bequeathed to us, Christians of today, called to witness to Christ at the beginning of a new millennium.

(18 June 2008)

Saint Joseph the Worker

Today, we are beginning the month of May with a liturgical Memorial very dear to the Christian people: that of Saint Joseph the Worker; and you know that my name is Joseph. Exactly fifty years ago it was established by Pope Pius XII of venerable memory to highlight the importance of work and of the presence of Christ and the Church in the working world. It is also necessary to witness in contemporary society to the "Gospel of work", of which John Paul II spoke in his Encyclical *Laborem Exercens*. I hope that work will be available, especially for young people, and that working conditions may be ever more respectful of the dignity of the human person.

(1 May 2005)

2 May

Saint Athanasius

Only a few years after his death, this authentic protagonist of the Christian tradition was already hailed as "the pillar of the Church" by Gregory Nazianzen, the great theologian and Bishop of Constantinople (*Orationes* 21, 26), and he has always been considered a model of orthodoxy in both East and West. As a result, it was not by chance that Gian Lorenzo Bernini placed his statue among those of the four holy Doctors of the Eastern and Western Churches—together with the images of Ambrose, John Chrysostom, and Augustine—which surround the Chair of Saint Peter in the marvelous apse of the Vatican Basilica.

Athanasius was undoubtedly one of the most important and revered early Church Fathers. But this great saint was above all the impassioned theologian of the Incarnation of the *Logos*, the Word of God who—as the Prologue of the Fourth Gospel says—"became flesh and dwelt among us" (Jn 1:14). For this very reason Athanasius was also the most important and tenacious adversary of the Arian heresy, which at that time threatened faith in Christ, reduced to a creature "halfway" between God and man, according to a recurring tendency in history which we also see manifested today in various forms. In all likelihood Athanasius was born in Alexandria, Egypt, in about the year 300 A.D. He received a good education before becoming a deacon and secretary to the Bishop of Alexandria, the great Egyptian metropolis. As a close collaborator of his Bishop, the young cleric took part with him in the Council of Nicaea, the first Ecumenical Council, convoked by the Emperor Constantine in May 325 A.D. to ensure Church unity. The Nicene Fathers were thus able to address various issues and primarily the serious problem that had arisen a few years earlier from the preaching of the Alexandrian priest Arius.

With his theory, Arius threatened authentic faith in Christ, declaring that the *Logos* was not a true God but a created God, a creature "halfway" between God and man who hence remained forever inaccessible to us. The Bishops gathered in Nicaea responded by developing and establishing the "Symbol of faith" ["Creed"] which, completed later at the First Council of Constantinople, has endured in the traditions of various Christian denominations and in the liturgy as the *Niceno-Constantinopolitan Creed.* In this fundamental text—which expresses the faith of the undivided Church and which we also recite today, every Sunday, in the Eucharistic celebration—the Greek term *homooúsios* is featured, in Latin *consubstantialis*: it means that the Son, the *Logos*, is "of the same substance" as the Father; he is God of God; he is his substance. Thus, the full divinity of the Son, which was denied by the Arians, was brought into the limelight.

In 328 A.D., when Bishop Alexander died, Athanasius succeeded him as Bishop of Alexandria. He showed straightaway that he was determined to reject any compromise with regard to the Arian theories condemned by the Council of Nicaea. His intransigence—tenacious and, if necessary, at times harsh—against those who opposed his episcopal appointment and especially against adversaries of the Nicene Creed, provoked the implacable hostility of the Arians and philo-Arians. Despite the unequivocal outcome of the Council, which clearly affirmed that the Son is of the same substance as the Father, these erroneous ideas shortly thereafter once again began to prevail—in this situation even Arius was rehabilitated—and they were upheld for political reasons by the Emperor Constantine himself and then by his son Constantius II. Moreover, Constantine was concerned not so much with theological truth but rather with the unity of the Empire and its political problems; he wished to politicize the faith, making it more accessible—in his opinion—to all his subjects throughout the Empire.

Thus, the Arian crisis, believed to have been resolved at Nicaea, persisted for decades with complicated events and painful divisions in the Church. At least five times—during the thirty years between 336 and 366 A.D.—Athanasius was obliged to abandon his city, spending seventeen years in exile and suffering for the faith. But during his forced absences from Alexandria, the Bishop was able to sustain and to spread in the West, first at Trier and then in Rome, the Nicene faith as well as the ideals of monasticism, embraced in Egypt by the great hermit Anthony with a choice of life to which Athanasius was always close. Saint Anthony, with his spiritual strength, was the most important champion of Saint Athanasius' faith. Reinstated in his See once and for all, the Bishop of Alexandria was able to devote himself to religious pacification and the reorganization of the Christian communities. He died on 2 May 373, the day when we celebrate his liturgical Memorial.

The most famous doctrinal work of the holy Alexandrian Bishop is his treatise: *De Incarnatione, On the Incarnation of the Word*, the divine *Logos* who was made flesh, becoming like one of us for our salvation. In this work Athanasius says with an affirmation that has rightly become famous that the Word of God "was made man so that we might be made God; and he manifested himself through a body so that we might receive the idea of the unseen Father; and he endured the insolence of men that we might inherit immortality" (54, 3). With his Resurrection, in fact, the Lord banished death from us like "straw from the fire" (8, 4). The fundamental idea of Athanasius' entire theological battle was precisely that God is accessible. He is not a secondary God; he is the true God, and it is through our communion with Christ that we can truly be united to God. He has really become "God-with-us".

Among the other works of this great Father of the Church—which remain largely associated with the events of the Arian crisis—let us remember the four epistles he addressed to his friend Serapion, Bishop of Thmuis, on the divinity of the Holy Spirit, which he clearly affirmed, and approximately thirty "Festal" Letters addressed at the beginning of each year to the Churches and monasteries of Egypt to inform them of the date of the Easter celebration but, above all, to guarantee the links between the faithful, reinforcing their faith and preparing them for this great Solemnity.

Lastly, Athanasius also wrote meditational texts on the Psalms, subsequently circulated widely, and, in particular, a work that constitutes the *bestseller* of early Christian literature: *The Life of Anthony*, that is, the biography of Saint Anthony Abbot. It was written shortly after this saint's death precisely while the exiled Bishop of Alexandria was staying with monks in the Egyptian desert. Athanasius was such a close friend of the great hermit that he received one of the two sheepskins which Anthony left as his legacy, together with the mantle that the Bishop of Alexandria himself had given to him. The exemplary biography of this figure dear to Christian tradition soon became very popular, almost immediately translated into Latin, in two editions, and then into various Oriental languages; it made an important contribution to the spread of monasticism in the East and in the West. It was not by chance that the interpretation of this text, in Trier, was at the center of a moving tale of the conversion of two imperial officials which Augustine incorporated into his *Confessions* (cf. 8, 6, 15) as the preamble to his own conversion.

Moreover, Athanasius himself showed he was clearly aware of the influence that Anthony's fine example could have on Christian people. Indeed, he wrote at the end of this work:

> The fact that his fame has been blazoned everywhere, that all regard him with wonder, and that those who have never seen him long for him is clear proof of his virtue and God's love of his soul. For not from writings or from worldly wisdom or through any art was Anthony renowned, but solely from his piety toward God. That this was the gift of God no one will deny. For from whence into Spain and into Gaul, how into Rome and Africa, was the man heard of who dwelt hidden in a mountain, unless it was God who makes his own known everywhere, who also promised this to Anthony at the beginning? For even if they work secretly, even if they wish to remain in obscurity, yet the Lord shows them as lamps to lighten all, that those who hear may thus know that the precepts of God are able to make men prosper and thus be zealous in the path of virtue. (*Life of Anthony* 93, 5–6)

Yes, brothers and sisters! We have many causes for which to be grateful to Saint Athanasius. His life, like that of Anthony and of countless other saints, shows us that "those who draw near to God do not withdraw from men, but rather become truly close to them" (*Deus Caritas Est*, no. 42).

(20 June 2007)

3 May

Saint Philip, Apostle

He always comes fifth in the lists of the Twelve (cf. Mt 10:3; Mk 3:18; Lk 6:14; Acts 1:13); hence, he is definitely among the first. Although Philip was of Jewish origin, his name is Greek, like that of Andrew, and this is a small sign of cultural openness that must not be underestimated. The information we have on him is provided by John's Gospel. Like Peter and Andrew, he is a native of Bethsaida (cf. Jn 1:44), a town that belonged to the Tetrarchy of a son of Herod the Great, who was also called Philip (cf. Lk 3:1).

The Fourth Gospel recounts that after being called by Jesus, Philip meets Nathanael and tells him: "We have found him of whom Moses in the law and also the prophets wrote, Jesus of Nazareth, the son of Joseph" (Jn 1:45). Philip does not give way to Nathanael's somewhat sceptical answer ("Can anything good come out of Nazareth?") and firmly retorts: "Come and see!" (Jn 1:46). In his dry but clear response, Philip displays the characteristics of a true witness: he is not satisfied with presenting the proclamation theoretically, but directly challenges the person addressing him by suggesting he have a personal experience of what he has been told. The same two verbs are used by Jesus when two disciples of John the Baptist approach him to ask him where he is staying. Jesus answers: "Come and see" (cf. Jn 1:38–39).

We can imagine that Philip is also addressing us with those two verbs that imply personal involvement. He is also saying to us what he said to Nathanael: "Come and see." The Apostle engages us to become closely acquainted with Jesus. In fact, friendship, true knowledge of the other person, needs closeness and indeed, to a certain extent, lives on it. Moreover, it should not be forgotten that according to what Mark writes, Jesus chose the Twelve primarily "to be with him" (Mk 3:14); that is, to share in his life and learn directly from him not only the style of his behavior, but above all who he really was. Indeed, only in this way, taking part in his life, could they get to know him and, subsequently, proclaim him. Later, in Paul's Letter to the Ephesians, one would read that what is important is to "learn Christ" (4:20): therefore, not only and not so much to listen to his teachings and words as rather to know him in person, that is, his humanity and his divinity, his mystery and his beauty. In fact, he is not only a Teacher but a Friend, indeed, a Brother. How will we be able to get to know him properly by being distant? Closeness, familiarity, and habit make us discover the true identity of Jesus Christ. The Apostle Philip reminds us precisely of this. And thus he invites us to "come" and "see", that is, to enter into contact by listening, responding, and communion of life with Jesus, day by day.

Then, on the occasion of the multiplication of the loaves, he received a request from Jesus as precise as it was surprising: that is, where could they buy bread to satisfy the hunger of all the people who were following him (cf. Jn 6:5). Then Philip very realistically answered: "Two hundred denarii would not buy enough bread for each of them to get a little" (Jn 6:7). Here one can see the practicality and realism of the Apostle, who can judge the effective implications of a situation. We then know how things went. We know that Jesus took the loaves and, after giving thanks, distributed them. Thus, he brought about the multiplication of the loaves. It is interesting, however, that it was to Philip himself that Jesus turned for some preliminary help with solving the problem: this is an obvious sign that he belonged to the close group that surrounded Jesus. On another occasion very important for future history, before the Passion some Greeks who had gone to Jerusalem for the Passover "came to Philip ... and said to him, 'Sir, we wish to see Jesus.' Philip went and told Andrew; Andrew went with Philip and they told Jesus" (cf. Jn 12:20–22). Once again, we have an indication of his special prestige within the Apostolic College. In this case, Philip acts above all as an intermediary between the request of some Greeks—he probably spoke Greek and could serve as an interpreter—and Jesus; even if he joined Andrew, the other Apostle with a Greek name, he was in any case the one whom the foreigners addressed. This teaches us always to be ready to accept questions and requests, wherever they come from, and to direct them to the Lord, the only one who can fully satisfy them. Indeed, it is important to know that the prayers of those who approach us are not ultimately addressed to us, but to the Lord: it is to him that we must direct anyone in need. So it is that each one of us must be an open road toward him!

There is then another very particular occasion when Philip makes his entrance. During the Last Supper, after Jesus affirmed that to know him was also to know the Father (cf. Jn 14:7), Philip quite ingenuously asks him: "Lord, show us the Father, and we shall be satisfied" (Jn 14:8). Jesus answered with a gentle rebuke: "Have I been with you so long, and yet you do not know me, Philip? He who has seen me has seen the Father; how can you say, 'Show us the Father'? Do you not believe that I am in the Father and the Father in me?... Believe me that I am in the Father and the Father in me" (Jn 14:9–11). These words are among the most exalted in John's Gospel. They contain a true and proper revelation. At the end of the Prologue to his Gospel, John says: "No one has ever seen God; the only Son, who is in the bosom of the Father, he has made him known" (Jn 1:18). Well, that declaration which is made by the Evangelist is taken up and confirmed by Jesus himself, but with a fresh nuance. In fact, whereas John's Prologue speaks of an explanatory intervention by Jesus through the words of his teaching, in his answer to Philip Jesus refers to his own Person as such, letting it be understood that it is possible to understand him not only through his words but, rather, simply through what he is. To express ourselves in accordance with the paradox of the Incarnation we can certainly say that God gave himself a human face, the Face of Jesus, and consequently, from now on, if we truly want to know the Face of God, all we have to do is to contemplate the Face of Jesus! In his Face we truly see who God is and what he looks like!

The Evangelist does not tell us whether Philip grasped the full meaning of Jesus' sentence. There is no doubt that he dedicated his whole life entirely to him. According to certain later accounts (*Acts of Philip* and others), our Apostle is said to have evangelized first Greece and then Frisia, where he is supposed to have died, in Hierapolis, by a torture described variously as crucifixion or stoning. Let us conclude our reflection by recalling the aim to which our whole life must aspire: to encounter Jesus as Philip encountered him, seeking to perceive in him God himself, the heavenly Father. If this commitment were lacking, we would be reflected back to ourselves as in a mirror and become more and more lonely! Philip teaches us instead to let ourselves be won over by Jesus, to be with him and also to invite others to share in this indispensable company; and in seeing, finding God, to find true life.

(6 September 2006)

3 May

Saint James, Apostle

He is ... included in the list of the Twelve Apostles personally chosen by Jesus and is always specified as "the son of Alphaeus" (Mt 10:3; Mk 3:18; Lk 5; Acts 1:13). He has often been identified with another James, called "the Younger" (cf. Mk 15:40), the son of a Mary (cf. *ibid.*), possibly "Mary the wife of Clopas", who stood, according to the Fourth Gospel, at the foot of the Cross with the Mother of Jesus (cf. Jn 19:25). He also came from Nazareth and was probably related to Jesus (cf. Mt 13:55; Mk 6:3); according to Semitic custom he is called "brother" (Mk 6:3; Gal 1:19). The book of the Acts of the Apostles emphasizes the prominent role that this latter James played in the Church of Jerusalem. At the Apostolic Council celebrated there after the death of James the Greater he declared, together with the others, that pagans could be received into the Church without first submitting to circumcision (cf. Acts 15:13). Saint Paul, who attributes a specific appearance of the Risen One to James (cf. 1 Cor 15:7), even named James before Cephas-Peter on the occasion of his visit to Jerusalem, describing him as a "pillar" of that Church on a par with Peter (cf. Gal 2:9). Subsequently, Judeo-Christians considered him their main reference point. The Letter that bears the name of James is also attributed to him and is included in the New Testament canon. In it, he is not presented as a "brother of the Lord" but as a "servant of God and of the Lord Jesus Christ" (Jas 1:1).

Among experts, the question of the identity of these two figures with the same name, James son of Alphaeus and James "the brother of the Lord", is disputed. With reference to the period of Jesus' earthly life, the Gospel traditions have not kept for us any account of either one of them. The Acts of the Apostles, on the other hand, reveal that a "James" played a very important role in the early Church, as we have already mentioned, after the Resurrection of Jesus (cf. Acts 12:17; 15:13–21; 21:18). His most important act was his intervention in the matter of the difficult relations between the Christians of Jewish origin and those of pagan origin: in this matter, together with Peter, he contributed to overcoming, or rather, to integrating the original Jewish dimension of Christianity with the need not to impose upon converted pagans the obligation to submit to all the norms of the Law of Moses. The Book of Acts has preserved for us the solution of compromise proposed precisely by James and accepted by all the Apostles present, according to which pagans who believed in Jesus Christ were to be asked only to abstain from the idolatrous practice of eating the meat of animals offered in sacrifice to the gods and from "impropriety", a term which probably alluded to irregular matrimonial unions. In practice, it was a question of adhering to only a few prohibitions of Mosaic Law held to be very important.

Thus, two important and complementary results were obtained, both of which are still valid today: on the one hand, the inseparable relationship that binds Christianity to the Jewish religion, as to a perennially alive and effective matrix, was recognized; and on the other, Christians of pagan origin were permitted to keep their own sociological identity which they would have lost had they been forced to observe the so-called "ceremonial precepts" of Moses. Henceforth, these precepts were no longer to be considered binding for converted pagans. In essence, this gave rise to a practice of reciprocal esteem and respect which, despite subsequent regrettable misunderstandings, aimed by its nature to safeguard what was characteristic of each one of the two parties.

The oldest information on the death of this James is given to us by the Jewish historian Flavius Josephus. In his *Jewish Antiquities* (20, 201ff.), written in Rome toward the end of the first century, he says that the death of James was decided with an illegal initiative by the High Priest Ananus, a son of the Ananias attested to in the Gospels; in the year 62, he profited from the gap between the deposition of one Roman Procurator (Festus) and the arrival of his successor (Albinus) to hand him over for stoning.

As well as the apocryphal Proto-Gospel of James, which exalts the holiness and virginity of Mary, Mother of Jesus, the Letter that bears his name is particularly associated with the name of this James. In the canon of the New Testament, it occupies the first place among the so-called "Catholic Letters", that is, those that were not addressed to any single particular Church—such as Rome, Ephesus, etc.—but to many Churches. It is quite an important writing which heavily insists on the need not to reduce our faith to a purely verbal or abstract declaration, but to express it in practice in good works. Among other things, he invites us to be constant in trials, joyfully accepted, and to pray with trust to obtain from God the gift of wisdom, thanks to which we succeed in understanding that the true values of life are not to be found in transient riches but rather in the ability to share our possessions with the poor and the needy (cf. Jas 1:27).

Thus, Saint James' Letter shows us a very concrete and practical Christianity. Faith must be fulfilled in life, above all, in love of neighbor and especially in dedication to the poor. It is against this background that the famous sentence must be read: "As the body apart from the spirit is dead, so faith apart from works is dead" (Jas 2:26). At times, this declaration by Saint James has been considered as opposed to the affirmations of Paul, who claims that we are justified by God not by virtue of our actions but through our faith (cf. Gal 2:16; Rom 3:28). However, if the two apparently contradictory sentences with their different perspectives are correctly interpreted, they actually complete each other. Saint Paul is opposed to the pride of man who thinks he does not need the love of God that precedes us; he is opposed to the pride of self-justification without grace, simply given and undeserved. Saint James, instead, talks about works as the normal fruit of faith: "Every sound tree bears good fruit, but the bad tree bears evil fruit", the Lord says (Mt 7:17). And Saint James repeats it and says it to us.

Lastly, the Letter of James urges us to abandon ourselves in the hands of God in all that we do: "If the Lord wills" (Jas 4:15). Thus, he teaches us not to presume to plan our lives autonomously and with self interest, but to make room for the inscrutable will of God, who knows what is truly good for us. In this way, Saint James remains an ever up-to-date teacher of life for each one of us.

(28 June 2006)

14 May

Saint Matthias, Apostle

We want to remember him who, after Easter, was elected in place of the betrayer. In the Church of Jerusalem two were proposed to the community, and then lots were cast for their names: "Joseph called Barsabbas, who was surnamed Justus, and Matthias" (Acts 1:23). Precisely the latter was chosen, hence, "he was enrolled with the eleven apostles" (Acts 1:26). We know nothing else about him except that he had been a witness to all Jesus' earthly events (cf. Acts 1:21–22), remaining faithful to him to the end. To the greatness of his fidelity was later added the divine call to take the place of Judas, almost compensating for his betrayal. We draw from this a final lesson: while there is no lack of unworthy and traitorous Christians in the Church, it is up to each of us to counterbalance the evil done by them with our clear witness to Jesus Christ, our Lord and Savior.

(18 October 2006)

19 May

Saint Maria Bernarda Bütler

At a very early age, Maria Bernarda Bütler, born in Auw in the Swiss canton of Aargau, experienced deep love for the Lord. As she herself said: "This is impossible to explain to someone who has not experienced the same thing." This love brought Verena Bütler, as she was then called, to enter the Capuchin Convent of Maria Hilf in Altstätten, where she made her final profession at the age of twenty-one. When she was forty, she received the call to the missions and went to Ecuador and then to Colombia.

On 29 October 1995, my venerable Predecessor John Paul II raised her to the honors of the altar, because of her life and her commitment to her neighbor.

Mother Maria Bernarda, a figure well-remembered and well-loved especially in Colombia, thoroughly understood that the banquet that the Lord has prepared for all people is represented in a very special way by the Eucharist.

In the Eucharist, Christ himself receives us as friends and gives himself to us at the table of the Bread and the Word of God, entering into deep communion with each one. The Eucharist is the source and pillar of the spirituality of this new Saint and of the missionary drive that impelled her to leave Switzerland, the land of her birth, to open

Translated in part by Andrew Matt.

herself to other horizons of evangelization in Ecuador and Colombia.

In the serious adversities that she was obliged to face, including exile, engraved in her heart she carried the exclamation of the Psalm we have heard today: "Even though I walk in the dark valley I fear no evil; for you are at my side" (Ps 23:4).

Thus, docile to the Word of God after Mary's example, she behaved like the servants mentioned in the Gospel narrative that we heard: she went everywhere proclaiming that the Lord invites everyone to his banquet. Thus she brought others to share in the love of God, to whom, throughout her life, she dedicated herself with faithfulness and joy.

Saint Maria Bernarda entrusted her life completely to God. In so doing she became an instrument of God's love, which she announced to the farthest frontiers of the earth. Following her example may we also commit ourselves to bearing the God of love and hope to all people.

(12 October 2008)

25 May

Saint Mary Magdalene de' Pazzi

Born in Florence on 2 April 1566 and baptized at the "beautiful Saint John" font with the name Caterina, Saint Mary Magdalene de' Pazzi showed a particular sensitivity to the supernatural from childhood and was attracted by intimate colloquy with God. As was the custom for children of noble families, her education was entrusted to the Dames of Malta, in whose monastery she received her First Holy Communion on 25 March 1576, and just some days later she consigned herself to the Lord forever with a promise of virginity. Returning to her family, she deepened her prayer life with the help of the Jesuit Fathers, who used to come to the palace. She cleverly did not allow herself to be conditioned by the worldly demands of an environment that, although Christian, was not sufficient to satisfy her desire to become more similar to her crucified Spouse. In this context she reached the decision to leave the world and enter the Carmel of Saint Mary of the Angels at Borgo San Frediano, where on 30 January 1583 she received the Carmelite habit and the name of Sister Mary Magdalene. In March of 1584, she fell gravely ill and asked to be able to make her profession ahead of time, and on 27 May, Feast of the Trinity, she was carried into the choir on her pallet, where she pronounced before the Lord her vows of chastity, poverty, and obedience forever.

From this moment an intense mystical season began which was also the source of the Saint's great ecstatic fame.

The Carmelites of Saint Mary of the Angels have five manuscripts in which are recorded the extraordinary experiences of their young Sister. "The Forty Days" of the summer of 1584 are followed by "The Colloquies" of the first half of the following year. The apex of the mystical knowledge that God granted of himself to Sister Mary Magdalene is found in "Revelations and Intelligences", eight days of splendid ecstasies from the vigil of Pentecost to the feast day of the Trinity in 1585. This was an intense experience that made her able at only nineteen years of age to span the whole mystery of salvation, from the Incarnation of the Word in the womb of Mary to the descent of the Holy Spirit on Pentecost. Five long years of interior purification followed—Mary Magdalene de' Pazzi speaks of it in the book of "The Probation"—in which her Spouse, the Word, takes away the sense of grace and leaves her like Daniel in the lions' den, amid many trials and great temptations. This is the context in which her ardent commitment to renew the Church takes place, after which, in the summer of 1586, splendors of light from on high came to show her the true state of the post-Tridentine era. Like Catherine of Siena, she felt "forced" to write some letters of entreaty to the Pope, Curial Cardinals, her Archbishop, and other ecclesial personages, for a decisive commitment to "The Renovation of the Church", as the title of the manuscript that contains them says. It consists of twelve letters dictated in ecstasy, perhaps never sent, but which remain as a testimony of her passion for the *Sponsa Verbi*.

With Pentecost of 1590 her difficult trial ended. She promised to dedicate herself with all her energy to the service of the community and in particular to the formation of novices. Sister Mary Magdalene had the gift to live communion with God in an ever more interior form, so as to become a reference point for the whole community, who still today continue to consider her "mother". The purified love that beat in her heart opened her to the desire for full conformity with Christ, her Spouse, even to sharing with him the "naked suffering" of the Cross. Her last three years of life were a true Calvary of suffering for her. Consumption began to manifest itself clearly: Sister Mary Magdalene was obliged to withdraw little by little from community life to immerse herself ever more in "naked suffering for love of God". She was oppressed by atrocious physical and spiritual pain which lasted until her death on Friday, 25 May 1607. She passed away at 3 P.M., while an unusual joy pervaded the entire monastery.

Within twenty years of her death, the Florentine Pontiff Urban VIII had already proclaimed her Blessed. Pope Clement IX inscribed her in the Roll of Saints on 28 April 1669. Her body has remained incorrupt and is the destination of constant pilgrimages. The monastery where the Saint lived is today the seat of the Archiepiscopal Seminary of Florence, which venerates her as their Patron, and the cell where she died has become a chapel in whose silence one can still feel her presence.

Saint Mary Magdalene de' Pazzi continues to be an inspiring spiritual figure for the Carmelites Nuns of the Ancient Observance. They see in her the "Sister" who has traveled the entire way of transforming union with God and who finds in Mary the "star" of the way to perfection. This great Saint has the gift of being a spiritual teacher for everyone, particularly for priests, for whom she always nourished a true passion.

I truly hope that the present jubilee celebrations commemorating her death will contribute to making ever better known this luminous figure, who manifests to all the dignity and beauty of the Christian vocation. As, while she was alive, grasping the bells she urged her Sisters with the cry:

"Come and love Love!" may the great Mystic, from Florence, from her Seminary, from the Carmelite monasteries that draw their inspiration from her, still make her voice heard in all the Church, spreading to every human creature the proclamation to love God.

(29 April 2007)

31 May

The Visitation of the Blessed Virgin Mary

On today's Feast of the Visitation, as in every passage of the Gospel, we see Mary docile to the divine plan and with an attitude of provident love for the brethren. In fact, the humble maiden from Nazareth, still amazed at what the Angel Gabriel had announced to her—that is, that she would be the mother of the promised Messiah—learned that her elderly kinswoman Elizabeth had in her old age also conceived a son. Mary immediately set out with haste for the house of her cousin, the Evangelist notes (cf. Lk 1:39), to offer her help at a time of special need. How can we fail to see that the hidden protagonist in the meeting between the young Mary and the by-then elderly Elizabeth is Jesus? Mary bears him in her womb as in a sacred tabernacle and offers him as the greatest gift to Zechariah, to Elizabeth, his wife, and also to the infant developing in her womb. "Behold", the mother of John the Baptist says, "when the voice of your greeting came to my ears, the babe in my womb leaped for joy" (Lk 1:44). Whoever opens his heart to the Mother encounters and welcomes the Son and is pervaded by his joy. True Marian devotion never obscures or diminishes faith and love for Jesus Christ Our Savior, the one Mediator between God and mankind. On the contrary, entrustment to Our Lady is a privileged path, tested by numerous saints, for a more faithful following of the Lord. Consequently, let us entrust ourselves to her with filial abandonment!

(31 May 2006)

1 June

Saint Justin Martyr

Saint Justin, Philosopher and Martyr, was the most important of the second-century apologist Fathers. The word
"apologist" designates those ancient Christian writers who
set out to defend the new religion from the weighty accusa-
tions of both pagans and Jews and to spread the Christian
doctrine in terms suited to the culture of their time. Thus,
the apologists had a twofold concern: that most properly
called "apologetic", to defend the newborn Christianity
(*apologhía* in Greek means, precisely, "defense"), and the
pro-positive, "missionary" concern, to explain the content
of the faith in a language and on a wavelength comprehen-
sible to their contemporaries.

Justin was born in about the year 100 near ancient
Shechem, Samaria, in the Holy Land; he spent a long time
seeking the truth, moving through the various schools of
the Greek philosophical tradition. Finally, as he himself
recounts in the first chapters of his *Dialogue with Tryphon*, a
mysterious figure, an old man he met on the seashore, initially led him into a crisis by showing him that it is impossible for the human being to satisfy his aspiration to the
divine solely with his own forces. He then pointed out to
him the ancient prophets as the people to whom to turn in
order to find the way to God and "true philosophy". In taking his leave, the old man urged him to pray that the gates
of light would be opened to him. The story foretells the

crucial episode in Justin's life: at the end of a long philosophical journey, a quest for the truth, he arrived at the Christian faith. He founded a school in Rome where, free of charge, he initiated students into the new religion, considered as the true philosophy. Indeed, in it he had found the truth and, hence, the art of living virtuously. For this reason he was reported and beheaded in about 165 during the reign of Marcus Aurelius, the philosopher-emperor to whom Justin had actually addressed one of his *Apologia*. These the two *Apologies* and the *Dialogue with the Hebrew, Tryphon*—are his only surviving works. In them, Justin intends above all to illustrate the divine project of creation and salvation, which is fulfilled in Jesus Christ, the *Logos*, that is, the eternal Word, eternal Reason, creative Reason. Every person as a rational being shares in the *Logos*, carrying within himself a "seed", and can perceive glimmers of the truth. Thus, the same *Logos* who revealed himself as a prophetic figure to the Hebrews of the ancient Law also manifested himself partially, in "seeds of truth", in Greek philosophy. Now, Justin concludes, since Christianity is the historical and personal manifestation of the *Logos* in his totality, it follows that "whatever things were rightly said among all men are the property of us Christians" (*Second Apology of Saint Justin Martyr* 13, 4). In this way, although Justin disputed Greek philosophy and its contradictions, he decisively oriented any philosophical truth to the *Logos*, giving reasons for the unusual "claim" to truth and universality of the Christian religion. If the Old Testament leaned toward Christ, just as the symbol is a guide to the reality represented, then Greek philosophy also aspired to Christ and the Gospel, just as the part strives to be united with the whole. And he said that these two realities, the Old Testament and Greek philosophy, are like two paths that lead to Christ, to the *Logos*. This is why Greek philosophy cannot be opposed to Gospel truth, and Christians can draw from it confidently as from a good of their own. Therefore, my venerable Predecessor, Pope John Paul II, described Saint Justin as a "pioneer of positive engagement with philosophical thinking—albeit with cautious discernment.... Although he continued to hold Greek philosophy in high esteem after his conversion, Justin claimed with power and clarity that he had found in Christianity 'the only sure and profitable philosophy' (*Dial.* 8, 1)" (*Fides et Ratio,* no. 38).

Overall, the figure and work of Justin mark the ancient Church's forceful option for philosophy, for reason, rather than for the religion of the pagans. With the pagan religion, in fact, the early Christians strenuously rejected every compromise. They held it to be idolatry, at the cost of being accused for this reason of "impiety" and "atheism". Justin in particular, especially in his first *Apology,* mercilessly criticized the pagan religion and its myths, which he considered to be diabolically misleading on the path of truth. Philosophy, on the other hand, represented the privileged area of the encounter between paganism, Judaism, and Christianity, precisely at the level of the criticism of pagan religion and its false myths. "Our philosophy ...": this is how another apologist, Bishop Melito of Sardis, a contemporary of Justin, came to define the new religion in a more explicit way (*Ap. Hist. Eccl.* 4, 26, 7).

In fact, the pagan religion did not follow the ways of the *Logos* but clung to myth, even if Greek philosophy recognized that mythology was devoid of consistency with the truth. Therefore, the decline of the pagan religion was inevitable: it was a logical consequence of the detachment of religion—reduced to an artificial collection of ceremonies, conventions, and customs—from the truth of being. Justin, and with him other apologists, adopted the clear stance taken by the Christian faith for the God of the philosophers against the false gods of the pagan religion. It was the choice of the *truth* of being against the myth of *custom*. Several decades after Justin, Tertullian defined the same option of Christians with a lapidary sentence that still applies: "*Dominus noster Christus veritatem se, non consuetudinem, cognominavit*—Christ has said that he is truth, not fashion" (*De Virgin. Vel.* 1, 1). It should be noted in this regard that the term *consuetudo*, used here by Tertullian in reference to the pagan religion, can be translated into modern languages with the expressions: "cultural fashion", "current fads".

In a time like ours, marked by relativism in the discussion on values and on religion—as well as in interreligious dialogue—this is a lesson that should not be forgotten. To this end, I suggest to you once again—and thus I conclude—the last words of the mysterious old man whom Justin the Philosopher met on the seashore: "Pray that, above all things, the gates of light may be opened to you; for these things cannot be perceived or understood by all, but only by the man to whom God and his Christ have imparted wisdom" (*Dial.* 7, 3).

(21 March 2007)

Saint Ephrem

Saint Ephrem the Syrian ... was born into a Christian family in Nisibis in about 306 A.D. He was Christianity's most important Syriac-speaking representative and uniquely succeeded in reconciling the vocations of theologian and poet. He was educated and grew up beside James, Bishop of Nisibis (303–338), and with him founded the theological school in his city. He was ordained a deacon and was intensely active in local Christian community life until 363, the year when Nisibis fell into Persian hands. Ephrem then emigrated to Edessa, where he continued his activity as a preacher. He died in this city in 373, a victim of the disease he contracted while caring for those infected with the plague. It is not known for certain whether he was a monk, but we can be sure in any case that he remained a deacon throughout his life and embraced virginity and poverty. Thus, the common and fundamental Christian identity appears in the specificity of his own cultural expression: faith, hope— the hope which makes it possible to live poor and chaste in this world, placing every expectation in the Lord—and lastly, charity, to the point of giving his life through nursing those sick with the plague.

Saint Ephrem has left us an important theological inheritance. His substantial opus can be divided into four categories: works written in ordinary prose (his polemic works or biblical commentaries); works written in poetic prose; homilies in verse; and lastly, hymns, undoubtedly Ephrem's most abundant production. He is a rich and interesting author in many ways, but especially from the theological point of view. It is the fact that theology and poetry converge in his work which makes it so special. If we desire to approach his doctrine, we must insist on this from the outset: namely, on the fact that he produces theology in poetical form. Poetry enabled him to deepen his theological reflection through paradoxes and images. At the same time, his theology became liturgy, became music; indeed, he was a great composer, a musician. Theology, reflection on the faith, poetry, song, and praise of God go together; and it is precisely in this liturgical character that the divine truth emerges clearly in Ephrem's theology. In his search for God, in his theological activity, he employed the way of paradoxes and symbols. He made ample use of contrasting images because they served to emphasize the mystery of God.

I cannot present much of his writing here, partly because his poetry is difficult to translate, but to give at least some idea of his poetical theology I would like to cite a part of two hymns. First of all, and also with a view to the approach of Advent, I shall propose to you *several* splendid images taken from his hymns *On the Nativity of Christ.* Ephrem expressed his wonder before the Virgin in inspired tones:

> The Lord entered her, and became a servant; the Word entered her, and became silent within her; thunder entered her, and his voice was still; the Shepherd of all entered her; he became a Lamb in her, and came forth bleating.
>
> The belly of your Mother changed the order of things, O you who order all! Rich he went in, he came out poor: the High One went into her [Mary], he came out lowly. Brightness went into her and clothed himself, and came forth a despised form....

He that gives food to all went in, and knew hunger. He
who gives drink to all went in, and knew thirst. Naked
and bare came forth from her the Clother of all things [in
beauty]. (Hymn *De Nativitate* 11:6–8)

To express the mystery of Christ, Ephrem uses a broad
range of topics, expressions, and images. In one of his
hymns he effectively links Adam (in Paradise) to Christ (in
the Eucharist):

It was by closing with the sword of the cherub that the
path to the tree of life was closed. But for the peoples, the
Lord of this tree gave himself as food in his (Eucharistic)
oblation.

The trees of the Garden of Eden were given as food
to the first Adam. For us, the gardener of the Garden in
person made himself food for our souls. Indeed, we had all
left Paradise together with Adam, who left it behind him.

Now that the sword has been removed here below (on
the Cross), replaced by the spear, we can return to it.
(*Hymn* 49:9–11)

To speak of the Eucharist, Ephrem used two images, embers
or burning coal and the pearl. The burning coal theme was
taken from the Prophet Isaiah (cf. 6:6). It is the image of
one of the seraphim who picks up a burning coal with tongs
and simply touches the lips of the Prophet with it in order to
purify them; the Christian, on the other hand, touches and
consumes the Burning Coal which is Christ himself:

In your bread hides the Spirit who cannot be consumed;
in your wine is the fire that cannot be swallowed. The
Spirit in your bread, fire in your wine: behold a wonder
heard from our lips.

The seraph could not bring himself to touch the glowing
coal with his fingers; it was Isaiah's mouth alone that it
touched; neither did the fingers grasp it nor the mouth

swallow it; but the Lord has granted us to do both these things. The fire came down with anger to destroy sinners, but the fire of grace descends on the bread and settles in it. Instead of the fire that destroyed man, we have consumed the fire in the bread and have been invigorated. (Hymn *De Fide* 10:8–10)

Here again is a final example of Saint Ephrem's hymns, where he speaks of the pearl as a symbol of the riches and beauty of faith:

I placed (the pearl), my brothers, on the palm of my hand, to be able to examine it. I began to look at it from one side and from the other: it looked the same from all sides. (Thus) is the search for the Son inscrutable, because it is all light. In its clarity I saw the Clear One who does not grow opaque; and in his purity, the great symbol of the Body of Our Lord, which is pure. In his indivisibility I saw the truth which is indivisible. (Hymn *On the Pearl* 1:2–3)

The figure of Ephrem is still absolutely timely for the life of the various Christian Churches. We discover him, in the first place, as a theologian who reflects poetically, on the basis of Holy Scripture, on the mystery of man's redemption brought about by Christ, the Word of God incarnate. His is a theological reflection expressed in images and symbols taken from nature, daily life, and the Bible. Ephrem gives his poetry and liturgical hymns a didactic and catechetical character: they are theological hymns yet at the same time suitable for recitation or liturgical song. On the occasion of liturgical feasts, Ephrem made use of these hymns to spread Church doctrine. Time has proven them to be an extremely effective catechetical instrument for the Christian community.

Ephrem's reflection on the theme of God the Creator is important: nothing in creation is isolated, and the world, next to Sacred Scripture, is a Bible of God. By using his freedom wrongly, man upsets the cosmic order. The role of women was important to Ephrem. The way he spoke of them was always inspired with sensitivity and respect: the dwelling place of Jesus in Mary's womb greatly increased women's dignity. Ephrem held that just as there is no redemption without Jesus, there is no Incarnation without Mary. The divine and human dimensions of the mystery of our redemption can already be found in Ephrem's texts; poetically and with fundamentally scriptural images, he anticipated the theological background and in some way the very language of the great Christological definitions of the fifth-century Councils.

Ephrem, honored by Christian tradition with the title "Harp of the Holy Spirit", remained a deacon of the Church throughout his life. It was a crucial and emblematic decision: he was a deacon, a servant, in his liturgical ministry and, more radically, in his love for Christ, whose praises he sang in an unparalleled way, and also in his love for his brethren, whom he introduced with rare skill to the knowledge of divine Revelation.

(28 November 2007)

11 June

Saint Barnabas, Apostle

Today let us turn our attention to some of Saint Paul's other collaborators. We must recognize that the Apostle is an eloquent example of a man open to collaboration: he did not want to do everything in the Church on his own but availed himself of many and very different colleagues. We cannot reflect on all these precious assistants because they were numerous. It suffices to recall, among others, Epaphras (cf. Col 1:7; 4:12; Phlm 23), Epaphroditus (cf. Phil 2:25; 4:18), Tychicus (cf. Acts 20:4; Eph 6:21; Col 4:7; 2 Tm 4:12; Ti 3:12), Urbanus (cf. Rom 16:9), Gaius and Aristarchus (cf. Acts 19:29; 20:4; 27:2; Col 4:10). And women such as Phoebe (Rom 16:1), Tryphaena and Tryphosa (cf. Rom 16:12), Persis, the mother of Rufus, whom Paul called "his mother and mine" (cf. Rom 16:12–13), not to mention married couples such as Prisca and Aquila (cf. Rom 16:3; 1 Cor 16:19; 2 Tm 4:19). Among this great array of Saint Paul's male and female collaborators, let us focus today on three of these people who played a particularly significant role in the initial evangelization: Barnabas, Silas, and Apollos.

Barnabas means "son of encouragement" (Acts 4:36) or "son of consolation". He was a Levite Jew, a native of Cyprus, and this was his nickname. Having settled in Jerusalem, he was one of the first to embrace Christianity after the Lord's Resurrection. With immense generosity, he sold a field which belonged to him and gave the money to the

Apostles for the Church's needs (Acts 4:37). It was he who vouched for the sincerity of Saul's conversion before the Jerusalem community that still feared its former persecutor (cf. Acts 9:27). Sent to Antioch in Syria, he went to meet Paul in Tarsus, where he had withdrawn, and spent a whole year with him there, dedicated to the evangelization of that important city in whose Church Barnabas was known as a prophet and teacher (cf. Acts 13:1). At the time of the first conversions of the Gentiles, therefore, Barnabas realized that Saul's hour had come. As Paul had retired to his native town of Tarsus, he went there to look for him. Thus, at that important moment, Barnabas, as it were, restored Paul to the Church; in this sense he gave back to her the Apostle to the Gentiles. The Church of Antioch sent Barnabas on a mission with Paul, which became known as the Apostle's first missionary journey. In fact, it was Barnabas' missionary voyage, since it was he who was really in charge of it and Paul had joined him as a collaborator, visiting the regions of Cyprus and Central and Southern Anatolia in present-day Turkey, with the cities of Attalia, Perga, Antioch of Pisidia, Iconium, Lystra, and Derbe (cf. Acts 13–14). Together with Paul, he then went to the so-called Council of Jerusalem, where after a profound examination of the question, the Apostles with the Elders decided to discontinue the practice of circumcision so that it was no longer a feature of the Christian identity (cf. Acts 15:1–35). It was only in this way that, in the end, they officially made possible the Church of the Gentiles, a Church without circumcision; we are children of Abraham simply through faith in Christ.

The two, Paul and Barnabas, disagreed at the beginning of the second missionary journey because Barnabas was determined to take with them as a companion John called Mark, whereas Paul was against it, since the young man had deserted them during their previous journey (cf. Acts 13:13;

15:36–40). Hence there are also disputes, disagreements, and controversies among saints. And I find this very comforting, because we see that the saints have not "fallen from Heaven". They are people like us, who also have complicated problems. Holiness does not consist in never having erred or sinned. Holiness increases the capacity for conversion, for repentance, for willingness to start again, and, especially, for reconciliation and forgiveness. So it was that Paul, who had been somewhat harsh and bitter with regard to Mark, in the end found himself with him once again. In Saint Paul's last Letters, to Philemon and in his Second Letter to Timothy, Mark actually appears as one of his "fellow workers". Consequently, it is not the fact that we have never erred but our capacity for reconciliation and forgiveness which makes us saints. And we can all learn this way of holiness. In any case, Barnabas, together with John Mark, returned to Cyprus (Acts 15:39) in about the year 49. From that moment we lose track of him. Tertullian attributes to him the Letter to the Hebrews. This is not improbable. Since he belonged to the tribe of Levi, Barnabas may have been interested in the topic of the priesthood; and the Letter to the Hebrews interprets Jesus' priesthood for us in an extraordinary way.

(31 January 2007)

22 June

Saint Paulinus of Nola

Paulinus, a contemporary of Saint Augustine to whom he was bound by a firm friendship, exercised his ministry at Nola in Campania, where he was a monk and later a priest and a Bishop. However, he was originally from Aquitaine in the South of France, to be precise, Bordeaux, where he was born into a high-ranking family. It was here, with the poet Ausonius as his teacher, that he received a fine literary education. He left his native region for the first time to follow his precocious political career, which was to see him rise while still young to the position of Governor of Campania. In this public office he attracted admiration for his gifts of wisdom and gentleness. It was during this period that grace caused the seed of conversion to grow in his heart. The incentive came from the simple and intense faith with which the people honored the tomb of a saint, Felix the Martyr, at the Shrine of present-day Cimitile. As the head of public government, Paulinus took an interest in this Shrine and had a hospice for the poor built and a road to facilitate access to it for the many pilgrims.

While he was doing his best to build the city on earth, he continued discovering the way to the city in Heaven. The encounter with Christ was the destination of a laborious journey, strewn with ordeals. Difficult circumstances which resulted from his loss of favor with the political authorities made the transience of things tangible to him. Once he had arrived at faith, he was to write: "The man without Christ is dust and shadow" (*Carm.* 10, 289). Anxious to shed light on the meaning of life, he went to Milan to attend the school of Ambrose. He then completed his Christian formation in his native land, where he was baptized by Bishop Delphinus of Bordeaux. Marriage was also a landmark on his journey of faith. Indeed, he married Therasia, a devout noblewoman from Barcelona, with whom he had a son. He would have continued to live as a good lay Christian had not the infant's death after only a few days intervened to rouse him, showing him that God had other plans for his life. Indeed, he felt called to consecrate himself to Christ in a rigorous ascetic life.

In full agreement with his wife, Therasia, he sold his possessions for the benefit of the poor and, with her, left Aquitaine for Nola. Here, the husband and wife settled beside the basilica of the patron saint, Felix, living henceforth in chaste brotherhood according to a form of life which also attracted others. The community's routine was typically monastic, but Paulinus, who had been ordained a priest in Barcelona, took it upon himself despite his priestly status to care for pilgrims. This won him the liking and trust of the Christian community, which chose Paulinus, upon the death of the Bishop in about 409, as his successor in the See of Nola. Paulinus intensified his pastoral activity, distinguished by special attention to the poor. He has bequeathed to us the image of an authentic Pastor of charity, as Saint Gregory the Great described him in chapter 3 of his *Dialogues*, in which he depicts Paulinus in the heroic gesture of offering himself as a prisoner in the place of a widow's son. The historical truth of this episode is disputed, but the figure of a Bishop with a great heart who knew how to make himself close to his people in the sorrowful trials of the barbarian invasions lives on.

Paulinus' conversion impressed his contemporaries. His teacher Ausonius, a pagan poet, felt "betrayed" and addressed bitter words to him, reproaching him, on the one hand, for his "contempt", considered insane, of material goods, and, on the other, for abandoning his literary vocation. Paulinus replied that giving to the poor did not mean contempt for earthly possessions but, rather, an appreciation of them for the loftiest aim of charity. As for literary commitments, what Paulinus had taken leave of was not his poetic talent—which he was to continue to cultivate—but poetic forms inspired by mythology and pagan ideals. A new aesthetic now governed his sensibility: the beauty of God incarnate, crucified, and risen, whose praises he now sang. Actually, he had not abandoned poetry but was henceforth to find his inspiration in the Gospel, as he says in this verse: "To my mind the only art is the faith, and Christ is my poetry" (*At nobis ars una fides, et musica Christus: Carm.* 20, 32).

Paulinus' poems are songs of faith and love in which the daily history of small and great events is seen as a history of salvation, a history of God with us. Many of these compositions, the so-called *Carmina natalicia*, are linked to the annual feast of Felix the Martyr, whom he had chosen as his heavenly Patron. Remembering Saint Felix, Paulinus desired to glorify Christ himself, convinced as he was that the Saint's intercession had obtained the grace of conversion for him: "In your light, joyful, I loved Christ" (*Carm.* 21, 373). He desired to express this very concept by enlarging the Shrine with a new basilica, which he had decorated in such a way that the paintings, described by suitable captions, would constitute a visual catechesis for pilgrims. Thus, he explained his project in a poem dedicated to another great catechist, Saint Nicetas of Remesiana, as he accompanied him on a visit to his basilicas: "I now want you to contemplate the paintings that unfold in a long series on the walls of the painted porticos. . . . It seemed to us useful to portray sacred themes in painting throughout the house of Felix, in the hope that when the peasants see the painted figure, these images will awaken interest in their astonished minds" (*Carm.* 27, vv. 511, 580–83). Today, it is still possible to admire the remains of these works which rightly place the Saint of Nola among the key figures of Christian archaeology.

Life in accordance with the ascetic discipline of Cimitile was spent in poverty and prayer and was wholly immersed in *lectio divina*. Scripture, read, meditated upon, and assimilated, was the light in whose brightness the Saint of Nola examined his soul as he strove for perfection. He told those who were struck by his decision to give up material goods that this act was very far from representing total conversion. "The relinquishment or sale of temporal goods possessed in this world is not the completion but only the beginning of the race in the stadium; it is not, so to speak, the goal, but only the starting point. In fact, the athlete does not win because he strips himself, for he undresses precisely in order to begin the contest, whereas he only deserves to be crowned as victorious when he has fought properly" (cf. *Ep.* 24, 7 to Sulpicius Severus).

After the ascetic life and the Word of God came charity; the poor were at home in the monastic community. Paulinus did not limit himself to distributing alms to them: he welcomed them as though they were Christ himself. He reserved a part of the monastery for them, and, by so doing, it seemed to him that he was not so much giving as receiving in the exchange of gifts between the hospitality offered and the prayerful gratitude of those assisted. He called the poor his "masters" (cf. *Ep.* 13, 11 to Pammachius) and, remarking that they were housed on the lower floor, liked to say that their prayers constituted the foundations of his house (cf. *Carm.* 21, 393–94).

Saint Paulinus did not write theological treatises, but his poems and ample correspondence are rich in a lived theology, woven from God's Word, constantly examined as a light for life. The sense of the Church as a mystery of unity emerges in particular from them. Paulinus lived communion above all through a pronounced practice of spiritual friendship. He was truly a master in this, making his life a crossroads of elect spirits: from Martin of Tours to Jerome, from Ambrose to Augustine, from Delphinus of Bordeaux to Nicetas of Remesiana, from Victricius of Rouen to Rufinus of Aquileia, from Pammachius to Sulpicius Severus and many others, more or less well known. It was in this atmosphere that the intense pages written to Augustine came into being. Over and above the content of the individual letters, one is impressed by the warmth with which the Saint of Nola sings of friendship itself as a manifestation of the one Body of Christ, enlivened by the Holy Spirit. Here is an important passage that comes at the beginning of the correspondence between the two friends: "It is not surprising if, despite being far apart, we are present to each other and, without being acquainted, know each other, because we are members of one body, we have one head, we are steeped in one grace, we live on one loaf, we walk on one road, and we dwell in the same house" (*Ep.* 6, 2). As can be seen, this is a very beautiful description of what it means to be Christian, to be the Body of Christ, to live within the Church's communion. The theology of our time has found the key to approaching the mystery of the Church precisely in the concept of communion. The witness of Saint Paulinus of Nola helps us to perceive the Church, as she is presented to us by the Second Vatican Council, as a sacrament of intimate union with God, hence, of unity among all of us and, lastly, among the whole human race (cf. *Lumen Gentium*, no. 1).

(12 December 2007)

24 June

The Birth of Saint John the Baptist

Saint John the Baptist [is] the only saint whose birth is commemorated because it marked the beginning of the fulfillment of the divine promises: John is that "prophet", identified with Elijah, who was destined to be the immediate precursor of the Messiah, to prepare the people of Israel for his coming (cf. Mt 11:14; 17:10–13). His Feast reminds us that our life is entirely and always "relative" to Christ and is fulfilled by accepting him, the Word, the Light, and the Bridegroom, whose voices, lamps, and friends we are (cf. Jn 1:1, 23; 1:7–8; 3:29). "He must increase, but I must decrease" (Jn 3:30): the Baptist's words are a program for every Christian.

(25 June 2006)

* * *

The liturgy invites us to celebrate the Solemnity of the Birth of Saint John the Baptist, whose life was totally directed to Christ, as was that of Mary, Christ's Mother. John the Baptist was the forerunner, the "voice" sent to proclaim the incarnate Word. Thus, commemorating his birth actually means celebrating Christ, the fulfillment of the promises of all the Prophets, among whom the greatest was the Baptist, called to "prepare the way" for the Messiah (cf. Mt 11:9–10).

All the Gospels introduce the narrative of Jesus' public life with the account of his baptism by John in the River

Jordan. Saint Luke frames the Baptist's entrance on the scene in a solemn historical setting. My book *Jesus of Nazareth* also begins with the Baptism of Jesus in the Jordan, an event which had enormous echoes in his day. People flocked from Jerusalem and every part of Judea to listen to John the Baptist and have themselves baptized in the river by him, confessing their sins (cf. Mk 1:5). The baptizing Prophet became so famous that many asked themselves whether he was the Messiah. The Evangelist, however, specifically denied this: "I am not the Christ" (Jn 1:20). Nevertheless, he was the first "witness" of Jesus, having received instructions from Heaven: "He on whom you see the Spirit descend and remain, this is he who baptizes with the Holy Spirit" (Jn 1:33). This happened precisely when Jesus, after receiving baptism, emerged from the water: John saw the Spirit descending upon him in the form of a dove. It was then that he "knew" the full reality of Jesus of Nazareth and began to make him "known to Israel" (Jn 1:31), pointing him out as the Son of God and Redeemer of man: "Behold, the Lamb of God, who takes away the sin of the world!" (Jn 1:29).

As an authentic prophet, John bore witness to the truth without compromise. He denounced transgressions of God's commandments, even when it was the powerful who were responsible for them. Thus, when he accused Herod and Herodias of adultery, he paid with his life, sealing with martyrdom his service to Christ, who is Truth in person. Let us invoke his intercession, together with that of Mary Most Holy, so that also in our day the Church will remain ever faithful to Christ and courageously witness to his truth and his love for all.

(24 June 2007)

25 June

Saint Maximus of Turin

Between the end of the fourth century and the beginning of
the fifth, another Father of the Church after Saint Ambrose
made a great contribution to the spread and consolidation
of Christianity in Northern Italy: Saint Maximus, whom
we come across in 398 as Bishop of Turin, a year after Saint
Ambrose's death. Very little is known about him; in com-
pensation, we have inherited a collection of about ninety of
his *Sermons*. It is possible to perceive in them the Bishop's
profound and vital bond with his city, which attests to an
evident point of contact between the episcopal ministry of
Ambrose and that of Maximus.

At that time serious tensions were disturbing orderly civil
coexistence. In this context, as Pastor and teacher, Maximus succeeded in obtaining the Christian people's support.
The city was threatened by various groups of barbarians.
They entered by the Eastern passes, which went as far as
the Western Alps. Turin was therefore permanently gar-
risoned by troops and at critical moments became a refuge
for the populations fleeing from the countryside and urban
centers where there was no protection. Maximus' interventions in the face of this situation testify to his commitment to respond to the civil degradation and disintegration.
Although it is still difficult to determine the social composition of those for whom the *Sermons* were intended, it
would seem that Maximus' preaching—to avoid the risk of

vagueness—was specifically addressed to a chosen nucleus of the Christian community of Turin, consisting of rich landowners who had property in the Turinese countryside and a house in the city. This was a clear-sighted pastoral decision by the Bishop, who saw this type of preaching as the most effective way to preserve and strengthen his own ties with the people.

To illustrate this view of Maximus' ministry in his city, I would like to point out, for example, *Sermons* 17 and 18, dedicated to an ever timely topic: wealth and poverty in Christian communities. In this context, too, the city was fraught with serious tensions. Riches were accumulated and hidden. "No one thinks about the needs of others", the Bishop remarked bitterly in his seventeenth *Sermon*. "In fact, not only do many Christians not share their own possessions, but they also rob others of theirs. Not only, I say, do they not bring the money they collect to the feet of the apostles, but in addition, they drag from priests' feet their own brethren who are seeking help." And he concluded: "In our cities there are many guests or pilgrims. Do what you have promised," adhering to faith, "so that what was said to Ananias will not be said to you as well: 'You have not lied to men, but to God'" (*Sermon* 17, 2–3).

In the next *Sermon*, the eighteenth, Maximus condemns the recurring forms of exploitation of others' misfortunes. "Tell me, Christian," the Bishop reprimands his faithful, "tell me why you snatched the booty abandoned by the plunderers? Why did you take home 'ill-gotten gains' as you yourself think, torn apart and contaminated?" "But perhaps", he continues, "you say you have purchased them, and thereby believe you are avoiding the accusation of avarice. However, this is not the way to equate purchasing with selling. It is a good thing to make purchases, but that means what is sold freely in times of peace, not goods looted during the sack of a city.... So act as a Christian and a citizen who purchases in order to repay" (*Sermon* 1, 3). Without being too obvious, Maximus thus managed to preach a profound relationship between a Christian's and a citizen's duties. In his eyes, living a Christian life also meant assuming civil commitments. Vice-versa, every Christian who, "despite being able to live by his own work, seizes the booty of others with the ferocity of wild beasts"; who "tricks his neighbor, who tries every day to nibble away at the boundaries of others, to gain possession of their produce", does not compare to a fox biting off the heads of chickens but rather to a wolf savaging pigs (*Sermon* 41, 4).

In comparison with the cautious, defensive attitude that Ambrose adopted to justify his famous project of redeeming prisoners of war, the historical changes that occurred in the relationship between the Bishop and the municipal institutions are clearly evident. By now sustained through legislation that invited Christians to redeem prisoners, Maximus, with the collapse of the civil authority of the Roman Empire, felt fully authorized in this regard to exercise true control over the city. This control was to become increasingly extensive and effective until it replaced the irresponsible evasion of the magistrates and civil institutions. In this context, Maximus not only strove to rekindle in the faithful the traditional love for their *hometown*, but he also proclaimed the precise duty to pay taxes, however burdensome and unpleasant they might appear (cf. *Sermon* 26, 2). In short, the tone and substance of the *Sermons* imply an increased awareness of the Bishop's political responsibility in the specific historical circumstances. He was "the lookout tower" posted in the city. Whoever could these watchmen be, Maximus wonders in *Sermon* 92, "other than the most blessed Bishops set on a lofty rock of wisdom, so to speak, to defend the peoples and to warn them about the evils approaching in the distance?" And in *Sermon* 89 the Bishop of Turin describes his tasks to his faithful, making a unique comparison between the Bishop's function and the function of bees: "Like the bee", he said, Bishops "observe bodily chastity, they offer the food of heavenly life using the sting of the law. They are pure in sanctifying, gentle in restoring, and severe in punishing." With these words, Saint Maximus described the task of the Bishop in his time.

In short, historical and literary analysis shows an increasing awareness of the political responsibility of the ecclesiastical authority in a context in which it continued de facto to replace the civil authority. Indeed, the ministry of the Bishop of Northwest Italy, starting with Eusebius, who dwelled in his Vercelli "like a monk", to Maximus of Turin, positioned "like a sentinel" on the highest rock in the city, developed along these lines. It is obvious that the contemporary historical, cultural, and social context is profoundly different. Today's context is rather the context outlined by my venerable Predecessor, Pope John Paul II, in the Post-Synodal Apostolic Exhortation *Ecclesia in Europa*, in which he offers an articulate analysis of the challenges and signs of hope for the Church in Europe today (nos. 6–22). In any case, regardless of the changed conditions, the believer's duties to his city and his homeland still remain valid. The intertwining of the obligations of the "honest citizen" with those of the "good Christian" has not in fact disappeared.

In conclusion, to highlight one of the most important aspects of the unity of Christian life, I would like to recall the words of the Pastoral Constitution *Gaudium et Spes*: consistency between faith and conduct, between Gospel and culture. The Council exhorts the faithful "to perform their duties faithfully in the spirit of the Gospel. It is a mistake to think that, because we have here no lasting city, but seek the city which is to come, we are entitled to shirk our earthly responsibilities; this is to forget that by our faith we are bound all the more to fulfill these responsibilities according to the vocation of each one" (no. 43). In following the magisterium of Saint Maximus and of many other Fathers, let us make our own the Council's desire that the faithful may be increasingly anxious to "carry out their earthly activity in such a way as to integrate human, domestic, professional, scientific, and technical enterprises with religious values, under whose supreme direction all things are ordered to the glory of God" (*ibid.*) and thus for the good of mankind.

(31 October 2007)

27 June

Saint Cyril of Alexandria

Linked to the Christological controversy which led to the Council of Ephesus in 431 and the last important representative of the Alexandrian tradition in the Greek Orient, Cyril was later defined as "the guardian of exactitude"—to be understood as guardian of the true faith—and even the "seal of the Fathers". These ancient descriptions express clearly a characteristic feature of Cyril: the Bishop of Alexandria's constant reference to earlier ecclesiastical authors (including, in particular, Athanasius), for the purpose of showing the continuity with tradition of theology itself. He deliberately, explicitly inserted himself into the Church's tradition, which he recognized as guaranteeing continuity with the Apostles and with Christ himself. Venerated as a saint in both East and West, in 1882 Saint Cyril was proclaimed a Doctor of the Church by Pope Leo XIII, who at the same time also attributed this title to another important exponent of Greek Patristics, Saint Cyril of Jerusalem. Thus are revealed the attention and love for the Eastern Christian traditions of this Pope, who later also chose to proclaim Saint John Damascene a Doctor of the Church, thereby showing that both the Eastern and Western traditions express the doctrine of Christ's one Church.

We have almost no information on Cyril's life prior to his election to the important See of Alexandria. He was a nephew of Theophilus, who had governed the Diocese of

Alexandria as Bishop since 385 A.D. with a prestigious and iron hand. It is likely that Cyril was born in this Egyptian metropolis between 370 and 380 A.D., was initiated into ecclesiastical life while he was still very young, and received a good education, both culturally and theologically. In 403, he went to Constantinople in the retinue of his powerful uncle. It was here that he took part in the so-called "Synod of the Oak", which deposed the Bishop of the city, John (later known as "Chrysostom"), and thereby marked the triumph of the Alexandrian See over its traditional rival, the See of Constantinople, where the Emperor resided. Upon his uncle Theophilus' death, the still young Cyril was elected in 412 as Bishop of the influential Church of Alexandria, which he governed energetically for thirty-two years, always seeking to affirm her primacy throughout the East, strong also because of her traditional bonds with Rome.

Two or three years later, in 417 or 418, the Bishop of Alexandria showed himself to be realistic in mending the broken communion with Constantinople, which had lasted by then since 406 as a consequence of Chrysostom's deposition. But the old conflict with the Constantinople See flared up again about ten years later, when in 428 Nestorius was elected, a severe and authoritarian monk trained in Antioch. The new Bishop of Constantinople, in fact, soon provoked opposition because he preferred to use as Mary's title in his preaching "Mother of Christ" (*Christotòkos*) instead of "Mother of God" (*Theotòkos*), already very dear to popular devotion. One reason for Bishop Nestorius' decision was his adherence to the Antiochean type of Christology, which, to safeguard the importance of Christ's humanity, ended by affirming the division of the Divinity. Hence, the union between God and man in Christ could no longer be true, so naturally it was no longer possible to speak of the "Mother of God".

The reaction of Cyril—at that time the greatest exponent of Alexandrian Christology, who intended, on the other hand, to stress the unity of Christ's person—was almost immediate, and from 429 he left no stone unturned, even addressing several letters to Nestorius himself. In the second of Cyril's letters to Nestorius (*PG* 77, 44–49), written in February 430, we read a clear affirmation of the duty of Pastors to preserve the faith of the People of God. This was his criterion, moreover, still valid today: the faith of the People of God is an expression of tradition; it is a guarantee of sound doctrine. This is what he wrote to Nestorius: "It is essential to explain the teaching and interpretation of the faith to the people in the most irreproachable way and to remember that those who cause scandal even to only one of the little ones who believe in Christ will be subjected to an unbearable punishment."

In the same letter to Nestorius—a letter which later, in 451, was to be approved by the Council of Chalcedon, the Fourth Ecumenical Council—Cyril described his Christological faith clearly: "Thus, we affirm that the natures are different that are united in one true unity, but from both has come only one Christ and Son; not because, due to their unity, the difference in their natures has been eliminated, but, rather, because divinity and humanity, reunited in an ineffable and indescribable union, have produced for us one Lord and Christ and Son." And this is important: true humanity and true divinity are really united in only one Person, Our Lord Jesus Christ. Therefore, the Bishop of Alexandria continued: "We will profess only one Christ and Lord, not in the sense that we worship the man together with the *Logos*, in order not to suggest the idea of separation by saying 'together', but in the sense that we worship only one and the same, because he is not extraneous to the *Logos*, his body, with which he also sits at his Father's side, not as if 'two sons' are sitting beside him, but only one, united with his own flesh."

And soon the Bishop of Alexandria, thanks to shrewd alliances, obtained the repeated condemnation of Nestorius: by the See of Rome, then with a series of twelve anathemas which he himself composed, and finally, by the Council held in Ephesus in 431, the Third Ecumenical Council. The assembly, which went on with alternating and turbulent events, ended with the first great triumph of devotion to Mary and with the exile of the Bishop of Constantinople, who had been reluctant to recognize the Blessed Virgin's right to the title of "Mother of God" because of an erroneous Christology that brought division to Christ himself. After thus prevailing against his rival and his doctrine, by 433 Cyril was nevertheless already able to achieve a theological formula of compromise and reconciliation with the Antiocheans. This is also significant: on the one hand is the clarity of the doctrine of faith, but in addition, on the other, the intense search for unity and reconciliation. In the following years he devoted himself in every possible way to defending and explaining his theological stance, until his death on 27 June 444.

Cyril's writings—truly numerous and already widely disseminated in various Latin and Eastern translations in his own lifetime, attested to by their instant success—are of the utmost importance for the history of Christianity. His commentaries on many of the New and Old Testament Books are important, including those on the entire Pentateuch, Isaiah, the Psalms, and the Gospels of John and Luke. Also important are his many doctrinal works, in which the defense of the Trinitarian faith against the Arian and Nestorian theses recurs. The basis of Cyril's teaching is the ecclesiastical tradition and in particular, as I mentioned, the writings of Athanasius, his great Predecessor in the See of Alexandria. Among Cyril's other writings, the books *Against Julian* deserve mention. They were the last great response to the anti-Christian controversies, probably dictated by the Bishop of Alexandria in the last years of his life to respond to the work *Against the Galileans*, composed many years earlier in 363 by the Emperor known as the "Apostate" for having abandoned the Christianity in which he was raised.

The Christian faith is first and foremost the encounter with Jesus, "a Person, which gives life a new horizon" (*Deus Caritas Est*, no. 1). Saint Cyril of Alexandria was an unflagging, staunch witness of Jesus Christ, the incarnate Word of God, emphasizing above all his unity, as he repeats in 433 in his first letter (*PG* 77, 228–237) to Bishop Succensus: "Only one is the Son, only one the Lord Jesus Christ, both before the Incarnation and after the Incarnation. Indeed, the *Logos* born of God the Father was not one Son and the one born of the Blessed Virgin another; but we believe that the very One who was born before the ages was also born according to the flesh and of a woman." Over and above its doctrinal meaning, this assertion shows that faith in Jesus the *Logos* born of the Father is firmly rooted in history because, as Saint Cyril affirms, this same Jesus came in time with his birth from Mary, the *Theotòkos*, and in accordance with his promise will always be with us. And this is important: God is eternal, he is born of a woman, and he stays with us every day. In this trust we live, in this trust we find the way for our life.

(3 October 2007)

Saint Irenaeus

Saint Irenaeus of Lyons. The biographical information on him comes from his own testimony, handed down to us by Eusebius in his fifth book on *Church History*. Irenaeus was in all probability born in Smyrna (today, Izmir in Turkey) in about 135–140, where in his youth, he attended the school of Bishop Polycarp, a disciple in his turn of the Apostle John. We do not know when he moved from Asia Minor to Gaul, but his move must have coincided with the first development of the Christian community in Lyons: here, in 177, we find Irenaeus listed in the college of presbyters. In that very year, he was sent to Rome bearing a letter from the community in Lyons to Pope Eleutherius. His mission to Rome saved Irenaeus from the persecution of Marcus Aurelius, which took a toll of at least forty-eight martyrs, including the ninety-year-old Bishop Pontinus of Lyons, who died from ill treatment in prison. Thus, on his return Irenaeus was appointed Bishop of the city. The new Pastor devoted himself without reserve to his episcopal ministry, which ended in about 202–203, perhaps with martyrdom.

Irenaeus was first and foremost a man of faith and a Pastor. Like a good Pastor, he had a good sense of proportion, a wealth of doctrine, and missionary enthusiasm. As a writer, he pursued a twofold aim: to defend true doctrine from the attacks of heretics and to explain the truth of the faith clearly. His two extant works—the five books of *The*

Detection and Overthrow of the False Gnosis and *Demonstration of the Apostolic Teaching* (which can also be called the oldest "catechism of Christian doctrine")—exactly corresponded with these aims. In short, Irenaeus can be defined as the champion in the fight against heresies. The second-century Church was threatened by the so-called *Gnosis*, a doctrine which affirmed that the faith taught in the Church was merely a symbolism for the simple who were unable to grasp difficult concepts; instead, the initiates, the intellectuals—*Gnostics*, they were called—claimed to understand what was behind these symbols and thus formed an elitist and intellectualist Christianity. Obviously, this intellectual Christianity became increasingly fragmented, splitting into different currents with ideas that were often bizarre and extravagant, yet attractive to many. One element these different currents had in common was "dualism": they denied faith in the one God and Father of all, Creator and Savior of man and of the world. To explain evil in the world, they affirmed the existence, besides the Good God, of a negative principle. This negative principle was supposed to have produced material things, matter.

Firmly rooted in the biblical doctrine of creation, Irenaeus refuted the Gnostic dualism and pessimism which debased corporeal realities. He decisively claimed the original holiness of matter, of the body, of the flesh no less than of the spirit. But his work went far beyond the confutation of heresy: in fact, one can say that he emerges as the first great Church theologian who created systematic theology; he himself speaks of the system of theology, that is, of the internal coherence of all faith. At the heart of his doctrine is the question of the "rule of faith" and its transmission. For Irenaeus, the "rule of faith" coincided in practice with the *Apostles' Creed*, which gives us the key for interpreting the Gospel, for interpreting the Creed in light of the Gospel.

The Creed, which is a sort of Gospel synthesis, helps us understand what it means and how we should read the Gospel itself.

In fact, the Gospel preached by Irenaeus is the one he was taught by Polycarp, Bishop of Smyrna, and Polycarp's Gospel dates back to the Apostle John, whose disciple Polycarp was. The true teaching, therefore, is not that invented by intellectuals, which goes beyond the Church's simple faith. The true Gospel is the one imparted by the Bishops, who received it in an uninterrupted line from the Apostles. They taught nothing except this simple faith, which is also the true depth of God's revelation. Thus, Irenaeus tells us, there is no secret doctrine concealed in the Church's common Creed. There is no superior Christianity for intellectuals. The faith publicly confessed by the Church is the common faith of all. This faith alone is apostolic; it is handed down from the Apostles, that is, from Jesus and from God. In adhering to this faith, publicly transmitted by the Apostles to their Successors, Christians must observe what their Bishops say and must give special consideration to the teaching of the Church of Rome, pre-eminent and very ancient. It is because of her antiquity that this Church has the greatest apostolicity; in fact, she originated in Peter and Paul, pillars of the Apostolic College. All Churches must agree with the Church of Rome, recognizing in her the measure of the true Apostolic Tradition, the Church's one common faith. With these arguments, summed up very briefly here, Irenaeus refuted the claims of these Gnostics, these intellectuals, from the start. First of all, they possessed no truth superior to that of the ordinary faith, because what they said was not of apostolic origin; it was invented by them. Secondly, truth and salvation are not the privilege or monopoly of the few, but are available to all through the preaching of the Successors of the Apostles, especially of the Bishop of Rome. In particular—once again disputing the "secret" character of the Gnostic tradition and noting its multiple and contradictory results—Irenaeus was concerned to describe the genuine concept of the Apostolic Tradition which we can sum up here in three points.

a. Apostolic Tradition is "public", not private or secret. Irenaeus did not doubt that the content of the faith transmitted by the Church is that received from the Apostles and from Jesus, the Son of God. There is no other teaching than this. Therefore, for anyone who wishes to know true doctrine, it suffices to know "the Tradition passed down by the Apostles and the faith proclaimed to men": a tradition and faith that "have come down to us through the succession of Bishops" (*Adversus Haereses* 3, 3, 3–4). Hence, the succession of Bishops, the personal principle, and Apostolic Tradition, the doctrinal principle, coincide.

b. Apostolic Tradition is "one". Indeed, whereas Gnosticism was divided into multiple sects, Church Tradition is one in its fundamental content, which—as we have seen—Irenaeus calls precisely *regula fidei* or *veritatis*: and thus, because it is one, it creates unity through the peoples, through the different cultures, through the different peoples; it is a common content like the truth, despite the diversity of languages and cultures. A very precious saying of Saint Irenaeus is found in his book *Adversus Haereses*:

> The Church, though dispersed throughout the world ... having received [this faith from the Apostles] ... as if occupying but one house, carefully preserves it. She also believes these points [of doctrine] just as if she had but one soul and one and the same heart, and she proclaims them and teaches them and hands them down with perfect harmony as if she possessed only one mouth. For, although the languages of the world are dissimilar, yet the import of the tradition is one and the same. For the Churches

which have been planted in Germany do not believe or hand down anything different, nor do those in Spain, nor those in Gaul, nor those in the East, nor those in Egypt, nor those in Libya, nor those which have been established in the central regions of the world. (1, 10, 1–2)

Already at that time—we are in the year 200—it was possible to perceive the Church's universality, her catholicity, and the unifying power of the truth that unites these very different realities, from Germany to Spain, to Italy, to Egypt, to Libya, in the common truth revealed to us by Christ.

c. Lastly, the Apostolic Tradition, as he says in the Greek language in which he wrote his book, is "pneumatic", in other words, spiritual, guided by the Holy Spirit: in Greek, the word for "spirit" is "*pneuma*". Indeed, it is a question of a transmission entrusted, not to the ability of more or less learned people, but to God's Spirit, who guarantees fidelity to the transmission of the faith. This is the "life" of the Church, what makes the Church ever young and fresh, fruitful with multiple charisms. For Irenaeus, Church and Spirit were inseparable: "This faith", we read again in the third book of *Adversus Haereses*, "which, having been received from the Church, we do preserve and which always, by the Spirit of God, renewing its youth as if it were some precious deposit in an excellent vessel, causes the vessel itself containing it to renew its youth also.... For where the Church is, there is the Spirit of God; and where the Spirit of God is, there is the Church and every kind of grace" (3, 24, 1).

As can be seen, Irenaeus did not stop at defining the concept of Tradition. His tradition, uninterrupted Tradition, is not traditionalism, because this Tradition is always enlivened from within by the Holy Spirit, who makes it live anew, causes it to be interpreted and understood in the vitality of the Church. Adhering to her teaching, the Church should transmit the faith in such a way that it must be what it appears, that is, "public", "one", "pneumatic", "spiritual". Starting with each one of these characteristics, a fruitful discernment can be made of the authentic transmission of the faith in the *today* of the Church. More generally, in Irenaeus' teaching, the dignity of man, body and soul, is firmly anchored in divine creation, in the image of Christ, and in the Spirit's permanent work of sanctification. This doctrine is like a "high road" in order to discern together with all people of good will the object and boundaries of the dialogue of values and to give an ever new impetus to the Church's missionary action, to the force of the truth which is the source of all true values in the world.

(28 March 2007)

29 June

Saints Peter and Paul, Apostles

"You are Peter, and on this rock I will build my Church" (Mt 16:18). What exactly was the Lord saying to Peter with these words? With them, what promise did he make to Peter and what task did he entrust to him? And what is he saying to us—to the Bishop of Rome, who is seated on the Chair of Peter, and to the Church today?

If we want to understand the meaning of Jesus' words, it is useful to remember that the Gospels recount for us three different situations in which the Lord, each time in a special way, transmits to Peter his future task. The task is always the same, but what the Lord was and is concerned with becomes clearer to us from the diversity of the situations and images used.

In the *Gospel according to Saint Matthew* that we have just heard, Peter makes his own confession to Jesus, recognizing him as the Messiah and Son of God. On the basis of this, his special task is conferred upon him through three images: the rock that becomes the foundation or cornerstone, the keys, and the image of binding and loosing. I do not intend here to interpret once again these three images that the Church down the ages has explained over and over again; rather, I would like to call attention to the geographical place and chronological context of these words. The promise is made at the sources of the Jordan, on the boundary of the Judaic Land, on the frontiers of the pagan world. The moment of the promise marks a crucial turning-point in Jesus' journey: the Lord now sets out for Jerusalem, and, for the first time, he tells the disciples that this journey to the Holy City is the journey to the Cross: "From that time Jesus began to show his disciples that he must go to Jerusalem and suffer many things from the elders and chief priests and scribes, and be killed, and on the third day be raised" (Mt 16:21). Both of these things go together and determine the inner place of the Primacy, indeed, of the Church in general: the Lord is continuously on his way toward the Cross, toward the lowliness of the servant of God, suffering and killed, but at the same time he is also on the way to the immensity of the world in which he precedes us as the Risen One, so that the light of his words and the presence of his love may shine forth in the world; he is on the way so that through him, the Crucified and Risen Christ, God himself, may arrive in the world. In this regard, Peter describes himself in his First Letter as "a witness of the sufferings of Christ as well as a partaker in the glory that is to be revealed" (I Pt 5:1). For the Church, Good Friday and Easter have always existed together; she is always both the mustard seed and the tree in whose boughs the birds of the air make their nests. The Church—and in her, Christ—still suffers today. In her, Christ is again and again taunted and slapped; again and again an effort is made to reject him from the world. Again and again the little barque of the Church is ripped apart by the winds of ideologies, whose waters seep into her and seem to condemn her to sink. Yet, precisely in the suffering Church, Christ is victorious. In spite of all, faith in him recovers ever new strength. The Lord also commands the waters today and shows that he is the Lord of the elements. He stays in his barque, in the little boat of the Church.

Thus, on the one hand, the weakness proper to human beings is revealed in Peter's ministry but, at the same time, also God's power: in the weakness of human beings itself the Lord shows his strength; he demonstrates that it is through frail human beings that he himself builds his Church. Let us now turn to the *Gospel according to Saint Luke,* which tells us that during the Last Supper, the Lord once again confers a special task upon Peter (cf. Lk 22:31–33). This time, the Lord's words addressed to Simon are found immediately after the Institution of the Most Blessed Eucharist. The Lord has just given himself to his followers under the species of bread and wine. We can see the Institution of the Eucharist as the true and proper founding act of the Church. Through the Eucharist, the Lord not only gives himself to his own but also gives them the reality of a new communion among themselves which is extended in time, "until he comes" (cf. I Cor 11:26). Through the Eucharist, the disciples become his living dwelling-place, which, as history unfolds, grows like the new and living temple of God in this world. Thus, immediately after the Institution of the Sacrament, Jesus speaks of what being disciples, of what the "ministry", means in the new community: he says that it is a commitment of service, just as he himself is among them as One who serves. And then he addresses Peter. He says that Satan has demanded to have him so that he may sift him like wheat. This calls to mind the passage in the *Book of Job,* where Satan asks God for the power to afflict Job. The devil—the slanderer of God and men—thereby wants to prove that no true religious feeling exists, but that in man every aim is always solely utilitarian. In the case of Job, God grants Satan the asked-for freedom precisely to be able by so doing to defend his creature—man—and himself. And this also happens with Jesus' disciples. God gives a certain liberty to Satan in all times. To us it oftentimes seems that God allows Satan too much freedom, that he grants him the power to distress us too terribly; and that this gets the better of our forces and oppresses us too heavily. Again and again we cry out to God: "Alas, look at the misery of your disciples! Ah, protect us!" In fact, Jesus continues: "I have prayed for you that your faith may not fail" (Lk 22:32). Jesus' prayer is the limit set upon the power of the devil. Jesus' prayer is the protection of the Church. We can seek refuge under this protection, cling to it and be safe. But—as he says in the Gospel—Jesus prays in a particular way for Peter: "... that your faith may not fail". Jesus' prayer is at the same time a promise and a duty. Jesus' prayer safeguards Peter's faith, that faith which he confessed at Caesarea Philippi: "You are the Christ, the Son of the living God" (Mt 16:16). And so, never let this faith be silenced; strengthen it over and over again, even in the face of the Cross and all the world's contradictions: this is Peter's task. Therefore, the point is that the Lord prays not only for Peter's personal faith, but for his faith as a service to others. This is exactly what he means with the words: "When you have turned again, strengthen your brethren" (Lk 22:32).

"When you have turned again": these words are at the same time a prophecy and a promise. They prophesy the weakness of Simon, who was to deny to a maid and a servant that he knew Christ. Through this fall, Peter—and with him the Church of all times—has to learn that one's own strength alone does not suffice to build and guide the Lord's Church. No one succeeds on his own. However capable and clever Peter may seem—already at the first moment of trial he fails. "When you have turned again": the Lord, who predicted his fall, also promises him conversion: "And the Lord turned and looked at Peter ..." (Lk 22:61). Jesus' look works the transformation and becomes Peter's salvation: "he went out and wept bitterly" (Lk 22:62). Let us implore ever anew this saving gaze of Jesus: for all those who have responsibility in the Church; for all who suffer the bewilderment of

these times; for the great and for the small: Lord, look at us
ever anew, pick us up every time we fall, and take us in your
good hands.

It is through the promise of his prayer that the Lord
entrusts to Peter the task for the brethren. Peter's responsibility is anchored in Jesus' prayer. It is this that gives him
the certainty that he will persevere through all human mis-
eries. And the Lord entrusts this task to him in the context of the Supper, in connection with the gift of the Most
Holy Eucharist. The Church, established in the Institution
of the Eucharist, in her inmost self is a Eucharistic community, hence, communion in the Body of the Lord. Peter's
task is to preside over this universal communion; to keep
it present in the world also as visible, incarnate unity. He,
together with the whole Church of Rome—as Saint Ignatius of Antioch said—must preside in charity: preside over
the community with that love which comes from Christ
and ever anew surpasses the limitations of the private sphere
to bring God's love to the ends of the earth.

The third reference to the Primacy is found in the *Gospel
according to Saint John* (21:15–19). The Lord is risen, and as the
Risen One he entrusts his flock to Peter. Here too, the Cross
and the Resurrection are interconnected. Jesus predicts to
Peter that he is to take the way of the Cross. In this Basilica
built over the tomb of Peter—a tomb of the poor—we see
that in this very way the Lord, through the Cross, is always
victorious. His power is not a power according to the ways of
this world. It is the power of goodness: of truth and of love,
which is stronger than death. Yes, his promise is true: the
powers of death, the gates of hell, will not prevail against the
Church which he built on Peter (cf. Mt 16:18) and which he,
in this very way, continues to build personally.

(29 June 2006)

The Most Sacred Heart of Jesus

The Solemnity of the Most Sacred Heart of Jesus [is] a devotion that is deeply rooted in the Christian people. In biblical language, "heart" indicates the center of the person where his sentiments and intentions dwell. In the Heart of the Redeemer we adore God's love for humanity, his will for universal salvation, his infinite mercy. Practicing devotion to the Sacred Heart of Christ therefore means adoring that Heart which, after having loved us to the end, was pierced by a spear and from high on the Cross poured out blood and water, an inexhaustible source of new life.

(5 June 2005)

* * *

It was traditional—and in some countries, still is—to consecrate families to the Sacred Heart, whose image they would keep in their homes. The devotion is rooted in the mystery of the Incarnation; it is precisely through the Heart of Jesus that the Love of God for humanity is sublimely manifested. This is why authentic devotion to the Sacred Heart has retained all its effectiveness and especially attracts souls thirsting for God's mercy, who find in it the inexhaustible source from which to draw the water of Life that can irrigate the deserts of the soul and make hope flourish anew.

The Solemnity of the Sacred Heart is also the World Day of Prayer for the Sanctification of Priests: I take the opportunity to invite all of you, dear brothers and sisters, to pray for priests always, so that they will be effective witnesses of Christ's love.

(25 June 2006)

The Immaculate Heart of Mary

The heart that resembles that of Christ more than any other is without a doubt the Heart of Mary, his Immaculate Mother, and for this very reason the liturgy holds them up together for our veneration. Responding to the Virgin's invitation at Fatima, let us entrust the whole world to her Immaculate Heart, which we contemplated yesterday in a special way, so that it may experience the merciful love of God and know true peace.

(5 June 2005)

3 JULY

Saint Thomas, Apostle

Ever present in the four lists [of Apostles] compiled by the
New Testament, in the first three Gospels [Saint Thomas]
is placed next to Matthew (cf. Mt 10:3; Mk 3:18; Lk 6:15),
whereas in Acts, he is found after Philip (cf. Acts 1:13).
His name derives from a Hebrew root, ta'am, which means
"paired, twin". In fact, John's Gospel several times calls him
"Didymus" (cf. Jn 11:16; 20:24; 21:2), a Greek nickname for,
precisely, "twin". The reason for this nickname is unclear.

It is above all the Fourth Gospel that gives us information that outlines some important traits of his personality.
The first concerns his exhortation to the other Apostles
when Jesus, at a critical moment in his life, decided to go to
Bethany to raise Lazarus, thus coming dangerously close to
Jerusalem (Mk 10:32). On that occasion Thomas said to his
fellow disciples: "Let us also go, that we may die with him"
(Jn 11:16). His determination to follow his Master is truly
exemplary and offers us a valuable lesson: it reveals his total
readiness to stand by Jesus, to the point of identifying his
own destiny with that of Jesus and of desiring to share with
him the supreme trial of death. In fact, the most important thing is never to distance oneself from Jesus. Moreover,
when the Gospels use the verb "to follow", it means that
where he goes, his disciple must also go. Thus, Christian life
is defined as a life with Jesus Christ, a life to spend together
with him. Saint Paul writes something similar when he

assures the Christians of Corinth: "You are in our hearts, to die together and to live together" (2 Cor 7:3). What takes place between the Apostle and his Christians must obviously apply first of all to the relationship between Christians and Jesus himself: dying together, living together, being in his Heart as he is in ours.

A second intervention by Thomas is recorded at the Last Supper. On that occasion, predicting his own imminent departure, Jesus announced that he was going to prepare a place for his disciples so that they could be where he is found; and he explains to them: "Where [I] am going you know the way" (Jn 14:4). It is then that Thomas intervenes, saying: "Lord, we do not know where you are going; how can we know the way?" (Jn 14:5). In fact, with this remark he places himself at a rather low level of understanding; but his words provide Jesus with the opportunity to pronounce his famous definition: "I am the Way, and the Truth, and the Life" (Jn 14:6). Thus, it is primarily to Thomas that he makes this revelation, but it is valid for all of us and for every age. Every time we hear or read these words, we can stand beside Thomas in spirit and imagine that the Lord is also speaking to us, just as he spoke to him. At the same time, his question also confers upon us the right, so to speak, to ask Jesus for explanations. We often do not understand him. Let us be brave enough to say: "I do not understand you, Lord; listen to me, help me to understand." In such a way, with this frankness which is the true way of praying, of speaking to Jesus, we express our meager capacity to understand and at the same time place ourselves in the trusting attitude of someone who expects light and strength from the One able to provide them.

Then, the proverbial scene of the doubting Thomas that occurred eight days after Easter is very well known. At first he did not believe that Jesus had appeared in his absence and said: "Unless I see in his hands the print of the nails, and place my finger in the mark of the nails, and place my hand in his side, I will not believe" (Jn 20:25). Basically, from these words emerges the conviction that Jesus can now be recognized by his wounds rather than by his face. Thomas holds that the signs that confirm Jesus' identity are now above all his wounds, in which he reveals to us how much he loved us. In this the Apostle is not mistaken. As we know, Jesus reappeared among his disciples eight days later, and this time Thomas was present. Jesus summons him: "Put your finger here, and see my hands; and put out your hand, and place it in my side; do not be faithless, but believing" (Jn 20:27). Thomas reacts with the most splendid profession of faith in the whole of the New Testament: "My Lord and my God!" (Jn 20:28). Saint Augustine comments on this: Thomas "saw and touched the man, and acknowledged the God whom he neither saw nor touched; but by the means of what he saw and touched, he now put far away from him every doubt, and believed the other" (*In ev. Jo.*, 121, 5). The Evangelist continues with Jesus' last words to Thomas: "Have you believed because you have seen me? Blessed are those who have not seen and yet believe" (Jn 20:29). This sentence can also be put into the present: "Blessed are those who do not see and yet believe." In any case, here Jesus spells out a fundamental principle for Christians who will come after Thomas, hence, for all of us. It is interesting to note that another Thomas, the great medieval theologian of Aquino, juxtaposed this formula of blessedness with the apparently opposite one recorded by Luke: "Blessed are the eyes which see what you see!" (Lk 10:23). However, Aquinas comments: "Those who believe without seeing are more meritorious than those who, seeing, believe" (*In Johann.*, XX *lectio*, VI, 2566). In fact, the Letter to the Hebrews, recalling the whole series of the ancient biblical Patriarchs who believed in God without seeing the fulfillment of his promises, defines faith as "the assurance of things hoped for, the conviction of things not seen" (Heb 11:1). The Apostle Thomas' case is important to us for at least three reasons: first, because it comforts us in our insecurity; second, because it shows us that every doubt can lead to an outcome brighter than any uncertainty; and, lastly, because the words that Jesus addressed to him remind us of the true meaning of mature faith and encourage us to persevere, despite the difficulty, along our journey of adhesion to him.

A final point concerning Thomas is preserved for us in the Fourth Gospel, which presents him as a witness of the Risen One in the subsequent event of the miraculous catch in the Sea of Tiberias (cf. Jn 21:2ff.). On that occasion, Thomas is even mentioned immediately after Simon Peter: an evident sign of the considerable importance that he enjoyed in the context of the early Christian communities. Indeed, the *Acts* and the *Gospel of Thomas*, both apocryphal works but in any case important for the study of Christian origins, were written in his name. Lastly, let us remember that an ancient tradition claims that Thomas first evangelized Syria and Persia (mentioned by Origen, according to Eusebius of Caesarea, *Hist. eccles.*, III, 1), then went on to Western India (cf. *Acts of Thomas*, 1–2 and 17ff.), from where also he finally reached Southern India. Let us end our reflection in this missionary perspective, expressing the hope that Thomas' example will never fail to strengthen our faith in Jesus Christ, Our Lord and Our God.

(27 September 2006)

8 JULY

Saints Aquila and Priscilla

The names Aquila and Priscilla are Latin, but the man and woman who bear them were of Hebrew origin. At least Aquila, however, geographically came from the diaspora of northern Anatolia, which faces the Black Sea—in today's Turkey—while Priscilla was probably a Jewish woman from Rome (cf. Acts 18:2). However, it was from Rome that they reached Corinth, where Paul met them at the beginning of the 50s. There he became associated with them, as Luke tells us, practicing the same trade of making tents or large draperies for domestic use, and he was even welcomed into their home (cf. Acts 18:3). The reason they came to Corinth was the decision taken by the Emperor Claudius to expel from Rome the city's Jewish residents. Concerning this event the Roman historian Suetonius tells us that the Hebrews were expelled because "they were rioting due to someone named Chrestus" (cf. "The Lives of the Twelve Caesars, Claudius", no. 25). One sees that he did not know the name well—instead of Christ he wrote "Chrestus"—and he had only a very confused idea of what had happened. In any case, there were internal discords within the Jewish community about the question if Jesus was the Christ. And for the Emperor these problems were the reason simply to expel all Jews from Rome. One can deduce that the couple had already embraced the Christian faith in the 40s, and now they had found in Paul someone who not only shared with them this faith—that Jesus is the Christ—but was also an Apostle, personally called by the Risen Lord. Therefore, their first encounter is at Corinth, where they welcomed him into their house and worked together making tents. In a second moment they transferred to Ephesus in Asia Minor. There they had a decisive role in completing the Christian formation of the Alexandrian Jew Apollo, about whom we spoke last Wednesday. Since he only knew the faith superficially, "Priscilla and Aquila ... took him and expounded to him the way of God more accurately" (Acts 18:26). When Paul wrote the First Letter to the Corinthians from Ephesus, together with his own greeting he explicitly sent those of "Aquila and Prisca, together with the church in their house" (16:19). Hence, we come to know the most important role that this couple played in the environment of the primitive Church: that of welcoming in their own house the group of local Christians when they gathered to listen to the Word of God and to celebrate the Eucharist. It is exactly this type of gathering that in Greek is called *ekklesía*—the Latin word is *ecclesia*, the Italian *chiesa*—which means convocation, assembly, gathering. In the house of Aquila and Priscilla, therefore, the Church gathered, the convocation of Christ, which celebrates here the Sacred Mysteries. Thus, we can see the very birth of the reality of the Church in the homes of believers. Christians, in fact, from the first part of the third century did not have their own places of worship. Initially it was the Jewish Synagogue, until the original symbiosis between the Old and New Testaments dissolved and the Church of the Gentiles was forced to give itself its own identity, always profoundly rooted in the Old Testament. Then, after this "break", they gathered in the homes of Christians that thus become "Church".

And finally, in the third century, true and proper buildings for Christian worship were born. But here, in the first half of the first century and in the second century, the homes of Christians become a true and proper "Church". As I said, together they read the Sacred Scripture and celebrate the Eucharist. That was what used to happen, for example, at Corinth, where Paul mentioned a certain "Gaius, who is host to me and to the whole church" (Rom 16:23), or at Laodicea, where the community gathered in the home of a certain Nympha (cf. Col 4:15), or at Colossae, where the meeting took place in the house of a certain Archippus (cf. Phlm 2).

Having returned subsequently to Rome, Aquila and Priscilla continue to carry out this precious function also in the capital of the Empire. In fact, Paul, writing to the Romans, sends this precise greeting: "Greet Prisca and Aquila, my fellow workers in Christ Jesus, who risked their necks for my life, to whom not only I but also all the churches of the Gentiles give thanks; greet also the church in their house" (Rom 16:3–5). What extraordinary praise for these two married persons in these words! And it is none other than Paul who extends it. He explicitly recognizes in them two true and important collaborators of his apostolate. The reference made to having risked their lives for him is probably linked to interventions in his favor during some prison stay, perhaps in the same Ephesus (cf. Acts 19:23; 1 Cor 15:32; 2 Cor 1:8–9). And to Paul's own gratitude even that of all the Churches of the Gentiles is joined. Even if the expression is perhaps somewhat hyperbolic, it lets one intuit how vast the radius of their action was and, therefore, their influence for the good of the Gospel.

Later hagiographic tradition has given a very singular importance to Priscilla, even if the problem of identifying her with the martyr Priscilla remains. In any case, here in Rome we have a Church dedicated to Saint Prisca on the Aventine Hill, near the Catacombs of Priscilla on Via Salaria. In this way, the memory of a woman who has certainly

been an active person and of great value in the history of
Roman Christianity is perpetuated. One thing is sure:
together with the gratitude of the early Church, of which
Saint Paul speaks, we must also add our own, since thanks
to the faith and apostolic commitment of the lay faithful,
of families, of spouses like Priscilla and Aquila, Christianity has reached our generation. It could not grow only due
to the Apostles who announced it. In order to take root
in the people's land and develop actively, the commitment
of these families, these spouses, these Christian communities, of these lay faithful was necessary in order to offer the
"humus" for the growth of the faith. As always, it is only in
this way that the Church grows. This couple in particular
demonstrates how important the action of Christian spouses
is. When they are supported by the faith and by a strong
spirituality, their courageous commitment for the Church
and in the Church becomes natural. The daily sharing of
their life prolongs and in some way is sublimated in the
assuming of a common responsibility in favor of the Mystical Body of Christ, even if just a little part of it. Thus it was
in the first generation and thus it will often be.

A further lesson we cannot neglect to draw from their
example: every home can transform itself into a little
church. Not only in the sense that in them must reign the
typical Christian love made of altruism and of reciprocal
care, but still more in the sense that the whole of family
life, based on faith, is called to revolve around the singular
lordship of Jesus Christ. Not by chance does Paul compare,
in the Letter to the Ephesians, the matrimonial relationship
to the spousal communion that happens between Christ and
the Church (cf. Eph 5:25–33). Even more, we can maintain that the Apostle indirectly models the life of the entire
Church on that of the family. And the Church, in reality, is
the family of God. Therefore, we honor Aquila and Priscilla

as models of conjugal life responsibly committed to the service of the entire Christian community. And we find in them the model of the Church, God's family for all times.

(7 February 2007)

11 July

Saint Benedict, Abbot, Patron of Europe

[This is] the feast of Saint Benedict, Patron of Europe, a saint and abbot particularly dear to me as you can guess from my choice of his name. Born in Norcia around 480, Benedict completed his first studies in Rome but, disappointed with city life, withdrew to Subiaco, where for about three years he lived in a grotto—the famous "Sacro Speco"—and dedicated himself entirely to God. Making use of the ruins of a cyclopean villa of the Emperor Nero at Subiaco, he built several monasteries together with his first followers. Thus, he brought into being a fraternal community founded on the primacy of love for Christ, in which prayer and work alternated harmoniously in praise of God. Some years later, he perfected the form of this project at Monte Cassino and wrote it down in the *Rule*, his only work that has come down to us. Seeking first of all the Kingdom of God, Benedict, perhaps unknowingly, scattered on the ashes of the Roman Empire the seed of a new civilization that would develop through an integration of Christian values with the classical heritage, on the one hand and, on the other, the Germanic and Slav cultures.

Today, I would like to emphasize one typical aspect of his spirituality. Benedict, unlike other great monastic missionaries of his time, did not found a monastic institution whose principal aim was the evangelization of the barbarian peoples; he pointed out to his followers the search for God as the fundamental and, indeed, one and only aim of life: "*Quaerere Deum*" [to seek God]. He knew, however, that when the believer enters into a profound relationship with God, he cannot be content with a mediocre life under the banner of a minimalistic ethic and a superficial religiosity. In this light one can understand better the expression that Benedict borrowed from Saint Cyprian and that in his *Rule* (IV, 21) sums up the monks' program of life: "*Nihil amori Christi praeponere*", "Prefer nothing to the love of Christ." *Holiness consists of this, a sound proposal for every Christian that has become a real and urgent pastoral need in our time, when we feel the need to anchor life and history to sound spiritual references.*

Mary Most Holy is a sublime and perfect model of holiness who lived in constant and profound communion with Christ. Let us invoke her intercession, together with Saint Benedict's, so that in our time too the Lord will multiply men and women who, through witnessing to an enlightened faith in their lives, may be the salt of the earth and the light of the world in this new millennium.

(10 July 2005)

* * *

Benedict, the Founder of Western Monasticism and also the Patron of my Pontificate. I begin with words that Saint Gregory the Great wrote about Saint Benedict: "The man of God who shone on this earth among so many miracles was just as brilliant in the eloquent exposition of his teaching" (cf. *II Dialogues* 36). The great Pope wrote these words in 592 A.D. The holy monk, who had died barely fifty years earlier, lived on in people's memories and especially in the flourishing religious Order he had founded. Saint Benedict of Norcia, with his life and his work, had a fundamental influence on the development of European civilization and culture. The most important source on Benedict's life is the second book of Saint Gregory the Great's *Dialogues*. It is not a biography in the classical sense. In accordance with the ideas of his time, by giving the example of a real man—Saint Benedict, in this case—Gregory wished to illustrate the ascent to the peak of contemplation which can be achieved by those who abandon themselves to God. He therefore gives us a model for human life in the climb toward the summit of perfection. Saint Gregory the Great also tells in this book of the *Dialogues* of many miracles worked by the Saint, and here too he does not wish merely to recount something curious but rather to show how God, by admonishing, helping, and even punishing, intervenes in the practical situations of man's life. Gregory's aim was to demonstrate that God is not a distant hypothesis placed at the origin of the world but is present in the life of man, of every man.

This perspective of the "biographer" is also explained in light of the general context of his time: straddling the fifth and sixth centuries, "the world was overturned by a tremendous crisis of values and institutions caused by the collapse of the Roman Empire, the invasion of new peoples, and the decay of morals." But in this terrible situation, here, in this very city of Rome, Gregory presented Saint Benedict as a "luminous star" in order to point the way out of the "black night of history" (cf. John Paul II, 18 May 1979). In fact, the Saint's work and particularly his *Rule* were to prove heralds of an authentic spiritual leaven which, in the course of the centuries, far beyond the boundaries of his country and time, changed the face of Europe following the fall of the political unity created by the Roman Empire, inspiring a new spiritual and cultural unity, that of the Christian faith shared by the peoples of the Continent. This is how the reality we call "Europe" came into being.

Saint Benedict was born around the year 480. As Saint Gregory said, he came *"ex provincia Nursiae"*—from the province of Norcia. His well-to-do parents sent him to study in Rome. However, he did not stay long in the Eternal City. As a fully plausible explanation, Gregory mentions that the young Benedict was put off by the dissolute life-style of many of his fellow students and did not wish to make the same mistakes. He wanted only to please God: *"soli Deo placere desiderans"* (*II Dialogues*, Prol. 1). Thus, even before he finished his studies, Benedict left Rome and withdrew to the solitude of the mountains east of Rome. After a short stay in the village of Enfide (today, Affile), where for a time he lived with a "religious community" of monks, he became a hermit in the neighboring locality of Subiaco. He lived there completely alone for three years in a cave which has been the heart of a Benedictine Monastery called the "Sacro Speco" (Holy Grotto) since the early Middle Ages. The period in Subiaco, a time of solitude with God, was a time of maturation for Benedict. It was here that he bore and overcame the three fundamental temptations of every human being: the temptation of self-affirmation and the desire to put oneself at the center, the temptation of sensuality, and, lastly, the temptation of anger and revenge. In fact, Benedict was convinced that only after overcoming these temptations would he be able to say a useful word to others about their own situations of neediness. Thus, having tranquilized his soul, he could be in full control of the drive of his ego and thus create peace around him. Only then did he decide to found his first monasteries in the Valley of the Anio, near Subiaco.

In the year 529, Benedict left Subiaco and settled in Monte Cassino. Some have explained this move as an escape from the intrigues of an envious local cleric. However, this attempt at an explanation hardly proved convincing since the latter's sudden death did not induce Benedict to return (*II Dialogues* 8). In fact, this decision was called for because he had entered a new phase of inner maturity and monastic experience. According to Gregory the Great, Benedict's exodus from the remote Valley of the Anio to Monte Cassino—a plateau dominating the vast surrounding plain which can be seen from afar—has a symbolic character: a hidden monastic life has its own *raison d'être*, but a monastery also has its public purpose in the life of the Church and of society, and it must give visibility to the faith as a force of life. Indeed, when Benedict's earthly life ended on 21 March 547, he bequeathed with his *Rule* and the Benedictine family he founded a heritage that bore fruit in the passing centuries and is still bearing fruit throughout the world.

Throughout the second book of his *Dialogues*, Gregory shows us how Saint Benedict's life was steeped in an atmosphere of prayer, the foundation of his existence. Without prayer there is no experience of God. Yet Benedict's spirituality was not an interiority removed from reality. In the anxiety and confusion of his day, he lived under God's gaze and in this very way never lost sight of the duties of daily life and of man with his practical needs. Seeing God, he understood the reality of man and his mission. In his *Rule* he describes monastic life as "a school for the service of the Lord" (Prol. 45) and advises his monks, "let nothing be preferred to the Work of God" [that is, the Divine Office, or the Liturgy of the Hours] (43, 3). However, Benedict states that in the first place prayer is an act of listening (Prol. 9–11), which must then be expressed in action. "The Lord is waiting every day for us to respond to his holy admonitions by our deeds" (Prol. 35). Thus, the monk's life becomes a fruitful symbiosis between action and contemplation, "so that God may be glorified in all things" (57, 9). In contrast with a facile and egocentric self-fulfillment, today often exalted, the first and indispensable commitment of a disciple of Saint Benedict is the sincere search for God (58, 7) on the path mapped out by the humble and obedient Christ (5, 13), whose love he must put before all else (4, 21; 72, 11), and in this way, in the service of the other, he becomes a man of service and peace. In the exercise of obedience practiced by faith inspired by love (5, 2), the monk achieves humility (5, 1), to which the *Rule* dedicates an entire chapter (7). In this way, man conforms ever more to Christ and attains true self-fulfillment as a creature in the image and likeness of God.

The obedience of the disciple must correspond with the wisdom of the Abbot, who, in the monastery, "is believed to hold the place of Christ" (2, 2; 63, 13). The figure of the Abbot, which is described above all in Chapter 2 of the *Rule* with a profile of spiritual beauty and demanding commitment, can be considered a self-portrait of Benedict, since, as Saint Gregory the Great wrote, "the holy man could not teach otherwise than as he himself lived" (cf. *II Dialogues* 36). The Abbot must be at the same time a tender father and a strict teacher (cf. 2, 24), a true educator. Inflexible against vices, he is nevertheless called above all to imitate the tenderness of the Good Shepherd (27, 8), to "serve rather than to rule" (64, 8) in order "to show them all what is good and holy by his deeds more than by his words" and "illustrate the divine precepts by his example" (2, 12). To be able to decide responsibly, the Abbot must also be a person who listens to "the brethren's views" (3, 2), because "the Lord often reveals to the youngest what is best" (3, 3). This provision makes a *Rule* written almost fifteen centuries ago surprisingly modern! A man with public responsibility even in small circles must always be a man who can listen and learn from what he hears.

Benedict describes the *Rule* he wrote as "minimal, just an initial outline" (cf. 73, 8); in fact, however, he offers useful guidelines not only for monks but for all who seek guidance on their journey toward God. For its moderation, humanity, and sober discernment between the essential and the secondary in the spiritual life, his *Rule* has retained its illuminating power even to today. By proclaiming Saint Benedict Patron of Europe on 24 October 1964, Paul VI intended to recognize the marvelous work the Saint achieved with his *Rule* for the formation of the civilization and culture of Europe. Having recently emerged from a century that was deeply wounded by two World Wars and the collapse of the great ideologies, now revealed as tragic utopias, Europe today is in search of its own identity. Of course, in order to create new and lasting unity, political, economic, and juridical instruments are important, but it is also necessary to awaken an ethical and spiritual renewal which draws on the Christian roots of the Continent; otherwise a new Europe cannot be built. Without this vital sap, man is exposed to the danger of succumbing to the ancient temptation of seeking to redeem himself by himself—a utopia which in different ways, in twentieth-century Europe, as Pope John Paul II pointed out, has caused "a regression without precedent in the tormented history of humanity" (*Address to the Pontifical Council for Culture*, 12 January 1990). Today, in seeking true progress, let us also listen to the *Rule* of Saint Benedict as a guiding light on our journey. The great monk is still a true master at whose school we can learn to become proficient in true humanism.

(9 April 2008)

16 July

Our Lady of Mount Carmel

The slopes of Carmel, a high ridge that runs down the eastern coast of the Mediterranean Sea at the altitude of Galilee, are dotted with numerous natural caves, beloved by hermits. The most famous of these men of God was the great Prophet Elijah, who in the ninth century before Christ strenuously defended the purity of faith in the one true God from contamination by idolatrous cults. Inspired by the figure of Elijah, the contemplative order of Carmelites arose. It is a religious family that counts among its members great saints such as Teresa of Avila, John of the Cross, Thérèse of the Child Jesus, and Teresa Benedicta of the Cross (in the world: Edith Stein). The Carmelites have spread among the Christian people devotion to Our Lady of Mount Carmel, holding her up as a model of prayer, contemplation, and dedication to God.

Indeed, Mary was the first, in a way which can never be equaled, to believe and experience that Jesus, the incarnate Word, is the summit, the peak of man's encounter with God. By fully accepting the Word, she "was blessedly brought to the holy Mountain" (cf. *Opening Prayer of the Memorial*) and lives forever with the Lord in body and soul. Today, I would like to entrust to the Queen of Mount Carmel all communities of contemplative life scattered throughout the world, especially those of the Carmelite Order, among which I recall the Monastery of Quart, not far from here, that I have had the opportunity to visit in these days. May Mary help every Christian to find God in the silence of prayer.

(16 July 2006)

18 July

Saint Simon of Lipnica

Simon of Lipnica, a great son of Poland, a witness of Christ, and a follower of the spirituality of Saint Francis of Assisi, lived in a distant age but precisely today is held up to the Church as a timely model of a Christian who—enlivened by the spirit of the Gospel—was ready to dedicate his life to his brethren. Thus, filled with the mercy he drew from the Eucharist, he did not hesitate to help the sick who were struck by the plague, and he himself contracted this disease which led to his death. Today in particular, let us entrust to his protection those who are suffering from poverty, illness, loneliness, and social injustice. Let us ask through his intercession for the grace of persevering and active love, for Christ and for our brothers and sisters.

(3 June 2007)

22 July

Saint Mary Magdalene

Saint Mary Magdalene [was] a disciple of the Lord who plays a lead role in the Gospels. Saint Luke lists her among the women who followed Jesus after being "healed of evil spirits and infirmities", explaining that "seven demons had gone out" from her (Lk 8:2). Magdalene would be present beneath the Cross with the Mother of Jesus and other women. In the early morning on the first day after the Sabbath she was to be the one to discover the empty tomb, beside which she stood weeping until the Risen Jesus appeared to her (cf. Jn 20:11). The story of Mary of Magdala reminds us all of a fundamental truth: a disciple of Christ is one who, in the experience of human weakness, has had the humility to ask for his help, has been healed by him, and has set out following closely after him, becoming a witness of the power of his merciful love that is stronger than sin and death.

(23 July 2006)

23 July

Saint Bridget, Patroness of Europe

Today, we are celebrating the Feast of Saint Bridget, one of the women saints whom John Paul II proclaimed Patroness of Europe. Saint Bridget traveled from Sweden to Italy, lived in Rome, and also went on pilgrimage to the Holy Land. With her witness she speaks of openness to different peoples and civilizations. Let us ask her to help humanity today to create large spaces for peace. May she obtain from the Lord in particular peace in the Holy Land, for which she felt such deep affection and veneration.

I also entrust the whole of humanity to the power of divine love, as I invite everyone to pray that the beloved populations of the Middle East may be able to abandon the way of armed conflict and, with the daring of dialogue, build a just and lasting peace. Mary, Queen of Peace, pray for us!

(23 July 2006)

25 July

Saint James, Apostle

The Apostle Saint James, John's brother, ... was the first martyr among the Apostles. He was one of the three closest to the Lord and took part in both the Transfiguration on Mount Tabor—with its beauty in which the splendor of the Lord's divinity shone out—and the anguish, the distress of the Lord on the Mount of Olives. Thus, he also learned that to bear the burden of the world the Son of God experienced all our suffering and is in solidarity with us. You know that the relics [of Saint James] are venerated at the famous Shrine of Compostela in Galicia, Spain, the destination of numerous pilgrimages from every part of Europe.

(24 July 2005)

* * *

The biblical lists of the Twelve mention two people with this name: James, son of Zebedee, and James, son of Alphaeus (cf. Mk 3:17, 18; Mt 10:2–3), who are commonly distinguished with the titles "James the Greater" and "James the Lesser". These titles are certainly not intended to measure their holiness, but simply to state the different importance they receive in the writings of the New Testament and, in particular, in the setting of Jesus' earthly life. Today we will focus our attention on the first of these two figures with the same name.

The name "James" is the translation of *Iakobos*, the Grecized form of the name of the famous Patriarch Jacob. The Apostle of this name was the brother of John and, in the above-mentioned lists, comes second, immediately after Peter, as occurs in Mark (3:17); or in the third place, after Peter and Andrew, as in the Gospels of Matthew (10:2) and Luke (6:14), while in the Acts he comes after Peter and John (1:13). This James belongs, together with Peter and John, to the group of the three privileged disciples whom Jesus admitted to important moments in his life....

James was able to take part, together with Peter and John, in Jesus' Agony in the Garden of Gethsemane and in the event of Jesus' Transfiguration. Thus, it is a question of situations very different from each other: in one case, James, together with the other two Apostles, experiences the Lord's glory and sees him talking to Moses and Elijah; he sees the divine splendor shining out in Jesus. On the other occasion, he finds himself face to face with suffering and humiliation; he sees with his own eyes how the Son of God humbles himself, making himself obedient unto death. The latter experience was certainly an opportunity for him to grow in faith, to adjust the unilateral, triumphalist interpretation of the former experience: he had to discern that the Messiah, whom the Jewish people were awaiting as a victor, was in fact surrounded not only by honor and glory, but also by suffering and weakness. Christ's glory was fulfilled precisely on the Cross, in his sharing in our sufferings.

This growth in faith was brought to completion by the Holy Spirit at Pentecost, so that James, when the moment of supreme witness came, would not draw back. Early in the first century, in the 40s, King Herod Agrippa, the grandson of Herod the Great, as Luke tells us, "laid violent hands upon some who belonged to the Church. He had James, the brother of John, killed by the sword" (Acts 12:1–2). The brevity of the news, devoid of any narrative detail, reveals, on the one hand, how normal it was for Christians to witness to the Lord with their own lives and, on the other, that James had a position of relevance in the Church of Jerusalem, partly because of the role he played during Jesus' earthly existence. A later tradition, dating back at least to Isidore of Seville, speaks of a visit he made to Spain to evangelize that important region of the Roman Empire. According to another tradition, it was his body instead that had been taken to Spain, to the city of Santiago de Compostela. As we all know, that place became the object of great veneration and is still the destination of numerous pilgrimages, not only from Europe but from the whole world. This explains the iconographical representation of Saint James with the pilgrim's staff and the scroll of the Gospel in hand, typical features of the traveling Apostle dedicated to the proclamation of the "Good News" and characteristics of the pilgrimage of Christian life.

Consequently, we can learn much from Saint James: promptness in accepting the Lord's call even when he asks us to leave the "boat" of our human securities, enthusiasm in following him on the paths that he indicates to us over and above any deceptive presumption of our own, readiness to witness to him with courage, if necessary to the point of making the supreme sacrifice of life. Thus James the Greater stands before us as an eloquent example of generous adherence to Christ. He, who initially had requested, through his mother, to be seated with his brother next to the Master in his Kingdom, was precisely the first to drink the chalice of the Passion and to share martyrdom with the Apostles.

And, in the end, summarizing everything, we can say that the journey, not only exterior but above all interior, from the mount of the Transfiguration to the mount of the Agony, symbolizes the entire pilgrimage of Christian life, among the persecutions of the world and the consolations of God, as the Second Vatican Council says. In following Jesus, like Saint James, we know that even in difficulties we are on the right path.

(21 June 2006)

26 July

Saint George Preca

George Preca, born in La Valletta on the Island of Malta, was a friend of Jesus and a witness to the holiness that derives from him. He was a priest totally dedicated to evangelization: by his preaching, his writings, his spiritual direction and the administration of the sacraments, and, first and foremost, by the example of his life. The Johannine expression *"Verbum caro factum est"* always directed his soul and his work, and thus the Lord could make use of him to give life to a praiseworthy institution, the "Society of Christian Doctrine", whose purpose is to guarantee parishes the qualified service of properly trained and generous catechists. As a profoundly priestly and mystical soul, he poured himself out in effusions of love for God, Jesus, the Virgin Mary, and the saints. He liked to repeat: "Lord God, how obliged to you I am! Thank you, Lord God, and forgive me, Lord God!" This is a prayer that we can also repeat and make our own. May Saint George Preca help the Church, in Malta and throughout the world, to be always a faithful echo of the voice of Christ, the incarnate Word.

(3 June 2007)

28 July

Saint Alphonsa of the Immaculate Conception
(Anna Muttathupadathu)

"He will swallow up death for ever, and the Lord God will wipe away tears from all faces" (Is 25:8). These words of the Prophet Isaiah contain the promise which sustained Alphonsa of the Immaculate Conception through a life of extreme physical and spiritual suffering.

This exceptional woman, who today is offered to the people of India as their first canonized saint, was convinced that her cross was the very means of reaching the heavenly banquet prepared for her by the Father.

By accepting the invitation to the wedding feast, and by adorning herself with the garment of God's grace through prayer and penance, she conformed her life to Christ's and now delights in the "rich fare and choice wines" of the heavenly kingdom (cf. Is 25:6).

She wrote, "I consider a day without suffering as a day lost." May we imitate her in shouldering our own crosses so as to join her one day in paradise....

Her heroic virtues of patience, fortitude, and perseverance in the midst of deep suffering remind us that God always gives us the strength we need to overcome every adversity.

(12 October 2008)

Translated in part by Andrew Matt.

31 July

Saint Ignatius of Loyola

Saint Ignatius of Loyola was first and foremost a man of God who in his life put God, his greatest glory and his greatest service, first. He was a profoundly prayerful man for whom the daily celebration of the Eucharist was the heart and crowning point of his day. Thus, he left his followers a precious spiritual legacy that must not be lost or forgotten. Precisely because he was a man of God, Saint Ignatius was a faithful servant of the Church, in which he saw and venerated the Bride of the Lord and the Mother of Christians. And the special vow of obedience to the Pope, which he himself describes as "our first and principal foundation" (*MI,* Series III, I., p. 162), was born from his desire to serve the Church in the most beneficial way possible.

(22 April 2006)

Saint Eusebius of Vercelli

Saint Eusebius of Vercelli [was] the first Bishop of Northern Italy of whom we have reliable information. Born in Sardinia at the beginning of the fourth century, he moved to Rome with his family at a tender age. Later, he was instituted lector: he thus came to belong to the clergy of the city at a time when the Church was seriously troubled by the Arian heresy. The high esteem that developed around Eusebius explains his election in 345 A.D. to the episcopal See of Vercelli. The new Bishop immediately began an intense process of evangelization in a region that was still largely pagan, especially in rural areas. Inspired by Saint Athanasius—who had written the *Life of Saint Anthony*, the father of monasticism in the East—he founded a priestly community in Vercelli that resembled a monastic community. This coenobium impressed upon the clergy of Northern Italy a significant hallmark of apostolic holiness and inspired important episcopal figures such as Limenius and Honoratus, successors of Eusebius in Vercelli, Gaudentius in Novara, Exuperantius in Tortona, Eustasius in Aosta, Eulogius in Ivrea, and Maximus in Turin, all venerated by the Church as saints.

With his sound formation in the Nicene faith, Eusebius did his utmost to defend the full divinity of Jesus Christ, defined by the Nicene *Creed* as "of one being with the Father". To this end, he allied himself with the great Fathers of the fourth century—especially Saint Athanasius, the standard bearer of Nicene orthodoxy—against the philo-Arian policies of the Emperor. For the Emperor, the simpler Arian faith appeared politically more useful as the ideology of the Empire. For him it was not truth that counted but rather political opportunism: he wanted to exploit religion as the bond of unity for the Empire. But these great Fathers resisted him, defending the truth against political expediency. Eusebius was consequently condemned to exile, as were so many other Bishops of the East and West: such as Athanasius himself, Hilary of Poitiers,... and Hosius of Cordoba. In Scythopolis, Palestine, to which he was exiled between 355 and 360, Eusebius wrote a marvelous account of his life. Here too, he founded a monastic community with a small group of disciples. It was also from here that he attended to his correspondence with his faithful in Piedmont, as can be seen in the second of the three *Letters* of Eusebius recognized as authentic. Later, after 360, Eusebius was exiled to Cappadocia and the Thebaid, where he suffered serious physical ill-treatment. After his death in 361, Constantius II was succeeded by the Emperor Julian, known as "the Apostate", who was not interested in making Christianity the religion of the Empire but merely wished to restore paganism. He rescinded the banishment of these Bishops and thereby also enabled Eusebius to be reinstated in his See. In 362 he was invited by Anastasius to take part in the Council of Alexandria, which decided to pardon the Arian Bishops as long as they returned to the secular state. Eusebius was able to exercise his episcopal ministry for another ten years, until he died, creating an exemplary relationship with his city which did not fail to inspire the pastoral service of other Bishops of Northern Italy, whom we shall reflect upon in future Catecheses, such as Saint Ambrose of Milan and Saint Maximus of Turin.

The Bishop of Vercelli's relationship with his city is illustrated in particular by two testimonies in his correspondence. The first is found in the *Letter* cited above, which Eusebius wrote from his exile in Scythopolis "to the beloved brothers and priests missed so much, as well as to the holy people with a firm faith of Vercelli, Novara, Ivrea, and Tortona" (*Second Letter: CCL* 9, 104). These first words, which demonstrate the deep emotion of the good Pastor when he thought of his flock, are amply confirmed at the end of the *Letter* in his very warm fatherly greetings to each and every one of his children in Vercelli, with expressions overflowing with affection and love. One should note first of all the explicit relationship that bound the Bishop to the *sanctae plebes* not only of *Vercellae /* Vercelli—the first and subsequently for some years the only Diocese in the Piedmont—but also of *Novaria /* Novara, *Eporedia /* Ivrea, and *Dertona /* Tortona, that is, of the Christian communities in the same Diocese which had become quite numerous and acquired a certain consistency and autonomy. Another interesting element is provided by the farewell with which the *Letter* concludes. Eusebius asked his sons and daughters to give his greeting "also to those who are outside the Church, yet deign to nourish feelings of love for us: *etiam hos, qui foris sunt et nos dignantur diligere*". This is an obvious proof that the Bishop's relationship with his city was not limited to the Christian population but also extended to those who—outside the Church—recognized in some way his spiritual authority and loved this exemplary man.

The second testimony of the Bishop's special relationship with his city comes from the *Letter* Saint Ambrose of Milan wrote to the Vercellians in about 394, more than twenty years after Eusebius' death (*Ep. extra collecitonem* 14: *Maur.* 63). The Church of Vercelli was going through a difficult period: she was divided and lacked a Bishop. Ambrose

frankly declared that he hesitated to recognize these Vercellians as descending from "the lineage of the holy fathers
who approved of Eusebius as soon as they saw him, without
ever having known him previously and even forgetting their
own fellow citizens". In the same *Letter*, the Bishop of Milan
attested to his esteem for Eusebius in the clearest possible
way: "Such a great man", he wrote in peremptory tones,
"well deserves to be elected by the whole of the Church."
Ambrose's admiration for Eusebius was based above all on
the fact that the Bishop of Vercelli governed his Diocese
with the witness of his life: "With the austerity of fasting he
governed his Church." Indeed, Ambrose was also fascinated,
as he himself admits, by the monastic ideal of the contemplation of God which, in the footsteps of the Prophet Elijah, Eusebius had pursued. First of all, Ambrose commented,
the Bishop of Vercelli gathered his clergy in *vita communis*
and educated its members in "the observance of the monastic rule, although they lived in the midst of the city". The
Bishop and his clergy were to share the problems of their
fellow citizens and did so credibly, precisely by cultivating at
the same time a different citizenship, that of Heaven (cf. Heb
13:14). And thus, they really built true citizenship and true
solidarity among all the citizens of Vercelli.

    While Eusebius was adopting the cause of the *sancta plebs*
of Vercelli, he lived a monk's life in the heart of the city,
opening the city to God. This trait, though, in no way
diminished his exemplary pastoral dynamism. It seems
among other things that he set up parishes in Vercelli for
an orderly and stable ecclesial service and promoted Marian
shrines for the conversion of the pagan populations in the
countryside. This "monastic feature", however, conferred
a special dimension on the Bishop's relationship with his
hometown. Just like the Apostles, for whom Jesus prayed at
his Last Supper, the Pastors and faithful of the Church "are

in the world" (Jn 17:11), but not "of the world". Therefore, Pastors, Eusebius said, must urge the faithful not to
consider the cities of the world as their permanent dwelling place but to seek the future city, the definitive heavenly
Jerusalem. This "eschatological reserve" enables Pastors and
faithful to preserve the proper scale of values without ever
submitting to the fashions of the moment and the unjust
claims of the current political power. The authentic scale of
values—Eusebius' whole life seems to say—does not come
from emperors of the past or of today but from Jesus Christ,
the perfect Man, equal to the Father in divinity, yet a man
like us. In referring to this scale of values, Eusebius never
tired of "warmly recommending" his faithful "to guard
the faith jealously, to preserve harmony, to be assiduous in
prayer" (*Second Letter, op. cit.*).

Dear friends, I too warmly recommend these perennial
values to you as I greet and bless you, using the very words
with which the holy Bishop Eusebius concluded his *Second
Letter*: "I address you all, my holy brothers and sisters, sons
and daughters, faithful of both sexes and of every age group,
so that you may ... bring our greeting also to those who are
outside the Church, yet deign to nourish feelings of love for
us" (*ibid.*).

(17 October 2007)

4 August

Saint John Mary Vianney

Throughout the year, the liturgy presents to us as examples
holy ministers of the Altar who have drawn strength from
the imitation of Christ in daily intimacy with him in the
celebration and adoration of the Eucharist....
Thinking of priests in love with the Eucharist, we cannot ... forget Saint John Mary Vianney, the humble parish
priest of Ars at the time of the French Revolution. With
the holiness of his life and his pastoral zeal, he succeeded
in making that little village a model Christian community,
enlivened by the Word of God and by the sacraments.

(18 September 2005)

The Transfiguration of the Lord

The mountain—Mount Tabor, like Sinai—is the place of nearness to God. Compared with daily life, it is the lofty space in which to breathe the pure air of creation. It is the place of prayer in which to stand in the Lord's presence like Moses and Elijah, who appeared beside the transfigured Jesus and spoke to him of the "exodus" that awaited him in Jerusalem, that is, his Pasch. The Transfiguration is a prayer event: in praying, Jesus is immersed in God, closely united to him, adhering with his own human will to the loving will of the Father, and thus light invades him and appears visibly as the truth of his being: he is God, Light of Light. Even Jesus' raiment becomes dazzling white. This is reminiscent of the white garment worn by neophytes. Those who are reborn in Baptism are clothed in light, anticipating heavenly existence (cf. Rv 7:9, 13). This is the crucial point: the Transfiguration is an anticipation of the Resurrection, but this presupposes death. Jesus expresses his glory to the Apostles so that they may have the strength to face the scandal of the Cross and understand that it is necessary to pass through many tribulations in order to reach the Kingdom of God. The Father's voice, which resounds from on high, proclaims Jesus his beloved Son as he did at the Baptism in the Jordan, adding: "Listen to him" (Mt 17:5). To enter eternal life requires listening to Jesus, following him on the way of the Cross, carrying in our heart like him the hope of the Resurrection. "Spe salvi", saved in hope. Today we can say: "Transfigured in hope".

(17 February 2008)

* * *

Mark the Evangelist recounts that Jesus took Peter, James, and John with him up a high mountain and was transfigured before them, becoming so dazzlingly bright that they were "whiter than the work of any bleacher could make them" (Mk 9:2–10). Today, the liturgy invites us to focus our gaze on this mystery of light. On the transfigured face of Jesus a ray of light which he held within shines forth. This same light was to shine on Christ's face on the day of the Resurrection. In this sense, the Transfiguration appears as a foretaste of the Paschal Mystery.

The Transfiguration invites us to open the eyes of our hearts to the mystery of God's light, present throughout salvation history. At the beginning of creation, the Almighty had already said: *"Fiat lux*—let there be light!"* (Gn 1:2), and the light was separated from the darkness. Like the other created things, light is a sign that reveals something of God: it is, as it were, a reflection of his glory which accompanies its manifestations. When God appears, "his brightness was like the light, rays flashed from his hand" (Heb 3:3ff.). Light, it is said in the Psalms, is the mantle with which God covers himself (cf. Ps 104[103]:2). In the Book of Wisdom, the symbolism of light is used to describe the very essence of God: wisdom, an outpouring of his glory, is "a reflection of eternal light" superior to any created light (cf. Wis 7:27, 29ff.). In the New Testament, it is Christ who constitutes the full manifestation of God's light. His Resurrection defeated the power of the darkness of evil forever. With the

Risen Christ, truth and love triumph over deceit and sin. In him, God's light henceforth illumines definitively human life and the course of history: "I am the light of the world," he says in the Gospel, "he who follows me will not walk in darkness, but will have the light of life" (Jn 8:12).

In our time too, we urgently need to emerge from the darkness of evil, to experience the joy of the children of light! May Mary ... obtain this gift for us.

(6 August 2006)

Saint Lawrence, Martyr

Today, we are celebrating the Memorial of Saint Lawrence, Martyr, a shining example of a Christian who lived his total attachment to the divine Master with courage and evangelical heroism. Dear friends, imitate his example and, like him, always be ready to respond faithfully to the Lord's call.

(10 August 2005)

* * *

Saint Lawrence [was] Archdeacon of Pope Saint Sixtus II and his reliable steward in the administration of the community's goods....

History confirms to us how glorious is the name of this Saint.... His concern for the poor, the generous service that he rendered to the Church of Rome in the context of assistance and charity, his fidelity to the Pope which he took to the point of desiring to follow him in the supreme trial of martyrdom and the heroic witness of pouring out his blood, which he suffered only a few days later, are facts well known to all.

Saint Leo the Great, in a beautiful homily, thus comments on the atrocious martyrdom of this "illustrious hero": "The flames could not overcome Christ's love, and the fire that burned outside was less keen than that which blazed within." And he adds: "The Lord desired to spread abroad his glory throughout the world, so that from the East to the West the dazzling brightness of his deacon's light does shine, and Rome is become as famous through Lawrence as Jerusalem was ennobled by Stephen" (Homily 85, 4: PL 54, 486)....

What better message can we glean from Saint Lawrence than that of holiness? He repeats to us that holiness, that is, going to meet Christ who comes ceaselessly to visit us, does not go out of fashion, on the contrary as time passes it shines brightly and expresses mankind's perennial striving for God....

May Lawrence, a heroic witness of the Crucified and Risen Christ, be for each person an example of docile adherence to the divine will, so that, as we heard the Apostle Paul remind the Corinthians, we too may live in such a way as to be found "guiltless" in the day of Our Lord (cf. 1 Cor 1:7–9).

(30 November 2008)

Saint Maximus the Confessor

The figure of one of the great Fathers of the Eastern Church
in later times. He is a monk, Saint Maximus, whose fearless
courage in witnessing to—"confessing"—even while suffering, the integrity of his faith in Jesus Christ, true God
and true man, Savior of the world, earned him Christian
tradition's title of *Confessor*. Maximus was born in Palestine,
the land of the Lord, in about 580. As a boy he was initiated into the monastic life and the study of the Scriptures
through the works of Origen, the great teacher who by the
third century had already "established" the exegetic tradition of Alexandria.

Maximus moved from Jerusalem to Constantinople and
from there, because of the barbarian invasions, sought refuge in Africa. Here he was distinguished by his extreme
courage in the defense of orthodoxy. Maximus refused to
accept any reduction of Christ's humanity. A theory had
come into being which held that there was only one will
in Christ, the divine will. To defend the oneness of Christ's
Person, people denied that he had his own true and proper
human will. And, at first sight, it might seem to be a good
thing that Christ had only one will. But Saint Maximus
immediately realized that this would destroy the mystery
of salvation, for humanity without a will, a man without a
will, is not a real man but an amputated man. Had this been
so, the man Jesus Christ would not have been a true man,

he would not have experienced the drama of being human, which consists, precisely, of conforming our will with the great truth of being. Thus Saint Maximus declared with great determination: Sacred Scripture does not portray to us an amputated man with no will but rather a true and complete man: God, in Jesus Christ, really assumed the totality of being human—obviously with the exception of sin— hence also a human will. And said like this, his point is clear: Christ either is or is not a man. If he is a man, he also has a will. But here the problem arises: do we not end up with a sort of dualism? Do we not reach the point of affirming two complete personalities: reason, will, sentiment? How is it possible to overcome dualism, to keep the completeness of the human being and yet succeed in preserving the unity of the Person of Christ, who was not schizophrenic? Saint Maximus demonstrates that man does not find his unity, the integration of himself or his totality, within himself but by surpassing himself, by coming out of himself. Thus, also in Christ, by coming out of himself, man finds himself in God, in the Son of God. It is not necessary to amputate man to explain the Incarnation; all that is required is to understand the dynamism of the human being who is fulfilled only by coming out of himself; it is in God alone that we find ourselves, our totality and our completeness. Hence, we see that the person who withdraws into himself is not a complete person, but the person who is open, who comes out of himself, becomes complete and finds himself, finds his true humanity, precisely in the Son of God. For Saint Maximus, this vision did not remain a philosophical speculation; he saw it realized in Jesus' actual life, especially in the drama of Gethsemane. In this drama of Jesus' agony, of the anguish of death, of the opposition between the human will not to die and the divine will which offers itself to death, in this drama of Gethsemane the whole human drama is played out, the drama of our redemption. Saint Maximus tells us that, and we know that this is true, Adam (and we ourselves are Adam) thought that the "no" was the peak of freedom. He thought that only a person who can say "no" is truly free; that if he is truly to achieve his freedom, man must say "no" to God; only in this way, he believed, could he at last be himself, could he reach the heights of freedom. The human nature of Christ also carried this tendency within it but overcame it, for Jesus saw that it was not the "no" that was the height of freedom. The height of freedom is the "yes", in conformity with God's will. It is only in the "yes" that man truly becomes himself; only in the great openness of the "yes", in the unification of his will with the divine, that man becomes immensely open, becomes "divine". What Adam wanted was to be like God, that is, to be completely free. But the person who withdraws into himself is not divine, is not completely free; he is freed by emerging from himself, it is in the "yes" that he becomes free; and this is the drama of Gethsemane: not my will but yours. It is by transferring the human will to the divine will that the real person is born; it is in this way that we are redeemed. This, in a few brief words, is the fundamental point of what Saint Maximus wanted to say, and here we see that the whole human being is truly at issue; the entire question of our life lies here. In Africa Saint Maximus was already having problems defending this vision of man and of God. He was then summoned to Rome. In 649 he took an active part in the Lateran Council, convoked by Pope Martin I to defend the two wills of Christ against the Imperial Edict which—*pro bono pacis*—forbade discussion of this matter. Pope Martin was made to pay dearly for his courage. Although he was in a precarious state of health, he was arrested and taken to Constantinople. Tried and condemned to death, the Pope obtained the commutation of his sentence to permanent exile in the Crimea, where he died on 16 September 655, after two long years of humiliation and torment.

It was Maximus' turn shortly afterward, in 662, as he too opposed the Emperor, repeating: "It cannot be said that Christ has a single will!" (cf. *PG* 91, 268–269). Thus, together with his two disciples, both called Anastasius, Maximus was subjected to an exhausting trial although he was then over eighty years of age. The Emperor's tribunal condemned him with the accusation of heresy, sentencing him to the cruel mutilation of his tongue and his right hand—the two organs through which, by words and writing, Maximus had fought the erroneous doctrine of the single will of Christ. In the end, thus mutilated, the holy monk was finally exiled to the region of Colchis on the Black Sea, where he died, worn out by the suffering he had endured, at the age of eighty-two, on 13 August that same year, 662.

In speaking of Maximus' life, we mentioned his literary opus in defense of orthodoxy. We referred in particular to the *Disputation with Pyrrhus*, formerly Patriarch of Constantinople: in this debate he succeeded in persuading his adversary of his errors. With great honesty, in fact, Pyrrhus concluded the *Disputation* with these words: "I ask forgiveness for myself and for those who have preceded me: by ignorance we arrived at these absurd ideas and arguments; and I ask that a way may be found to cancel these absurdities, saving the memory of those who erred" (*PG* 91, 352). Also several dozen important works have been handed down to us, among which the *Mystagogia* is outstanding. This is one of Saint Maximus' most important writings, which gathers his theological thought in a well-structured synthesis.

Saint Maximus' thought was never merely theological, speculative, or introverted because its target was always the practical reality of the world and its salvation. In this context in which he had to suffer, he could not escape into purely theoretical and philosophical affirmations. He had to seek the meaning of life, asking himself: who am I? What is the world? God entrusted to man, created in his image and likeness, the mission of unifying the cosmos. And just as Christ unified the human being in himself, the Creator unified the cosmos in man. He showed us how to unify the cosmos in the communion of Christ and thus truly arrived at a redeemed world. Hans Urs von Balthasar, one of the greatest theologians of the twentieth century, referred to this powerful saving vision when—"relaunching" Maximus—he defined his thought with the vivid expression *Kosmische Liturgie*, "cosmic liturgy". Jesus, the one Savior of the world, is always at the center of this solemn "liturgy". The efficacy of his saving action, which definitively unified the cosmos, is guaranteed by the fact that in spite of being God in all things, he is also integrally a man and has the "energy" and will of a man.

The life and thought of Maximus were powerfully illumined by his immense courage in witnessing to the integral reality of Christ, without any reduction or compromise. And thus it becomes clear who man really is and how we should live in order to respond to our vocation. We must live united to God in order to be united to ourselves and to the cosmos, giving the cosmos itself and humanity their proper form. Christ's universal "yes" also shows us clearly how to put all the other values in the right place. We think of values that are justly defended today, such as tolerance, freedom, and dialogue. But a tolerance that no longer distinguishes between good and evil would become chaotic and self-destructive, just as a freedom that did not respect the freedom of others or find the common measure of our respective liberties would become anarchy and destroy authority. Dialogue that no longer knows what to discuss becomes empty chatter. All these values are important and fundamental but can remain true values only if they have the point of reference that unites them and gives them true authenticity. This reference point is the synthesis between God and the cosmos, the figure of Christ in which we learn the truth about ourselves and thus where to rank all other values, because we discover their authentic meaning. Jesus Christ is the reference point that gives light to all other values. This was the conclusion of the great Confessor's witness. And it is in this way, ultimately, that Christ indicates that the cosmos must become a liturgy, the glory of God, and that worship is the beginning of the true transformation, of the true renewal of the world.

I would therefore like to conclude with a fundamental passage from one of Saint Maximus' works: "We adore one Son together with the Father and the Holy Spirit, as it was in the beginning before all time, is now, and ever shall be, for all time and for the time after time. Amen!" (*PG* 91, 269).

(25 June 2008)

The Assumption of the Blessed Virgin Mary

The Christian tradition has placed, as we know, in the heart of summer a most ancient and suggestive Marian feast, the Solemnity of the Assumption of the Blessed Virgin Mary. Like Jesus, risen from the dead and ascended to the right hand of the Father, so Mary, having finished the course of her earthly existence, was assumed into Heaven. Today, the liturgy reminds us of this consoling truth of faith, while it sings the praises of the one who has been crowned with incomparable glory. We read today in the verse from the Apocalypse proposed by the Church for our meditation: "And a great portent appeared in heaven, a woman clothed with the sun, with the moon under her feet, and on her head a crown of twelve stars" (12:1). In this woman, resplendent with light, the Fathers of the Church have recognized Mary. In her triumph the Christian people, pilgrims in history, catch a glimpse of the fulfillment of its longing and a certain sign of its hope.

Mary is an example and support for all believers: she encourages us not to lose confidence before the difficulties and inevitable problems of every day. She assures us of her help and reminds us that it is essential to seek and think of "the things above, not those of the earth" (cf. Col 3:2). Caught up in daily activities we risk, in fact, thinking that here, in this world in which we are only passing through, is the ultimate goal of human existence. Instead, Paradise is the true goal of our earthly pilgrimage. How different our days would be if they were animated by this perspective! It was this way for the saints. Their lives witnessed to what they lived, with their hearts continually directed to God. Earthly realities are lived properly because the eternal truth of divine love illuminates them.

(15 August 2006)

20 August

Saint Bernard, Abbot

Today, the calendar mentions among the day's saints Bernard of Clairvaux, a great Doctor of the Church who lived between the eleventh and twelfth centuries (1091–1153). His example and teachings are proving more useful than ever, even in our time. Having withdrawn from the world after a period of intense inner travail, he was elected abbot of the Cistercian Monastery of Clairvaux at age twenty-five, remaining its guide for thirty-eight years until his death. His dedication to silence and contemplation did not prevent him from carrying out intense apostolic activity. He was also exemplary in his commitment to battle against his impetuous temperament, as well as in his humility, by which he recognized his own limitations and shortcomings.

The riches and merits of his theology do not lie in having taken new paths, but rather in being able to propose the truths of the faith in a style so clear and incisive that it fascinated those listening and prepared their souls for recollection and prayer. In every one of his writings, one senses the echo of a rich interior experience, which he succeeded in communicating to others with a surprising capacity for persuasion. For him, love is the greatest strength of the spiritual life. God, who is love, creates man out of love and out of love redeems him. The salvation of all human beings, mortally wounded by original sin and burdened by personal sins, consists in being firmly attached to divine love, which was fully revealed to us in Christ Crucified and Risen.

In his love, God heals our will and our sick understanding, raising them to the highest degree of union with him, that is, to holiness and mystical union. Saint Bernard deals with this, among other things, in his brief but substantial *Liber de Diligendo Deo*. There is then another writing of his that I would like to point out, *De Consideratione,* addressed to Pope Eugene III. Here, in this very personal book, the dominant theme is the importance of inner recollection— and he tells this to the Pope—an essential element of piety. It is necessary, the Saint observes, to beware of the dangers of excessive activity whatever one's condition and office, because, as he said to the Pope of that time and to all Popes, to all of us, many occupations frequently lead to "hardness of heart"; "they are none other than suffering of spirit, loss of understanding, dispersion of grace" (II, 3). This warning applies to every kind of occupation, even those inherent in the government of the Church. In this regard, Bernard addresses provocative words to the Pontiff, a former disciple of his at Clairvaux: "See", he writes, "where these accursed occupations can lead you, if you continue to lose yourself in them ... without leaving anything of yourself to yourself" (*ibid.*). How useful this appeal to the primacy of prayer and contemplation is also for us! May we too be helped to put this into practice in our lives by Saint Bernard, who knew how to harmonize the monk's aspiration to the solitude and tranquility of the cloister with the pressing needs of impor- tant and complex missions at the service of the Church.

Let us entrust this desire, not easy to find, that is, the equilibrium between interiority and necessary work, to the intercession of Our Lady, whom he loved from childhood with such a tender and filial devotion as to deserve the title: "Marian Doctor". Let us now invoke her so that she may obtain the gift of true and lasting peace for the whole world. In one of his famous discourses, Saint Bernard compares Mary to the Star that navigators seek so as not to lose their course: "Whoever you are who perceive yourself during this mortal existence to be drifting in treacherous waters at the mercy of the winds and the waves rather than walking on firm ground, turn your eyes not away from the splendor of this guiding star, unless you wish to be submerged by the storm!... Look at the star, call upon Mary.... With her for a guide, you will never go astray;... under her protection, you have nothing to fear; if she walks before you, you will not grow weary; if she shows you favor, you will reach the goal" (Hom. Super Missus Est II, 17).

(20 August 2006)

* * *

Saint Bernard of Clairvaux [is] called "the last of the Fathers" of the Church because once again in the twelfth century he renewed and brought to the fore the important theology of the Fathers. We do not know in any detail about the years of his childhood; however, we know that he was born in 1090 in Fontaines, France, into a large and fairly well-to-do family. As a very young man he devoted himself to the study of the so-called liberal arts—especially grammar, rhetoric, and dialectics—at the school of the canons of the Church of Saint-Vorles at Châtillon-sur-Seine; and the decision to enter religious life slowly matured within him. At the age of about twenty, he entered Cîteaux, a new monastic foundation that was more flexible in comparison with the ancient and venerable monasteries of the period while at the same time stricter in the practice of the evangelical counsels. A few years later, in 1115, Bernard was sent by Stephen

Harding, the third Abbot of Cîteaux, to found the monastery of Clairvaux. Here the young Abbot—he was only twenty-five years old—was able to define his conception of monastic life and set about putting it into practice. In looking at the discipline of other monasteries, Bernard firmly recalled the need for a sober and measured life, at table as in clothing and monastic buildings, and recommended the support and care of the poor. In the meantime the community of Clairvaux became ever more numerous, and its foundations multiplied.

In those same years before 1130, Bernard started a prolific correspondence with many people of both important and modest social status. To the many *Epistolae* of this period must be added numerous *Sermones*, as well as *Sententiae* and *Tractatus*. Bernard's great friendship with William, Abbot of Saint-Thierry, and with William of Champeaux, among the most important figures of the twelfth century, also dates to this period. From 1130 on, Bernard began to concern himself with many serious matters of the Holy See and of the Church. For this reason he was obliged to leave his monastery ever more frequently, and he sometimes also traveled outside France. He founded several women's monasteries and engaged in a lively correspondence with Peter the Venerable, Abbot of Cluny.... In his polemical writings he targeted in particular Abelard, a great thinker who had conceived of a new approach to theology, introducing above all the dialectic and philosophical method in the construction of theological thought. On another front, Bernard combated the heresy of the Cathars, who despised matter and the human body and consequently despised the Creator. On the other hand, he felt it was his duty to defend the Jews and condemned the ever more widespread outbursts of anti-Semitism. With regard to this aspect of his apostolic action, several decades later Rabbi Ephraim of Bonn addressed a vibrant tribute to Bernard. In the same period the holy Abbot wrote his most famous works, such as the celebrated *Sermons on the Song of Songs [In Canticum Sermones]*. In the last years of his life—he died in 1153—Bernard was obliged to curtail his journeys but did not entirely stop traveling. He made the most of this time to review definitively the whole collection of his *Letters*, *Sermons*, and *Treatises*. Worthy of mention is a quite unusual book that he completed in this same period, in 1145, when Bernardo Pignatelli, a pupil of his, was elected Pope with the name of Eugene III. On this occasion, Bernard, as his spiritual father, dedicated to his spiritual son the text *De Consideratione* [Five Books on Consideration] which contains teachings on how to be a good Pope. In this book, which is still appropriate reading for the Popes of all times, Bernard did not only suggest how to be a good Pope, but also expressed a profound vision of the mystery of the Church and of the mystery of Christ which is ultimately resolved in contemplation of the mystery of the Triune God. "The search for this God who is not yet sufficiently sought must be continued," the holy Abbot wrote, "yet it may be easier to search for him and find him in prayer rather than in discussion. So let us end the book here, but not the search" (XIV, 32: *PL* 182, 808) and journey on toward God.

I would now like to reflect on only two of the main aspects of Bernard's rich doctrine: they concern Jesus Christ and Mary Most Holy, his Mother. His concern for the Christian's intimate and vital participation in God's love in Jesus Christ brings no new guidelines to the scientific status of theology. However, in a more decisive manner than ever, the Abbot of Clairvaux embodies the theologian, the contemplative, and the mystic. Jesus alone—Bernard insists in the face of the complex dialectical reasoning of his time—Jesus alone is "honey in the mouth, song to the ear, jubilation in the heart (*mel in ore, in aure melos, in corde iubilum*)". The title *Doctor Mellifluus*, attributed to Bernard by tradition, stems precisely from this; indeed, his praise of Jesus Christ "flowed like honey". In the exhausting battles between Nominalists and Realists—two philosophical currents of the time—the Abbot of Clairvaux never tired of repeating that only one name counts, that of Jesus of Nazareth. "All food of the soul is dry", he professed, "unless it is moistened with this oil; insipid, unless it is seasoned with this salt. What you write has no savor for me unless I have read Jesus in it" (*In Canticum Sermones* XV, 6: PL 183, 847). For Bernard, in fact, true knowledge of God consisted in a personal, profound experience of Jesus Christ and of his love. And, dear brothers and sisters, this is true for every Christian: faith is first and foremost a personal, intimate encounter with Jesus; it is having an experience of his closeness, his friendship, and his love. It is in this way that we learn to know him ever better, to love him, and to follow him more and more. May this happen to each one of us!

In his well-known *Sermon on the Sunday in the Octave of the Assumption*, the holy Abbot described with passionate words Mary's intimate participation in the redeeming sacrifice of her Son. "O Blessed Mother," he exclaimed, "a sword has truly pierced your soul! . . . So deeply has the violence of pain pierced your soul that we may rightly call you more than a martyr, for in you participation in the Passion of the Son by far surpasses in intensity the physical sufferings of martyrdom" (14: PL 183, 437–438). Bernard had no doubts: "*per Mariam ad Iesum*", through Mary we are led to Jesus. He testifies clearly to Mary's subordination to Jesus, in accordance with the foundation of traditional Mariology. Yet the text of the *Sermon* also documents the Virgin's privileged place in the economy of salvation, subsequent to the Mother's most particular participation (*compassio*) in the sacrifice of the Son. It is not for nothing that a century and a half after Bernard's death, Dante Alighieri, in the last canticle of the *Divine Comedy*, was to put on the lips of the *Doctor Mellifluus* the sublime prayer to Mary: "Virgin Mother, daughter of your own Son, / humble and exalted more than any creature, / fixed term of the eternal counsel" (*Paradise* XXXIII, vv. 1ff.).

These reflections, characteristic of a person in love with Jesus and Mary as was Bernard, are still a salutary stimulus not only to theologians but to all believers. Some claim to have solved the fundamental questions on God, on man, and on the world with the power of reason alone. Saint Bernard, on the other hand, solidly grounded on the Bible and on the Fathers of the Church, reminds us that without a profound faith in God, nourished by prayer and contemplation, by an intimate relationship with the Lord, our reflections on the divine mysteries risk becoming an empty intellectual exercise and losing their credibility. Theology refers us back to the "knowledge of the saints", to their intuition of the mysteries of the living God, and to their wisdom, a gift of the Holy Spirit, which become a reference point for theological thought. Together with Bernard of Clairvaux, we too must recognize that man seeks God better and finds him more easily "in prayer than in discussion". In the end, the truest figure of a theologian and of every evangelizer remains the Apostle John, who laid his head on the Teacher's breast.

I would like to conclude these reflections on Saint Bernard with the invocations to Mary that we read in one of his beautiful homilies. "In danger, in distress, in uncertainty", he says, "think of Mary, call upon Mary. She never leaves your lips, she never departs from your heart; and so that you may obtain the help of her prayers, never forget the example of her life. If you follow her, you cannot falter; if you pray to her, you cannot despair; if you think of her, you cannot err.

If she sustains you, you will not stumble; if she protects you, you have nothing to fear; if she guides you, you will never flag; if she is favorable to you, you will attain your goal ..." (*Hom. II super Missus est*, 17: PL 183, 70–71).

(21 October 2009)

24 August

Saint Bartholomew, Apostle

In the ancient lists of the Twelve he always comes before Matthew, whereas the name of the Apostle who precedes him varies; it may be Philip (cf. Mt 10:3; Mk 3:18; Lk 6:14) or Thomas (cf. Acts 1:13). His name is clearly a patronymic, since it is formulated with an explicit reference to his father's name. Indeed, it is probably a name with an Aramaic stamp, *bar Talmay*, which means precisely: "son of Talmay".

We have no special information about Bartholomew; indeed, his name always and only appears in the lists of the Twelve mentioned above and is therefore never central to any narrative. However, it has traditionally been identified with Nathanael: a name that means "God has given". This Nathanael came from Cana (cf. Jn 21:2), and he may therefore have witnessed the great "sign" that Jesus worked in that place (cf. Jn 2:1–11). It is likely that the identification of the two figures stems from the fact that Nathanael is placed in the scene of his calling, recounted in John's Gospel, next to Philip, in other words, the place that Bartholomew occupies in the lists of the Apostles mentioned in the other Gospels. Philip told this Nathanael that he had found "him of whom Moses in the law and also the prophets wrote, Jesus of Nazareth, the son of Joseph" (Jn 1:45). As we know, Nathanael's retort was rather strongly prejudiced: "Can anything good come out of Nazareth?" (Jn 1:46). In its own way, this form of protestation is important for us. Indeed, it makes us see that according to Judaic expectations the Messiah could not come from such an obscure village as, precisely, Nazareth (see also Jn 7:42). But at the same time Nathanael's protest highlights God's freedom, which baffles our expectations by causing him to be found in the very place where we least expect him. Moreover, we actually know that Jesus was not exclusively "from Nazareth" but was born in Bethlehem (cf. Mt 2:1; Lk 2:4) and came ultimately from Heaven, from the Father who is in Heaven.

Nathanael's reaction suggests another thought to us: in our relationship with Jesus we must not be satisfied with words alone. In his answer, Philip offers Nathanael a meaningful invitation: "Come and see!" (Jn 1:46). Our knowledge of Jesus needs above all a first-hand experience: someone else's testimony is of course important, for normally the whole of our Christian life begins with the proclamation handed down to us by one or more witnesses. However, we ourselves must then be personally involved in a close and deep relationship with Jesus; in a similar way, when the Samaritans had heard the testimony of their fellow citizen whom Jesus had met at Jacob's well, they wanted to talk to him directly, and after this conversation they told the woman: "It is no longer because of your words that we believe, for we have heard for ourselves, and we know that this is indeed the Savior of the world" (Jn 4:42).

Returning to the scene of Nathanael's vocation, the Evangelist tells us that when Jesus sees Nathanael approaching, he exclaims: "Behold, an Israelite indeed, in whom there is no guile!" (Jn 1:47). This is praise reminiscent of the text of a Psalm: "Blessed is the man ... in whose spirit there is no deceit" (32[31]:2), but provokes the curiosity of Nathanael, who answers in amazement: "How do you know me?" (Jn 1:48). Jesus' reply cannot immediately be understood. He says: "Before Philip called you, when you

were under the fig tree, I saw you" (Jn 1:48). We do not
know what had happened under this fig tree. It is obvious
that it had to do with a decisive moment in Nathanael's life.
His heart is moved by Jesus' words; he feels understood and
he understands: "This man knows everything about me,
he knows and is familiar with the road of life; I can truly
trust this man." And so he answers with a clear and beautiful confession of faith: "Rabbi, you are the Son of God!
You are the King of Israel!" (Jn 1:49). In this confession
is conveyed a first important step in the journey of attachment to Jesus. Nathanael's words shed light on a twofold,
complementary aspect of Jesus' identity: he is recognized
both in his special relationship with God the Father, of
whom he is the Only-Begotten Son, and in his relationship
with the People of Israel, of whom he is the declared King,
precisely the description of the awaited Messiah. We must
never lose sight of either of these two elements because if
we only proclaim Jesus' heavenly dimension, we risk making him an ethereal and evanescent being; and if, on the
contrary, we recognize only his concrete place in history,
we end by neglecting the divine dimension that properly
qualifies him.

    We have no precise information about Bartholomew-
Nathanael's subsequent apostolic activity. According to
information handed down by Eusebius, the fourth-century
historian, a certain Pantaenus is supposed to have discovered
traces of Bartholomew's presence even in India (cf. *Hist.
eccles.*, V, 10, 3). In later tradition, as from the Middle Ages,
the account of his death by flaying became very popular.
Only think of the famous scene of the *Last Judgment* in the
Sistine Chapel in which Michelangelo painted Saint Bartholomew, who is holding his own skin in his left hand, on
which the artist left his self-portrait. Saint Bartholomew's
relics are venerated here in Rome in the Church dedicated

to him on the Tiber Island, where they are said to have been brought by the German Emperor Otto III in the year 983.

To conclude, we can say that despite the scarcity of information about him, Saint Bartholomew stands before us to tell us that attachment to Jesus can also be lived and witnessed to without performing sensational deeds. Jesus himself, to whom each one of us is called to dedicate his own life and death, is and remains extraordinary.

(4 October 2006)

Saint Monica

Today, 27 August, we commemorate Saint Monica, and tomorrow we will be commemorating Saint Augustine, her son: their witnesses can be of great comfort and help to so many families also in our time. Monica, who was born into a Christian family at Tagaste, today Souk-Aharàs in Algeria, lived her mission as a wife and mother in an exemplary way, helping her husband, Patricius, to discover the beauty of faith in Christ and the power of evangelical love, which can overcome evil with good. After his premature death, Monica courageously devoted herself to caring for her three children, including Augustine, who initially caused her suffering with his somewhat rebellious temperament. As Augustine himself was to say, his mother gave birth to him twice; the second time required a lengthy spiritual travail of prayers and tears, but it was crowned at last with the joy of seeing him not only embrace the faith and receive Baptism, but also dedicate himself without reserve to the service of Christ. How many difficulties there are also today in family relations and how many mothers are in anguish at seeing their children setting out on wrong paths! Monica, a woman whose faith was wise and sound, invites them not to lose heart but to persevere in their mission as wives and mothers, keeping firm their trust in God and clinging with perseverance to prayer.

As for Augustine, his whole life was a passionate search for the truth. In the end, not without a long inner torment, he found in Christ the ultimate and full meaning of his own life and of the whole of human history. In adolescence, attracted by earthly beauty, he "flung himself" upon it—as he himself confides (cf. *Confessions* 10, 27–38)—with selfish and possessive behavior that caused his pious mother great pain. But through a toilsome journey and thanks also to her prayers, Augustine became always more open to the fullness of truth and love until his conversion, which happened in Milan under the guidance of the Bishop, Saint Ambrose. He thus remained the model of the journey toward God, supreme Truth and supreme Good. "Late have I loved you," he wrote in the famous book of the *Confessions*, "beauty, ever ancient and ever new, late have I loved you. You were within me, and I was outside of you, and it was there that I sought you.... You were with me, and I was not with you.... You called, you cried out, you pierced my deafness. You shone, you struck me down, and you healed my blindness" (*ibid.*). May Saint Augustine obtain the gift of a sincere and profound encounter with Christ for all those young people who, thirsting for happiness, are seeking it on the wrong paths and getting lost in blind alleys.

Saint Monica and Saint Augustine invite us to turn confidently to Mary, Seat of Wisdom. Let us entrust Christian parents to her so that, like Monica, they may accompany their children's progress with their own example and prayers. Let us commend youth to the Virgin Mother of God so that, like Augustine, they may always strive for the fullness of Truth and Love which is Christ: he alone can satisfy the deepest desires of the human heart.

(27 August 2006)

28 August

Saint Augustine

Saint Augustine. This man of passion and faith, of the highest intelligence and tireless in his pastoral care, a great saint and Doctor of the Church, is often known, at least by hearsay, even by those who ignore Christianity or who are not familiar with it, because he left a very deep mark on the cultural life of the West and on the whole world. Because of his special importance, Saint Augustine's influence was widespread. It could be said, on the one hand, that all the roads of Latin Christian literature led to Hippo (today Annaba, on the coast of Algeria), the place where he was Bishop from 395 to his death in 430, and, on the other, that from this city of Roman Africa, many other roads of later Christianity and of Western culture itself branched out.

A civilization has seldom encountered such a great spirit who was able to assimilate Christianity's values and exalt its intrinsic wealth, inventing ideas and forms that were to nourish the future generations, as Paul VI also stressed: "It may be said that all the thought-currents of the past meet in his works and form the source which provides the whole doctrinal tradition of succeeding ages" (Inaugural *Address* at the Patristic Institute of the "Augustinianum", 4 May 1970; *L'Osservatore Romano* English edition, 21 May 1970, p. 8). Augustine is also the Father of the Church who left the greatest number of works. Possidius, his biographer, said that it seemed impossible that one man could have written so many things in his lifetime. We shall speak of these different works at one of our meetings soon. Today, we shall focus on his life, which is easy to reconstruct from his writings, in particular the *Confessions*, his extraordinary spiritual autobiography written in praise of God. This is his most famous work; and rightly so, since it is precisely Augustine's *Confessions*, with their focus on interiority and psychology, that constitute a unique model in Western literature, and not only Western, even non-religious literature, up to modern times. This attention to the spiritual life, to the mystery of the "I", to the mystery of God who is concealed in the "I", is something quite extraordinary, without precedent, and remains forever, as it were, a spiritual "peak".

But to come back to his life: Augustine was born in Tagaste in the Roman Province of Numidia, Africa, on 13 November 354 to Patricius, a pagan who later became a catechumen, and Monica, a fervent Christian. This passionate woman, venerated as a saint, exercised an enormous influence on her son and raised him in the Christian faith. Augustine had also received the salt, a sign of acceptance in the catechumenate, and was always fascinated by the figure of Jesus Christ; indeed, he said that he had always loved Jesus but had drifted further and further away from ecclesial faith and practice, as also happens to many young people today.

Augustine also had a brother, Navigius, and a sister whose name is unknown to us and who, after being widowed, subsequently became the head of a monastery for women. As a boy with a very keen intelligence, Augustine received a good education, although he was not always an exemplary student. However, he learned grammar well, first in his native town and then in Madaura, and from 370, he studied rhetoric in Carthage, the capital of Roman Africa. He mastered Latin perfectly but was not quite as successful with Greek and did not learn Punic, spoken by his contemporaries. It was in Carthage itself that for the first time Augustine read the *Hortensius*, a writing by Cicero later lost, an event that can be placed at the beginning of his journey toward conversion. In fact, Cicero's text awoke within him love for wisdom, as, by then a Bishop, he was to write in his *Confessions*: "The book changed my feelings", to the extent that "every vain hope became empty to me, and I longed for the immortality of wisdom with an incredible ardor in my heart" (III, 4, 7).

However, since he was convinced that without Jesus the truth cannot be said effectively to have been found and since Jesus' Name was not mentioned in this book, immediately after he read it he began to read Scripture, the Bible. But it disappointed him. This was not only because the Latin style of the translation of the Sacred Scriptures was inadequate but also because to him their content itself did not seem satisfying. In the scriptural narratives of wars and other human vicissitudes, he discovered neither the loftiness of philosophy nor the splendor of the search for the truth which is part of it. Yet he did not want to live without God and thus sought a religion which corresponded to his desire for the truth and also with his desire to draw close to Jesus. Thus, he fell into the net of the Manichaeans, who presented themselves as Christians and promised a totally rational religion. They said that the world was divided into two principles: good and evil. And in this way the whole complexity of human history can be explained. Their dualistic morals also pleased Saint Augustine, because it included a very high morality for the elect: and those like him who adhered to it could live a life better suited to the situation of the time, especially for a young man. He therefore became a Manichaean, convinced at that time that he had found the synthesis between rationality and the search for the truth and love of Jesus Christ. Manichaeanism also offered him a concrete advantage in life: joining the Manichaeans facilitated the prospects of a career. By belonging to that religion, which included so many influential figures, he was able to continue his relationship with a woman and to advance in his career. By this woman he had a son, Adeodatus, who was very dear to him and very intelligent, who was later to be present during the preparation for Baptism near Lake Como, taking part in those "Dialogues" which Saint Augustine has passed down to us. The boy unfortunately died prematurely. Having been a grammar teacher since his twenties in the city of his birth, Augustine soon returned to Carthage, where he became a brilliant and famous teacher of rhetoric. However, with time Augustine began to distance himself from the faith of the Manichaeans. They disappointed him precisely from the intellectual viewpoint since they proved incapable of dispelling his doubts. He moved to Rome and then to Milan, where the imperial court resided at that time and where he obtained a prestigious post through the good offices and recommendations of the Prefect of Rome, Symmacus, a pagan hostile to Saint Ambrose, Bishop of Milan.

In Milan, Augustine acquired the habit of listening—at first for the purpose of enriching his rhetorical store of knowledge—to the eloquent preaching of Bishop Ambrose, who had been a representative of the Emperor for Northern Italy. The African rhetorician was fascinated by the words of the great Milanese Prelate; and not only by his rhetoric. It was above all the content that increasingly touched Augustine's heart. The great difficulty with the Old Testament, because of its lack of rhetorical beauty and lofty philosophy, was resolved in Saint Ambrose's preaching through his typological interpretation of the Old Testament: Augustine realized that the whole of the Old Testament was a journey toward Jesus Christ. Thus, he found the key to understanding the beauty and even the philosophical depth of the Old

Testament and grasped the whole unity of the mystery of Christ in history as well as the synthesis between philosophy, rationality, and faith in the *Logos*, in Christ, the Eternal Word who was made flesh.

Augustine soon realized that the allegorical interpretation of Scripture and the Neo-Platonic philosophy practiced by the Bishop of Milan enabled him to solve the intellectual difficulties which, when he was younger during his first approach to the biblical texts, had seemed insurmountable to him.

Thus, Augustine followed his reading of the philosophers' writings by reading Scripture anew, especially the Pauline Letters. His conversion to Christianity on 15 August 386 therefore came at the end of a long and tormented inner journey—of which we shall speak in another Catechesis— and the African moved to the countryside, north of Milan by Lake Como—with his mother, Monica, his son, Adeodatus, and a small group of friends—to prepare himself for Baptism. So it was that at the age of thirty-two Augustine was baptized by Ambrose in the Cathedral of Milan on 24 April 387, during the Easter Vigil.

After his Baptism, Augustine decided to return to Africa with his friends, with the idea of living a community life of the monastic kind at the service of God. However, while awaiting their departure in Ostia, his mother fell ill unexpectedly and died shortly afterward, breaking her son's heart. Having returned to his homeland at last, the convert settled in Hippo for the very purpose of founding a monastery. In this city on the African coast he was ordained a priest in 391, despite his reticence, and with a few companions began the monastic life which had long been in his mind, dividing his time between prayer, study, and preaching. All he wanted was to be at the service of the truth. He did not feel he had a vocation to pastoral life but realized later that God was calling him to be a pastor among others and thus to offer people the gift of the truth. He was ordained a Bishop in Hippo four years later, in 395. Augustine continued to deepen his study of Scripture and of the texts of the Christian tradition and was an exemplary Bishop in his tireless pastoral commitment: he preached several times a week to his faithful, supported the poor and orphans, supervised the formation of the clergy and the organization of men's and women's monasteries. In short, the former rhetorician asserted himself as one of the most important exponents of Christianity of that time. He was very active in the government of his Diocese—with remarkable, even civil, implications—in the more than thirty-five years of his Episcopate, and the Bishop of Hippo actually exercised a vast influence in his guidance of the Catholic Church in Roman Africa and, more generally, in the Christianity of his time, coping with religious tendencies and tenacious, disruptive heresies such as Manichaeism, Donatism, and Pelagianism, which endangered the Christian faith in the one God, rich in mercy.

And Augustine entrusted himself to God every day until the very end of his life: smitten by fever, while for almost three months his Hippo was being besieged by vandal invaders, the Bishop—his friend Possidius recounts in his *Vita Augustini*—asked that the penitential psalms be transcribed in large characters "and that the sheets be attached to the wall, so that while he was bedridden during his illness he could see and read them, and he shed constant hot tears" (31, 2). This is how Augustine spent the last days of his life. He died on 28 August 430, when he was not yet seventy-six.

(9 January 2008)

Saint Gregory the Great

[The] exceptional, I would say, almost unique figure [of Saint Gregory the Great, Pope and Doctor of the Church (ca. 540–604)] is an example to hold up both to pastors of the Church and to public administrators: indeed, he was first Prefect and then Bishop of Rome. As an imperial official, he was so distinguished for his administrative talents and moral integrity that he served in the highest civil office, *Praefectus Urbis,* when he was only thirty years old. Within him, however, the vocation to the monastic life was maturing; he embraced it in 574, upon his father's death. The Benedictine *Rule* then became the backbone of his existence. Even when the Pope sent him as his Representative to the Emperor of the East in Constantinople, he maintained a simple and poor monastic life-style.

Called back to Rome, Gregory, although living in a monastery, was a close collaborator of Pope Pelagius II, and when the Pope died, the victim of a plague epidemic, Gregory was acclaimed by all as his Successor. He sought in every way to escape this appointment but in the end was obliged to yield. He left the cloister reluctantly and dedicated himself to the community, aware of doing his duty and being a simple and poor "servant of the servants of God". "He is not really humble," he wrote, "who understands that he must be a leader of others by decree of the divine will and yet disdains this pre-eminence. If, on the contrary, he submits to divine dispositions and does not have the vice of obstinacy and is prepared to benefit others with those gifts when the highest dignity of governing souls is imposed on him, he must flee from it with his heart, but against his will, he must obey" (*Pastoral Rule*, I, 6). It is like a dialogue that the Pope has with himself at that time. With prophetic foresight, Gregory intuited that a new civilization was being born from the encounter of the Roman legacy with so-called "barbarian" peoples, thanks to the cohesive power and moral elevation of Christianity. Monasticism was proving to be a treasure not only for the Church but for the whole of society.

With delicate health but strong moral character Saint Gregory the Great carried out intense pastoral and civil action. He left a vast collection of letters, wonderful homilies, a famous commentary on the Book of Job, and writings on the life of Saint Benedict, as well as numerous liturgical texts, famous for the reform of song that was called "Gregorian", after him. However, his most famous work is certainly the *Pastoral Rule*, which had the same importance for the clergy as the *Rule* of Saint Benedict had for monks in the Middle Ages. The life of a pastor of souls must be a balanced synthesis of contemplation and action, inspired by the love "that rises wonderfully to high things when it is compassionately drawn to the low things of neighbors; and the more kindly it descends to the weak things of this world, the more vigorously it recurs to the things on high" (II, 5). In this ever timely teaching, the Fathers of the Second Vatican Council found inspiration to outline the image of today's Pastor. Let us pray to the Virgin Mary that the example and teaching of Saint Gregory the Great may be followed by pastors of the Church and also by those in charge of civil institutions.

(3 September 2006)

* * *

Today I would like to present the figure of one of the greatest Fathers in the history of the Church, one of four Doctors
of the West, Pope Saint Gregory, who was Bishop of Rome
from 590 to 604 and who earned the traditional title of *Mag-
nus* / the Great. Gregory was truly a great Pope and a great
Doctor of the Church! He was born in Rome about 540
into a rich patrician family of the *gens Anicia*, who were distinguished not only for their noble blood but also for their
adherence to the Christian faith and for their service to the
Apostolic See. Two Popes came from this family: Felix III
(483–492), the great-great grandfather of Gregory, and Aga-
petus (535–536). The house in which Gregory grew up stood
on the Clivus Scauri, surrounded by majestic buildings that
attested to the greatness of ancient Rome and the spiritual
strength of Christianity. The example of his parents, Gord-
ian and Sylvia, both venerated as Saints, and those of his
father's sisters, Aemiliana and Tharsilla, who lived in their
own home as consecrated virgins following a path of prayer
and self-denial, inspired lofty Christian sentiments in him.

In the footsteps of his father, Gregory entered early into an
administrative career which reached its climax in 572, when
he became Prefect of the city. This office, complicated by
the sorry times, allowed him to apply himself on a vast range
to every type of administrative problem, drawing light for
future duties from them. In particular, he retained a deep
sense of order and discipline: having become Pope, he advised
Bishops to take as a model for the management of ecclesial
affairs diligence and respect for the law like civil functionar-
ies. Yet this life could not have satisfied him since, shortly
after, he decided to leave every civil assignment in order to
withdraw to his home to begin the monastic life, transforming his family home into the monastery of Saint Andrew
on the Coelian Hill. This period of monastic life, the life of
permanent dialogue with the Lord in listening to his Word,

constituted a perennial nostalgia to which he referred ever anew and ever more in his homilies. In the midst of the pressure of pastoral worries, he often recalled it in his writings as a happy time of recollection in God, dedication to prayer, and peaceful immersion in study. Thus, he could acquire that deep understanding of Sacred Scripture and of the Fathers of the Church that later served him in his work.

But the cloistered withdrawal of Gregory did not last long. The precious experience that he gained in civil administration during a period marked by serious problems, the relationships he had had in this post with the Byzantines, and the universal respect that he acquired induced Pope Pelagius to appoint him deacon and to send him to Constantinople as his "apocrisarius"—today one would say "Apostolic Nuncio"— in order to help overcome the last traces of the Monophysite controversy and above all to obtain the Emperor's support in the effort to check the Lombard invaders. The stay at Constantinople, where he resumed monastic life with a group of monks, was very important for Gregory, since it permitted him to acquire direct experience of the Byzantine world as well as to approach the problem of the Lombards, who would later put his ability and energy to the test during the years of his Pontificate. After some years he was recalled to Rome by the Pope, who appointed him his secretary. They were difficult years: the continual rain, flooding due to overflowing rivers, the famine that afflicted many regions of Italy as well as Rome. Finally, even the plague broke out, which claimed numerous victims, among whom was also Pope Pelagius II. The clergy, people, and senate were unanimous in choosing Gregory as his Successor to the See of Peter. He tried to resist, even attempting to flee, but to no avail: finally, he had to yield. The year was 590.

Recognizing the will of God in what had happened, the new Pontiff immediately and enthusiastically set to work.

From the beginning he showed a singularly enlightened vision of the reality with which he had to deal, an extraordinary capacity for work confronting both ecclesial and civil affairs, a constant and even balance in making decisions, at times with courage, imposed on him by his office. Abundant documentation has been preserved from his governance thanks to the *Register* of his Letters (approximately 800), reflecting the complex questions that arrived on his desk on a daily basis. They were questions that came from Bishops, Abbots, clergy, and even from civil authorities of every order and rank. Among the problems that afflicted Italy and Rome at that time was one of special importance both in the civil and ecclesial spheres: the Lombard question. The Pope dedicated all possible energy to it in view of a truly peaceful solution. Contrary to the Byzantine Emperor, who assumed that the Lombards were only uncouth individuals and predators to be defeated or exterminated, Saint Gregory saw this people with the eyes of a good pastor and was concerned with proclaiming the word of salvation to them, establishing fraternal relationships with them in view of a future peace founded on mutual respect and peaceful coexistence between Italians, Imperials, and Lombards. He was concerned with the conversion of the young people and the new civil structure of Europe: the Visigoths of Spain, the Franks, the Saxons, the immigrants in Britain, and the Lombards were the privileged recipients of his evangelizing mission. Yesterday we celebrated the liturgical Memorial of Saint Augustine of Canterbury, the leader of a group of monks Gregory assigned to go to Britain to evangelize England.

The Pope—who was a true peacemaker—deeply committed himself to establishing an effective peace in Rome and in Italy by undertaking intense negotiations with Agilulf, the Lombard King. This negotiation led to a period of truce that lasted for about three years (598–601), after which, in 603, it was possible to stipulate a more stable armistice. This positive result was obtained also thanks to the parallel contacts that, meanwhile, the Pope undertook with Queen Theodolinda, a Bavarian princess who, unlike the leaders of other Germanic peoples, was Catholic, deeply Catholic. A series of Letters of Pope Gregory to this Queen has been preserved in which he reveals his respect and friendship for her. Theodolinda, little by little, was able to guide the King to Catholicism, thus preparing the way to peace. The Pope also was careful to send her relics for the Basilica of Saint John the Baptist which she had had built in Monza and did not fail to send his congratulations and precious gifts for the same Cathedral of Monza on the occasion of the birth and baptism of her son, Adaloald. The series of events concerning this Queen constitutes a beautiful testimony to the importance of women in the history of the Church. Gregory constantly focused on three basic objectives: to limit the Lombard expansion in Italy; to preserve Queen Theodolinda from the influence of schismatics and to strengthen the Catholic faith; and to mediate between the Lombards and the Byzantines in view of an accord that guaranteed peace in the Peninsula and at the same time permitted the evangelization of the Lombards themselves. Therefore, in the complex situation his focus was constantly twofold: to promote understanding on the diplomatic-political level and to spread the proclamation of the true faith among the peoples.

Along with his purely spiritual and pastoral action, Pope Gregory also became an active protagonist in multifaceted social activities. With the revenues from the Roman See's substantial patrimony in Italy, especially in Sicily, he bought and distributed grain, assisted those in need, helped priests, monks, and nuns who lived in poverty, paid the ransom for citizens held captive by the Lombards, and purchased armistices and truces. Moreover, whether in Rome or other parts of Italy, he carefully carried out administrative reorganization, giving precise instructions so that the goods of the Church, useful for her sustenance and evangelizing work in the world, were managed with absolute rectitude and according to the rules of justice and mercy. He demanded that the tenants on Church territory be protected from dishonest agents and, in cases of fraud, quickly compensated, so that the face of the Bride of Christ was not soiled with dishonest profits.

Gregory carried out this intense activity notwithstanding his poor health, which often forced him to remain in bed for days on end. The fasts practiced during the years of monastic life had caused him serious digestive problems. Furthermore, his voice was so feeble that he was often obliged to entrust the reading of his homilies to the deacon, so that the faithful present in the Roman Basilicas could hear him. On feast days he did his best to celebrate the *Missarum sollemnia*, that is, the solemn Mass, and then he met personally with the People of God, who were very fond of him, because they saw in him the authoritative reference from whom to draw security: not by chance was the title *consul Dei* quickly attributed to him. Notwithstanding the very difficult conditions in which he had to work, he gained the faithful's trust, thanks to his holiness of life and rich humanity, achieving truly magnificent results for his time and for the future. He was a man immersed in God: his desire for God was always alive in the depths of his soul, and precisely because of this he was always close to his neighbor, to the needy people of his time. Indeed, during a desperate period of havoc, he was able to create peace and give hope. This man of God shows us the true sources of peace, from which true hope comes. Thus, he becomes a guide also for us today.

(28 May 2008)

Saint John Chrysostom

Throughout the year, the liturgy presents to us as examples holy ministers of the Altar who have drawn strength from the imitation of Christ in daily intimacy with him in the celebration and adoration of the Eucharist. A few days ago, we commemorated Saint John Chrysostom, Patriarch of Constantinople at the end of the fourth century. He was described as "golden-mouthed" because of his extraordinary eloquence; he was also called "Doctor of the Eucharist" because of the vastness and depth of his teaching on the Most Holy Sacrament. The "Divine Liturgy" which is most frequently celebrated in the Eastern Church and which bears his name as well as his motto: "a man full of zeal suffices to transform a people", shows the effectiveness of Christ's action through his ministers.

(18 September 2005)

* * *

It can be said that John of Antioch, nicknamed "Chrysostom", that is, "golden-mouthed", because of his eloquence, is also still alive today because of his works. An anonymous copyist left in writing that "they cross the whole globe like flashes of lightening." Chrysostom's writings also enable us, as they did the faithful of his time whom his frequent exiles deprived of his presence, to live with his books, despite his absence. This is what he himself suggested in a letter when he was in exile (*To Olympias*, Letter 8, 45).

He was born in about the year 349 A.D. in Antioch, Syria (today Antakya in Southern Turkey). He carried out his priestly ministry there for about eleven years, until 397, when, appointed Bishop of Constantinople, he exercised his episcopal ministry in the capital of the Empire prior to his two exiles, which succeeded one close upon the other—in 403 and 407. Let us limit ourselves today to examining the years Chrysostom spent in Antioch.

He lost his father at a tender age and lived with Anthusa, his mother, who instilled in him exquisite human sensitivity and a deep Christian faith. After completing his elementary and advanced studies crowned by courses in philosophy and rhetoric, he had as his teacher Libanius, a pagan and the most famous rhetorician of that time. At his school John became the greatest orator of late Greek antiquity. He was baptized in 368 and trained for the ecclesiastical life by Bishop Meletius, who instituted him as lector in 371. This event marked Chrysostom's official entry into the ecclesiastical *cursus*. From 367 to 372, he attended the *Asceterius*, a sort of seminary in Antioch, together with a group of young men, some of whom later became Bishops, under the guidance of the exegete Diodore of Tarsus, who initiated John into the literal and grammatical exegesis characteristic of Antiochean tradition.

He then withdrew for four years to the hermits on the neighboring Mount Silpius. He extended his retreat for a further two years, living alone in a cave under the guidance of an "old hermit". In that period, he dedicated himself unreservedly to meditating on "the laws of Christ", the Gospels, and especially the Letters of Paul. Having fallen ill, he found it impossible to care for himself unaided and therefore had to return to the Christian community in Antioch (cf. Palladius, *Dialogue on the Life of Saint John Chrysostom* 5). The Lord, his biographer explains, intervened with the illness at the right moment to enable John to follow his true vocation. In fact, he himself was later to write that were he to choose between the troubles of Church government and the tranquility of monastic life, he would have preferred pastoral service a thousand times (cf. *On the Priesthood* 6, 7): it was precisely to this that Chrysostom felt called. It was here that he reached the crucial turning point in the story of his vocation: a full-time pastor of souls! Intimacy with the Word of God, cultivated in his years at the hermitage, had developed in him an irresistible urge to preach the Gospel, to give to others what he himself had received in his years of meditation. The missionary ideal thus launched him into pastoral care, his heart on fire.

Between 378 and 379, he returned to the city. He was ordained a deacon in 381 and a priest in 386 and became a famous preacher in his city's churches. He preached homilies against the Arians, followed by homilies commemorating the Antiochean martyrs and other important liturgical celebrations: this was an important teaching of faith in Christ and also in the light of his saints. The year 387 was John's "heroic year", that of the so-called "revolt of the statues". As a sign of protest against levied taxes, the people destroyed the Emperor's statues. It was in those days of Lent and the fear of the Emperor's impending reprisal that Chrysostom gave his twenty-two vibrant *Homilies on the Statues*, whose aim was to induce repentance and conversion. This was followed by a period of serene pastoral care (387–397).

Chrysostom is among the most prolific of the Fathers: seventeen treatises, more than seven hundred authentic homilies, commentaries on Matthew and on Paul (Letters to the Romans, Corinthians, Ephesians, and Hebrews),

and 241 letters are extant. He was not a speculative theologian. Nevertheless, he passed on the Church's tradition
and reliable doctrine in an age of theological controversies,
sparked above all by Arianism or, in other words, the denial
of Christ's divinity. He is therefore a trustworthy witness
of the dogmatic development achieved by the Church from
the fourth to the fifth centuries. His is a perfectly pastoral
theology in which there is constant concern for consistency
between thought expressed via words and existential experience. It is this in particular that forms the main theme of the
splendid catecheses with which he prepared catechumens to
receive Baptism. On approaching death, he wrote that the
value of man lies in "exact knowledge of true doctrine and
in rectitude of life" (*Letter from Exile*). Both these things,
knowledge of truth and rectitude of life, go hand in hand:
knowledge has to be expressed in life. All his discourses
aimed to develop in the faithful the use of intelligence, of
true reason, in order to understand and to put into practice
the moral and spiritual requirements of faith.

John Chrysostom was anxious to accompany his writings
with the person's integral development in his physical, intellectual, and religious dimensions. The various phases of his
growth are compared to as many seas in an immense ocean:
"The first of these seas is childhood" (*Homily* 81, 5 *on Matthew's Gospel*). Indeed, "it is precisely at this early age that
inclinations to vice or virtue are manifest." Thus, God's law
must be impressed upon the soul from the outset "as on a
wax tablet" (*Homily* 3, 1 *on John's Gospel*): This is indeed the
most important age. We must bear in mind how fundamentally important it is that the great orientations which give
man a proper outlook on life truly enter him in this first
phase of life. Chrysostom therefore recommended: "From
the tenderest age, arm children with spiritual weapons and
teach them to make the Sign of the Cross on their forehead

with their hand" (*Homily, 12, 7 on First Corinthians*). Then come adolescence and youth: "Following childhood is the sea of adolescence, where violent winds blow ..., for concupiscence ... grows within us" (*Homily 81, 5 on Matthew's Gospel*). Lastly comes engagement and marriage: "Youth is succeeded by the age of the mature person who assumes family commitments: this is the time to seek a wife" (*ibid.*). He recalls the aims of marriage, enriching them—referring to virtue and temperance—with a rich fabric of personal relationships. Properly prepared spouses therefore bar the way to divorce: everything takes place with joy, and children can be educated in virtue. Then when the first child is born, he is "like a bridge; the three become one flesh, because the child joins the two parts" (*Homily 12, 5 on the Letter to the Colossians*), and the three constitute "a family, a Church in miniature" (*Homily 20, 6 on the Letter to the Ephesians*).

Chrysostom's preaching usually took place during the liturgy, the "place" where the community is built with the Word and the Eucharist. The assembly gathered here expresses the one Church (*Homily 8, 7 on the Letter to the Romans*), the same Word is addressed everywhere to all (*Homily 24, 2 on First Corinthians*), and Eucharistic Communion becomes an effective sign of unity (*Homily 32, 7 on Matthew's Gospel*). His pastoral project was incorporated into the Church's life, in which the lay faithful assume the priestly, royal, and prophetic office with Baptism. To the lay faithful he said: "Baptism will also make you king, priest, and prophet" (*Homily 3, 5 on Second Corinthians*). From this stems the fundamental duty of the mission, because each one is to some extent responsible for the salvation of others: "This is the principle of our social life ... not to be solely concerned with ourselves!" (*Homily 9, 2 on Genesis*). This all takes place between two poles: the great Church and the "Church in miniature", the family, in a reciprocal relationship. As you can see, dear brothers and sisters, Chrysostom's lesson on the authentically Christian presence of the lay faithful in the family and in society is still more timely than ever today. Let us pray to the Lord to make us docile to the teachings of this great Master of the faith.

(19 September 2007)

The Exaltation of the Holy Cross

The liturgical Feast of the Triumph of the Cross. In the Year dedicated to the Eucharist this feast acquires a particular significance: it invites us to meditate on the deep and indissoluble bond that unites the Eucharistic Celebration and the mystery of the Cross. Every Holy Mass, in fact, actualizes the redeeming sacrifice of Christ. "Every priest who celebrates Holy Mass", our beloved John Paul II wrote in the Encyclical *Ecclesia de Eucharistia,* "together with the Christian community which takes part in it, is led back in spirit" to Golgotha and to the "hour" of his death on the Cross (no. 4). The Eucharist is therefore the memorial of the entire Paschal Mystery: the Passion, death, descent into hell, Resurrection, and Ascension into Heaven; and the Cross is the moving manifestation of the act of infinite love with which the Son of God saved mankind and the world from sin and death. For this reason, the sign of the Cross is the fundamental act of our prayer, of Christian prayer. Making the sign of the Cross—as we will do during the Blessing— means saying a visible and public "yes" to the One who died and rose for us, to God who in the humility and weakness of his love is the Almighty, stronger than all the power and intelligence of the world.

After the consecration of Holy Mass, the assembly of the faithful, aware of being in the real presence of the Crucified and Risen Christ, exclaims: "Christ has died, Christ is risen, Christ will come again." With the eyes of faith, the Community recognizes the living Jesus by the signs of his Passion and with Thomas can repeat, full of wonder: "My Lord and my God!" (Jn 20:28). The Eucharist is a mystery of death and of glory like the Crucifixion, which is not an accident on the journey but the way by which Christ entered into his glory (cf. Lk 24:26) and reconciled the whole of humanity, overcoming all enmity. This is why the liturgy invites us to pray with trusting hope: *Mane nobiscum, Domine!* Stay with us, Lord, who has redeemed the world with your Holy Cross!

Mary, present on Calvary beneath the Cross, is also present with the Church and as Mother of the Church in each one of our Eucharistic Celebrations (cf. *Ecclesia de Eucharistia*, no. 57). No one better than she, therefore, can teach us to understand and live Holy Mass with faith and love, uniting ourselves with Christ's redeeming sacrifice. When we receive Holy Communion, like Mary and united to her, we too clasp the wood that Jesus with his love transformed into an instrument of salvation and pronounce our "Amen", our "Yes" to Love, crucified and risen.

(11 September 2005)

Our Lady of Sorrows

I would like to reflect on two recent and important liturgical events: the Feast of the Exaltation of the Holy Cross, celebrated on 14 September, and the Memorial of Our Lady of Sorrows, celebrated the following day. These two liturgical celebrations can be summed up visually in the traditional image of the Crucifixion, which portrays the Virgin Mary at the foot of the Cross, according to the description of the Evangelist John, the only one of the Apostles who stayed by the dying Jesus. But what does exalting the Cross mean? Is it not maybe scandalous to venerate a shameful form of execution? The Apostle Paul says: "We preach Christ crucified, a stumbling block to Jews and folly to Gentiles" (I Cor 1:23). Christians, however, do not exalt just any cross but the Cross which Jesus sanctified with his sacrifice, the fruit and testimony of immense love. Christ on the Cross pours out his Blood to set humanity free from the slavery of sin and death. Therefore, from being a sign of malediction, the Cross was transformed into a sign of blessing, from a symbol of death into a symbol par excellence of the Love that overcomes hatred and violence and generates immortal life. "*O Crux ave, spes unica!* O Cross, our only hope!" Thus sings the liturgy.

The Evangelist recounts: Mary was standing by the Cross (cf. Jn 19:25–27). Her sorrow is united with that of her Son. It is a sorrow full of faith and love. The Virgin on Calvary participates in the saving power of the suffering of Christ, joining her "fiat", her "yes", to that of her Son. Dear brothers and sisters, spiritually united to Our Lady of Sorrows, let us also renew our "yes" to God, who chose the Way of the Cross in order to save us. This is a great mystery which continues and will continue to take place until the end of the world and which also asks for our collaboration. May Mary help us to take up our cross every day and follow Jesus faithfully on the path of obedience, sacrifice, and love.

(17 September 2006)

Saint Cyprian

An excellent African Bishop of the third century, Saint Cyprian [was] "the first Bishop in Africa to obtain the crown of martyrdom". His fame, Pontius the Deacon, his first biographer, attests, is also linked to his literary corpus and pastoral activity during the thirteen years between his conversion and his martyrdom (cf. *Life and Passion of Saint Cyprian* 19, 1; 1, 1). Cyprian was born in Carthage into a rich pagan family. After a dissipated youth, he converted to Christianity at the age of thirty-five. He himself often told of his spiritual journey, "When I was still lying in darkness and gloomy night", he wrote a few months after his Baptism,

> I used to regard it as extremely difficult and demanding to do what God's mercy was suggesting to me. I myself was held in bonds by the innumerable errors of my previous life, from which I did not believe I could possibly be delivered, so I was disposed to acquiesce in my clinging vices and to indulge my sins.... But after that, by the help of the water of new birth, the stain of my former life was washed away, and a light from above, serene and pure, was infused into my reconciled heart ... a second birth restored me to a new man. Then, in a wondrous manner every doubt began to fade.... I clearly understood that what had first lived within me, enslaved by the vices of the flesh, was earthly and that what, instead, the Holy Spirit had wrought within me was divine and heavenly. (*Ad Donatum* 3–4)

Immediately after his conversion, despite envy and resistance, Cyprian was chosen for the priestly office and raised to the dignity of Bishop. In the brief period of his episcopacy, he had to face the first two persecutions sanctioned by imperial decree: that of Decius (250) and that of Valerian (257–258). After the particularly harsh persecution of Decius, the Bishop had to work strenuously to restore order to the Christian community. Indeed, many of the faithful had abjured or at any rate had not behaved correctly when put to the test. They were the so-called *lapsi*—that is, the "fallen"—who ardently desired to be readmitted to the community. The debate on their readmission actually divided the Christians of Carthage into laxists and rigorists. These difficulties were compounded by a serious epidemic of the plague, which swept through Africa and gave rise to anguished theological questions both within the community and in the confrontation with pagans. Lastly, the controversy between Saint Cyprian and Stephen, Bishop of Rome, concerning the validity of Baptism administered to pagans by heretical Christians, must not be forgotten.

In these truly difficult circumstances, Cyprian revealed his choice gifts of government: he was severe but not inflexible with the *lapsi*, granting them the possibility of forgiveness after exemplary repentance. Before Rome, he staunchly defended the healthy traditions of the African Church; he was deeply human and steeped with the most authentic Gospel spirit when he urged Christians to offer brotherly assistance to pagans during the plague; he knew how to maintain the proper balance when reminding the faithful—excessively afraid of losing their lives and their earthly possessions—that true life and true goods are not those of this world; he was implacable in combating corrupt morality and the sins that devastated moral life, especially avarice. "Thus he spent his days", Pontius the Deacon tells at this point, "when at the bidding of the proconsul, the officer with his soldiers all of a sudden came unexpectedly upon him in his grounds" (*Life and Passion of Saint Cyprian* 15, 1). On that day, the holy Bishop was arrested and, after being questioned briefly, courageously faced martyrdom in the midst of his people.

The numerous treatises and letters that Cyprian wrote were always connected with his pastoral ministry. Little inclined to theological speculation, he wrote above all for the edification of the community and to encourage the good conduct of the faithful. Indeed, the Church was easily his favorite subject. Cyprian distinguished between the *visible*, hierarchical *Church* and the *invisible* mystical *Church* but forcefully affirmed that the Church is one, founded on Peter. He never wearied of repeating that "if a man deserts the Chair of Peter upon whom the Church was built, does he think that he is in the Church?" (cf. *De unit.* [*On the unity of the Catholic Church*] 4). Cyprian knew well that "outside the Church there is no salvation", and said so in strong words (*Epistles* 4, 4 and 73, 21); and he knew that "no one can have God as Father who does not have the Church as mother" (*De unit.* 6). An indispensable characteristic of the Church is unity, symbolized by Christ's seamless garment (*ibid.*, 7): Cyprian said that this unity is founded on Peter (*ibid.*, 4) and finds its perfect fulfillment in the Eucharist (*Epistle* 63, 13). "God is one and Christ is one", Cyprian cautioned, "and his Church is one, and the faith is one, and the Christian people is joined into a substantial unity of body by the cement of concord. Unity cannot be severed. And what is one by its nature cannot be separated" (*De unit.* 23).

We have spoken of his thought on the Church, but, lastly, let us not forget Cyprian's teaching on prayer. I am particularly fond of his treatise on the Our Father, which has been a great help to me in understanding and reciting the

Lord's Prayer better. Cyprian teaches that it is precisely in the Lord's Prayer that the proper way to pray is presented to Christians. And he stresses that this prayer is in the plural in order that "the person who prays it might not pray for himself alone. "Our prayer", he wrote, "is public and common; and when we pray, we pray not for one, but for the whole people, because we, the whole people, are one" (*De Dom. orat.* [*Treatise on the Lord's Prayer*] 8). Thus, personal and liturgical prayer seem to be strongly bound. Their unity stems from the fact that they respond to the same Word of God. The Christian does not say "*my* Father" but "*our* Father", even in the secrecy of a closed room, because he knows that in every place, on every occasion, he is a member of one and the same Body.

"Therefore let us pray, beloved Brethren," the Bishop of Carthage wrote,

> as God our Teacher has taught us. It is a trusting and intimate prayer to beseech God with his own Word, to raise to his ears the prayer of Christ. Let the Father acknowledge the words of his Son when we pray, and let him also who dwells within our breast himself dwell in our voice.... But let our speech and petition when we pray be under discipline, observing quietness and modesty. Let us consider that we are standing in God's sight. We must please the divine eyes both with the position of the body and with the measure of voice.... Moreover, when we meet together with the brethren in one place and celebrate divine sacrifices with God's priest, we ought to be mindful of modesty and discipline—not to throw abroad our prayers indiscriminately, with unsubdued voices, or to cast to God with tumultuous wordiness a petition that ought to be commended to God by modesty; for God is the hearer, not of the voice, but of the heart (*non vocis sed cordis auditor est*). (3–4)

Today too, these words still apply and help us to celebrate the Holy Liturgy well.

Ultimately, Cyprian placed himself at the root of that fruitful theological and spiritual tradition which sees the "heart" as the privileged place for prayer. Indeed, in accordance with the Bible and the Fathers, the heart is the intimate depths of man, the place in which God dwells. In it occurs the encounter in which God speaks to man, and man listens to God; man speaks to God, and God listens to man. All this happens through one divine Word. In this very sense—re-echoing Cyprian—Smaragdus, Abbot of Saint Michael on the Meuse in the early years of the ninth century, attests that prayer "is the work of the heart, not of the lips, because God does not look at the words but at the heart of the person praying" (*Diadema monachorum* [*Diadem of the monks*] 1).

Dear friends, let us make our own this receptive heart and "understanding mind" of which the Bible (cf. 1 Kgs 3:9) and the Fathers speak. How great is our need for it! Only then will we be able to experience fully that God is our Father and that the Church, the holy Bride of Christ, is truly our Mother.

(6 June 2007)

Saint Matthew, Apostle and Evangelist

To tell the truth, it is almost impossible to paint a complete picture of [Saint Matthew] because the information we have of him is scarce and fragmentary. What we can do, however, is to outline not so much his biography as, rather, the profile of him that the Gospel conveys.

To begin with, he always appears in the lists of the Twelve chosen by Jesus (cf. Mt 10:3; Mk 3:18; Lk 6:15; Acts 1:13). His name in Hebrew means "gift of God". The first canonical Gospel, which goes under his name, presents him to us in the list of the Twelve, labeled very precisely: "the tax collector" (Mt 10:3). Thus, Matthew is identified with the man sitting at the tax office whom Jesus calls to follow him: "As Jesus passed on from there, he saw a man called Matthew sitting at the tax office; and he said to him, 'Follow me.' And he rose and followed him" (Mt 9:9). Mark (cf. 2:13–17) and Luke (cf. 5:27–30) also tell of the calling of the man sitting at the tax office, but they call him "Levi". To imagine the scene described in Matthew 9:9, it suffices to recall Caravaggio's magnificent canvas, kept here in Rome at the Church of Saint Louis of the French. A further biographical detail emerges from the Gospels: in the passage that immediately precedes the account of the call, a miracle that Jesus worked at Capernaum is mentioned (cf. Mt 9:1–8; Mk 2:1–12) and the proximity to the Sea of Galilee, that is, the Lake of Tiberias (cf. Mk 2:13–14). It is possible to deduce from this that Matthew exercised the function of tax collector at Capernaum, which was exactly located "by the sea" (Mt 4:13), where Jesus was a permanent guest at Peter's house.

On the basis of these simple observations that result from the Gospel, we can advance a pair of thoughts. The first is that Jesus welcomes into the group of his close friends a man who, according to the concepts in vogue in Israel at that time, was regarded as a public sinner. Matthew, in fact, not only handled money deemed impure because of its provenance from people foreign to the People of God, but he also collaborated with an alien and despicably greedy authority whose tributes, moreover, could be arbitrarily determined. This is why the Gospels several times link "tax collectors and sinners" (Mt 9:10; Lk 15:1), as well as "tax collectors and prostitutes" (Mt 21:31). Furthermore, they see publicans as an example of miserliness (cf. Mt 5:46: they only like those who like them) and mention one of them, Zacchaeus, as "a chief tax collector, and rich" (Lk 19:2), whereas popular opinion associated them with "extortioners, the unjust, adulterers" (Lk 18:11). A first fact strikes one based on these references: Jesus does not exclude anyone from his friendship. Indeed, precisely while he is at table in the home of Matthew-Levi, in response to those who expressed shock at the fact that he associated with people who had so little to recommend them, he made the important statement: "Those who are well have no need of a physician, but those who are sick; I came not to call the righteous, but sinners" (Mk 2:17).

The good news of the Gospel consists precisely in this: offering God's grace to the sinner! Elsewhere, with the famous words of the Pharisee and the publican who went up to the Temple to pray, Jesus actually indicates an anonymous tax collector as an appreciated example of humble trust in divine mercy: while the Pharisee is boasting of his own moral perfection, the "tax collector ... would not even lift up his eyes to heaven, but beat his breast, saying, 'God, be merciful to me a sinner!'" And Jesus comments: "I tell you, this man went down to his house justified rather than the other; for every one who exalts himself will be humbled, but he who humbles himself will be exalted" (Lk 18:13–14). Thus, in the figure of Matthew, the Gospels present to us a true and proper paradox: those who seem to be the farthest from holiness can even become a model of the acceptance of God's mercy and offer a glimpse of its marvelous effects in their own lives. Saint John Chrysostom makes an important point in this regard: he notes that only in the account of certain calls is the work of those concerned mentioned. Peter, Andrew, James, and John are called while they are fishing, while Matthew, while he is collecting tithes. These are unimportant jobs, Chrysostom comments, "because there is nothing more despicable than the tax collector, and nothing more common than fishing" (*In Matth. Hom.: PL* 57, 363). Jesus' call, therefore, also reaches people of a low social class while they go about their ordinary work.

Another reflection prompted by the Gospel narrative is that Matthew responds instantly to Jesus' call: "he rose and followed him." The brevity of the sentence clearly highlights Matthew's readiness in responding to the call. For him it meant leaving everything, especially what guaranteed him a reliable source of income, even if it was often unfair and dishonorable. Evidently, Matthew understood that familiarity with Jesus did not permit him to pursue activities of which God disapproved. The application to the present day is easy to see: it is not permissible today either to be attached to things that are incompatible with the following of Jesus, as is the case with riches dishonestly achieved. Jesus once said, mincing no words: "If you would be perfect, go, sell what you possess and give to the poor, and you will have treasure in heaven; and come, follow me" (Mt 19:21). This is exactly what Matthew did: he rose and followed him! In this "he rose", it is legitimate to read detachment from a sinful situation and, at the same time, a conscious attachment to a new, upright life in communion with Jesus.

Lastly, let us remember that the tradition of the ancient Church agrees in attributing to Matthew the paternity of the First Gospel. This had already begun with Bishop Papias of Hierapolis in Frisia, in about the year 130. He writes: "Matthew set down the words (of the Lord) in the Hebrew tongue, and everyone interpreted them as best he could" (in Eusebius of Caesarea, *Hist. Eccl.*, III, 39, 16). Eusebius, the historian, adds this piece of information: "When Matthew, who had first preached among the Jews, decided also to reach out to other peoples, he wrote down the Gospel he preached in his mother tongue; thus, he sought to put in writing, for those whom he was leaving, what they would be losing with his departure" (*ibid.*, III, 24, 6). The Gospel of Matthew written in Hebrew or Aramaic is no longer extant, but in the Greek Gospel that we possess we still continue to hear, in a certain way, the persuasive voice of the publican Matthew, who, having become an Apostle, continues to proclaim God's saving mercy to us. And let us listen to Saint Matthew's message, meditating upon it ever anew also to learn to stand up and follow Jesus with determination.

(30 August 2006)

Saint Pio of Pietrelcina

Throughout the year, the liturgy presents to us as examples holy ministers of the Altar who have drawn strength from the imitation of Christ in daily intimacy with him in the celebration and adoration of the Eucharist....

In our own age, the figure of Padre Pio, Saint Pio of Pietrelcina, whom we will commemorate this Friday [23 September], stands out. When he celebrated Holy Mass he relived the mystery of Calvary with such intensity so as to edify the faith and devotion of all. Moreover, the stigmata which God gave to him showed how closely he was conformed to the Crucified Jesus.

(18 September 2005)

Saint Gregory the Illuminator

More than eighteen centuries ago, this great Saint formed the Armenians into a Christian people, indeed, the first people officially to call themselves Christian. The conversion of the Armenians is an event that has profoundly marked the Armenian identity, not only on the personal level, but as an entire nation. This Saint is celebrated as the "Illuminator", a term that emphasizes the double function that Saint Gregory had in the history of the Armenian conversion. "Illumination" is a term used in Christian parlance to indicate the passage from darkness to the light of Christ. And, in truth, the great Illuminator is really Christ himself, whose light radiates through the entire existence of whoever welcomes him and follows him faithfully. Now, Saint Gregory was called the Illuminator precisely because the face of Christ was reflected in him in an extraordinary way. The word "illumination" also carries a further meaning in the Armenian context: it points to the light that derives from the diffusion of culture through teaching. This immediately brings to mind those monk-teachers who, through their preaching and following in the footsteps of Saint Gregory, spread the light of Gospel truth that reveals to man the very truth of his own being, thereby releasing rich cultural and spiritual resources.

(22 January 2008)

Translated by Andrew Matt.

Saint Jerome

Saint Jerome [was] a Church Father who centered his life on the Bible: he translated it into Latin, commented on it in his works, and, above all, strove to live it in practice throughout his long earthly life, despite the well-known difficult, hot-tempered character with which nature had endowed him.

Jerome was born into a Christian family in about 347 A.D. in Stridon. He was given a good education and was even sent to Rome to fine-tune his studies. As a young man he was attracted by the worldly life (cf. *Ep.* 22, 7), but his desire for and interest in the Christian religion prevailed. He received Baptism in about 366 and opted for the ascetic life. He went to Aquileia and joined a group of fervent Christians that had formed around Bishop Valerian and which he described as almost "a choir of blesseds" (*Chron. ad ann.* 374). He then left for the East and lived as a hermit in the Desert of Chalcis, south of Aleppo (*Ep.* 14, 10), devoting himself assiduously to study. He perfected his knowledge of Greek, began learning Hebrew (cf. *Ep.* 125, 12), and transcribed codices and Patristic writings (cf. *Ep.* 5, 2). Meditation, solitude, and contact with the Word of God helped his Christian sensibility to mature. He bitterly regretted the indiscretions of his youth (cf. *Ep.* 22, 7) and was keenly aware of the contrast between the pagan mentality and the Christian life: a contrast made famous by the dramatic and lively "vision"—of which he has left us an account—in which it seemed to him that he was being scourged before God because he was "Ciceronian rather than Christian" (cf. *Ep.* 22, 30).

In 382 he moved to Rome: here, acquainted with his fame as an ascetic and his ability as a scholar, Pope Damasus engaged him as secretary and counselor; the Pope encouraged him, for pastoral and cultural reasons, to embark on a new Latin translation of the biblical texts. Several members of the Roman aristocracy, especially noblewomen such as Paula, Marcella, Asella, Lea, and others, desirous of committing themselves to the way of Christian perfection and of deepening their knowledge of the Word of God, chose him as their spiritual guide and teacher in the methodical approach to the sacred texts. These noblewomen also learned Greek and Hebrew.

After the death of Pope Damasus, Jerome left Rome in 385 and went on pilgrimage, first to the Holy Land, a silent witness of Christ's earthly life, and then to Egypt, the favorite country of numerous monks (cf. *Contra Rufinum* 3, 22; *Ep.* 108, 6–14). In 386 he stopped in Bethlehem, where a monastery for men and a monastery for women were built through the generosity of the noblewoman Paula as well as a hospice for pilgrims bound for the Holy Land, "remembering Mary and Joseph who had found no room there" (*Ep.* 108, 14). He stayed in Bethlehem until he died, continuing to do a prodigious amount of work: he commented on the Word of God; he defended the faith, vigorously opposing various heresies; he urged the monks on to perfection; he taught classical and Christian culture to young students; he welcomed with a pastor's heart pilgrims who were visiting the Holy Land. He died in his cell close to the Grotto of the Nativity on 30 September 419–20.

Jerome's literary studies and vast erudition enabled him to revise and translate many biblical texts: an invaluable undertaking for the Latin Church and for Western culture. On the basis of the original Greek and Hebrew texts, and thanks to the comparison with previous versions, he revised the four Gospels in Latin, then the Psalter and a large part of the Old Testament. Taking into account the original Hebrew and Greek texts of the Septuagint, the classical Greek version of the Old Testament that dates back to pre-Christian times, as well as the earlier Latin versions, Jerome was able, with the assistance later of other collaborators, to produce a better translation: this constitutes the so-called *"Vulgate"*, the "official" text of the Latin Church which was recognized as such by the Council of Trent and which, after the recent revision, continues to be the "official" Latin text of the Church. It is interesting to point out the criteria which the great biblicist abided by in his work as a translator. He himself reveals them when he says that he respects even the order of the words of the Sacred Scriptures, for in them, he says, "the order of the words is also a mystery" (*Ep.* 57, 5), that is, a revelation. Furthermore, he reaffirms the need to refer to the original texts: "Should an argument on the New Testament arise between Latins because of interpretations of the manuscripts that fail to agree, let us turn to the original, that is, to the Greek text in which the New Testament was written. Likewise, with regard to the Old Testament, if there are divergences between the Greek and Latin texts we should have recourse to the original Hebrew text; thus, we shall be able to find in the streams all that flows from the source" (*Ep.* 106, 2). Jerome also commented on many biblical texts. For him the commentaries had to offer multiple opinions "so that the shrewd reader, after reading the different explanations and hearing many opinions—to be accepted or rejected—may judge which is the most reliable and, like an expert moneychanger, may reject the false coin" (*Contra Rufinum* 1, 16).

Jerome refuted with energy and liveliness the heretics who contested the tradition and faith of the Church. He also demonstrated the importance and validity of Christian literature, which had by then become a real culture that deserved to be compared with classical literature: he did so by composing his *De Viris Illustribus*, a work in which Jerome presents the biographies of more than a hundred Christian authors. Further, he wrote biographies of monks, illustrating, alongside other spiritual paths, the monastic ideal. In addition, he translated various works by Greek authors. Lastly, in the important *Epistulae*, a masterpiece of Latin literature, Jerome emerges with the profile of a man of culture, an ascetic, and a guide of souls.

What can we learn from Saint Jerome? It seems to me, this above all; to love the Word of God in Sacred Scripture. Saint Jerome said: "Ignorance of the Scriptures is ignorance of Christ." It is therefore important that every Christian live in contact and in personal dialogue with the Word of God given to us in Sacred Scripture. This dialogue with Scripture must always have two dimensions: on the one hand, it must be a truly personal dialogue because God speaks with each one of us through Sacred Scripture, and it has a message for each one. We must not read Sacred Scripture as a word of the past but as the Word of God that is also addressed to us, and we must try to understand what it is that the Lord wants to tell us. However, to avoid falling into individualism, we must bear in mind that the Word of God has been given to us precisely in order to build communion and to join forces in the truth on our journey toward God. Thus, although it is always a personal Word, it is also a Word that builds community, that builds the Church. We must therefore read it in communion with the living Church. The privileged place for reading and listening to the Word of God is the liturgy, in which, celebrating the Word and making Christ's Body present in the Sacrament, we actualize the Word in our lives and make it present among us. We must never forget that the Word of God transcends time. Human opinions come and go. What is very modern today will be very antiquated tomorrow. On the other hand, the Word of God is the Word of eternal life; it bears within it eternity and is valid forever. By carrying the Word of God within us, we therefore carry within us eternity, eternal life.

I thus conclude with a word Saint Jerome once addressed to Saint Paulinus of Nola. In it the great exegete expressed this very reality, that is, in the Word of God we receive eternity, eternal life. Saint Jerome said: "Seek to learn on earth those truths which will remain ever valid in Heaven" (*Ep.* 53, 10).

(7 November 2007)

Saint Ignatius of Antioch

Today, we will be speaking of Saint Ignatius, who was the third Bishop of Antioch from 70 to 107, the date of his martyrdom. At that time, Rome, Alexandria, and Antioch were the three great metropolises of the Roman Empire. The Council of Nicaea mentioned three "primacies": Rome, but also Alexandria and Antioch participated in a certain sense in a "primacy". Saint Ignatius was Bishop of Antioch, which today is located in Turkey. Here in Antioch, as we know from the Acts of the Apostles, a flourishing Christian community developed. Its first Bishop was the Apostle Peter—or so tradition claims—and it was there that the disciples were *"for the first time called Christians"* (Acts 11:26). Eusebius of Caesarea, a fourth-century historian, dedicated an entire chapter of his *Church History* to the life and literary works of Ignatius (cf. 3, 36). Eusebius writes: "The Report says that he [Ignatius] was sent from Syria to Rome and became food for wild beasts on account of his testimony to Christ. And as he made the journey through Asia under the strictest military surveillance" (he called the guards "ten leopards" in his *Letter to the Romans* 5, 1), "he fortified the parishes in the various cities where he stopped by homilies and exhortations and warned them above all to be especially on their guard against the heresies that were then beginning to prevail and exhorted them to hold fast to the tradition of the Apostles." The first place Ignatius stopped on the way to

his martyrdom was the city of Smyrna, where Saint Polycarp, a disciple of Saint John, was Bishop. Here, Ignatius
wrote four letters, respectively to the Churches of Ephesus,
Magnesia, Tralli, and Rome. "Having left Smyrna", Eusebius continues, Ignatius reached Troas and "wrote again":
two letters to the Churches of Philadelphia and Smyrna and
one to Bishop Polycarp. Thus, Eusebius completes the list of
his letters, which have come down to us from the Church
of the first century as a precious treasure. In reading these
texts, one feels the freshness of the faith of the generation
which had still known the Apostles. In these letters, the
ardent love of a saint can also be felt. Lastly, the martyr traveled from Troas to Rome, where he was thrown to fierce
wild animals in the Flavian Amphitheater.

No Church Father has expressed the longing for *union*
with Christ and for *life* in him with the intensity of Ignatius.
We therefore read the Gospel passage on the vine, which
according to John's Gospel is Jesus. In fact, two spiritual
"currents" converge in Ignatius, that of Paul, straining with
all his might for *union* with Christ, and that of John, concentrated on *life* in him. In turn, these two currents translate into the *imitation* of Christ, whom Ignatius several times
proclaimed as "my" or "our God". Thus, Ignatius implores
the Christians of Rome not to prevent his martyrdom since
he is impatient "to attain to Jesus Christ". And he explains,
"It is better for me to die on behalf of Jesus Christ than to
reign over all the ends of the earth.... Him I seek, who
died for us: him I desire, who rose again for our sake....
Permit me to be an imitator of the Passion of my God!"
(*Romans* 5–6). One can perceive in these words on fire with
love the pronounced Christological "realism" typical of the
Church of Antioch, more focused than ever on the Incarnation of the Son of God and on his true and concrete humanity: "Jesus Christ", Saint Ignatius wrote to the Smyrnaeans,

"was *truly* of the seed of David", "he was *truly* born of a virgin" "and was *truly* nailed [to the Cross] for us" (1, 1).

Ignatius' irresistible longing for union with Christ was the foundation of a real "mysticism of unity". He describes himself: "I therefore did what befitted me as a man devoted to unity" (*Philadelphians* 8, 1). For Ignatius unity was first and foremost a prerogative of God, who, since he exists as Three Persons, is One in absolute unity. Ignatius often used to repeat that God is unity and that in God alone is unity found in its pure and original state. Unity to be brought about on this earth by Christians is no more than an imitation as close as possible to the divine archetype. Thus, Ignatius reached the point of being able to work out a vision of the Church strongly reminiscent of certain expressions in Clement of Rome's Letter to the Corinthians. For example, he wrote to the Christians of Ephesus: "It is fitting that you should concur with the will of your Bishop, which you also do. For your justly renowned presbytery, worthy of God, is fitted as exactly to the Bishop as the strings are to the harp. Therefore, in your concord and harmonious love, Jesus Christ is sung. And man by man, you become a choir, that being harmonious in love and taking up the song of God in unison you may with one voice sing to the Father ..." (4, 1–2). And after recommending to the Smyrnaeans: "Let no man do anything connected with Church without the Bishop", he confides to Polycarp:

> I offer my life for those who are submissive to the Bishop, to the presbyters and to the deacons, and may I along with them obtain my portion in God! Labor together with one another; strive in company together; run together; suffer together; sleep together; and awake together as the stewards and associates and servants of God. Please him under whom you fight and from whom you receive your wages. Let none of you be found a deserter. Let your Baptism endure

as your arms; your faith as your helmet; your love as your spear; your patience as a complete panoply. (*Polycarp* 6, 1–2)

Overall, it is possible to grasp in the *Letters* of Ignatius a sort of constant and fruitful dialectic between two characteristic aspects of Christian life: on the one hand, the hierarchical structure of the Ecclesial Community and, on the other, the fundamental unity that binds all the faithful in Christ. Consequently, their roles cannot be opposed to one another. On the contrary, the insistence on communion among believers and of believers with their Pastors was constantly reformulated in eloquent images and analogies: the harp, strings, intonation, the concert, the symphony. The special responsibility of Bishops, priests, and deacons in building the community is clear. This applies, first of all, to their invitation to love and unity. "Be one", Ignatius wrote to the Magnesians, echoing the prayer of Jesus at the Last Supper: "one supplication, one mind, one hope in love.... Therefore, all run together as into one temple of God, as to one altar, as to one Jesus Christ who came forth from one Father and is with and has gone to one" (7, 1–2). Ignatius was the first person in Christian literature to attribute to the Church the adjective "catholic" or "universal": "Wherever Jesus Christ is," he said, "there is the Catholic Church" (*Smyrnaeans* 8, 2). And precisely in the service of unity to the Catholic Church, the Christian community of Rome exercised a sort of primacy of love: "The Church which presides in the place of the region of the Romans, and which is worthy of God, worthy of honor, worthy of the highest happiness ... and which presides over love, is named from Christ and from the Father ..." (*Romans*, Prologue).

As can be seen, Ignatius is truly the "Doctor of Unity": unity of God and unity of Christ (despite the various heresies gaining ground which separated the human and the divine in Christ), unity of the Church, unity of the faithful in "faith and love, to which nothing is to be preferred" (*Smyrnaeans* 6, 1). Ultimately, Ignatius' realism invites the faithful of yesterday and today, invites us all, to make a gradual synthesis between *configuration to Christ* (union with him, life in him) and *dedication to his Church* (unity with the Bishop, generous service to the community and to the world). To summarize, it is necessary to achieve a synthesis between *communion* of the Church within herself and *mission*, the proclamation of the Gospel to others, until the other speaks through one dimension and believers increasingly "have obtained the inseparable Spirit, who is Jesus Christ" (*Magnesians* 15). Imploring from the Lord this "grace of unity" and in the conviction that the whole Church presides in charity (cf. *Romans*, Prologue), I address to you yourselves the same hope with which Ignatius ended his *Letter to the Trallians*: "Love one another with an undivided heart. Let my spirit be sanctified by yours, not only now, but also when I shall attain to God.... In [Jesus Christ] may you be found unblemished" (13). And let us pray that the Lord will help us to attain this unity and to be found at last unstained, because it is love that purifies souls.

(14 March 2007)

Saint Severinus Boethius

Boethius, born in Rome in about 480 from the noble Anicius lineage, entered public life when he was still young and by age twenty-five was already a senator. Faithful to his family's tradition, he devoted himself to politics, convinced that it would be possible to temper the fundamental structure of Roman society with the values of the new peoples. And in this new time of cultural encounter he considered it his role to reconcile and bring together these two cultures, the classical Roman and the nascent Ostrogoth culture. Thus, he was also politically active under Theodoric, who at the outset held him in high esteem. In spite of this public activity, Boethius did not neglect his studies and dedicated himself in particular to acquiring a deep knowledge of philosophical and religious subjects. However, he also wrote manuals on arithmetic, geometry, music, and astronomy, all with the intention of passing on the great Greco-Roman culture to the new generations, to the new times. In this context, in his commitment to fostering the encounter of cultures, he used the categories of Greek philosophy to present the Christian faith, here too seeking a synthesis between the Hellenistic-Roman heritage and the Gospel message. For this very reason Boethius was described as the last representative of ancient Roman culture and the first of the medieval intellectuals.

His most famous work is undoubtedly *De Consolatione Philosophiae*, which he wrote in prison to help explain his unjust detention. In fact, he had been accused of plotting against King Theodoric for having taken the side of his friend Senator Albinus in a court case. But this was a pretext. Actually, Theodoric, an Arian and a barbarian, suspected that Boethius was sympathizing with the Byzantine Emperor Justinian. Boethius was tried and sentenced to death. He was executed on 23 October 524, when he was only forty-four years old. It is precisely because of his tragic end that he can also speak from the heart of his own experience to contemporary man, and especially to the multitudes who suffer the same fate because of the injustice inherent in so much of "human justice". Through this work, *De Consolatione Philosophiae*, he sought consolation, enlightenment, and wisdom in prison. And he said that precisely in this situation he knew how to distinguish between apparent goods, which disappear in prison, and true goods, such as genuine friendship, which even in prison do not disappear. The loftiest good is God: Boethius—and he teaches us this—learned not to sink into a fatalism that extinguishes hope. He teaches us that it is not the event but Providence that governs, and Providence has a face. It is possible to speak to Providence because Providence is God. Thus, even in prison, he was left with the possibility of prayer, of dialogue with the One who saves us. At the same time, even in this situation he retained his sense of the beauty of culture and remembered the teaching of the great ancient Greek and Roman philosophers, such as Plato, Aristotle—he had begun to translate these Greeks into Latin—Cicero, Seneca, and also poets, such as Tibullus and Virgil.

Boethius held that philosophy, in the sense of the quest for true wisdom, was the true medicine of the soul (Bk I). On the other hand, man can experience authentic happiness only within his own interiority (Bk II). Boethius thus succeeded in finding meaning by thinking of his own personal tragedy in the light of a sapiential text of the Old Testament (Wis 7:30—8:1), which he cites: "Against wisdom evil does not prevail. She reaches mightily from one end of the earth to the other, and she orders all things well" (Bk III, 12: *PL* 63, 780). The so-called prosperity of the wicked is therefore proven to be false (Bk IV), and the providential nature of *adversa fortuna* is highlighted. Life's difficulties not only reveal how transient and short-lived life is, but are even shown to serve for identifying and preserving authentic relations among human beings. *Adversa fortuna*, in fact, makes it possible to discern false friends from true and makes one realize that nothing is more precious to the human being than a true friendship. The fatalistic acceptance of a condition of suffering is nothing short of perilous, the believer Boethius added, because "it eliminates at its roots the very possibility of prayer and of theological hope, which form the basis of man's relationship with God" (Bk V, 3: *PL* 63, 842).

The final peroration of *De Consolatione Philosophiae* can be considered a synthesis of the entire teaching that Boethius addressed to himself and all who might find themselves in his same conditions. Thus, in prison he wrote: "So combat vices, dedicate yourselves to a virtuous life oriented by hope, which draws the heart upward until it reaches Heaven with prayers nourished by humility. Should you refuse to lie, the imposition you have suffered can change into the enormous advantage of always having before your eyes the supreme Judge, who sees and knows how things truly are" (Bk V, 6: *PL* 63, 862). Every prisoner, regardless of the reason why he ended up in prison, senses how burdensome this particular human condition is, especially when it is brutalized, as it was for Boethius, by recourse to torture. Then particularly absurd is the condition of those like Boethius—whom the city of Pavia recognizes and celebrates in the liturgy as a martyr of the faith—who are tortured to death for no other reason than their own ideals and political and religious convictions. Boethius, the symbol of an immense number of people unjustly imprisoned in all ages and on all latitudes, is in fact an objective entrance way that gives access to contemplation of the mysterious Crucified One of Golgotha.

(12 March 2008)

Saints Simon and Jude, Apostles

Let us examine two of the Twelve Apostles: Simon the Cananaean and Jude Thaddaeus (not to be confused with Judas Iscariot). Let us look at them together, not only because they are always placed next to each other in the lists of the Twelve (cf. Mt 10:3, 4; Mk 3:18; Lk 6:15; Acts 1:13), but also because there is very little information about them, apart from the fact that the New Testament canon preserves one Letter attributed to Jude Thaddaeus.

Simon is given a nickname that varies in the four lists: while Matthew and Mark describe him as a "Cananaean", Luke instead describes him as a "Zealot". In fact, the two descriptions are equivalent because they mean the same thing: indeed, in Hebrew the verb *qanà'* means "to be jealous, ardent" and can be said both of God, since he is jealous with regard to his Chosen People (cf. Ex 20:5), and of men who burn with zeal in serving the one God with unreserved devotion, such as Elijah (cf. 1 Kgs 19:10). Thus, it is highly likely that even if this Simon was not exactly a member of the nationalist movement of Zealots, he was at least marked by passionate attachment to his Jewish identity, hence, for God, his People, and divine Law. If this was the case, Simon was worlds apart from Matthew, who, on the contrary, had an activity behind him as a tax collector that was frowned upon as entirely impure. This shows that Jesus called his disciples and collaborators, without exception, from the most varied social and religious backgrounds. It was people who interested him, not social classes or labels! And the best thing is that in the group of his followers, despite their differences, they all lived side by side, overcoming imaginable difficulties: indeed, what bound them together was Jesus himself, in whom they all found themselves united with one another. This is clearly a lesson for us who are often inclined to accentuate differences and even contrasts, forgetting that in Jesus Christ we are given the strength to get the better of our continual conflicts. Let us also bear in mind that the group of the Twelve is the prefiguration of the Church, where there must be room for all charisms, peoples, and races, all human qualities that find their composition and unity in communion with Jesus.

Then with regard to Jude Thaddaeus, this is what tradition has called him, combining two different names: in fact, whereas Matthew and Mark call him simply "Thaddaeus" (Mt 10:3; Mk 3:18), Luke calls him "Judas, the son of James" (Lk 6:16; Acts 1:13). The nickname "Thaddaeus" is of uncertain origin and is explained either as coming from the Aramaic *taddà'*, which means "breast" and would therefore suggest "magnanimous", or as an abbreviation of a Greek name, such as "Teodòro, Teòdoto". Very little about him has come down to us. John alone mentions a question he addressed to Jesus at the Last Supper: Thaddaeus says to the Lord: "Lord, how is it that you will manifest yourself to us and not to the world?" This is a very timely question which we also address to the Lord: why did not the Risen One reveal himself to his enemies in his full glory in order to show that it is God who is victorious? Why did he manifest himself only to his disciples? Jesus' answer is mysterious and profound. The Lord says: "If a man loves me, he will keep my word, and my Father will love him, and we will come to him and make our home with him" (Jn 14:22–23).

This means that the Risen One must be seen, must be perceived also by the heart, in a way so that God may take up his abode within us. The Lord does not appear as a thing. He desires to enter our lives, and therefore his manifestation is a manifestation that implies and presupposes an open heart. Only in this way do we see the Risen One.

The paternity of one of those New Testament Letters known as "catholic", since they are not addressed to a specific local Church but intended for a far wider circle, has been attributed to Jude Thaddaeus. Actually, it is addressed "to those who are called, beloved in God the Father and kept for Jesus Christ" (v. 1). A major concern of this writing is to put Christians on guard against those who make a pretext of God's grace to excuse their own licentiousness and corrupt their brethren with unacceptable teachings, introducing division within the Church "in their dreamings" (v. 8). This is how Jude defines their doctrine and particular ideas. He even compares them to fallen angels and, mincing no words, says that "they walk in the way of Cain" (v. 11). Furthermore, he brands them mercilessly as "waterless clouds, carried along by winds; fruitless trees in late autumn, twice dead, uprooted; wild waves of the sea, casting up the foam of their own shame; wandering stars for whom the nether gloom of darkness has been reserved for ever" (vv. 12–13).

Today, perhaps, we are no longer accustomed to using language that is so polemic, yet that tells us something important. In the midst of all the temptations that exist, with all the currents of modern life, we must preserve our faith's identity. Of course, the way of indulgence and dialogue, on which the Second Vatican Council happily set out, should certainly be followed firmly and consistently. But this path of dialogue, while so necessary, must not make us forget our duty to rethink and to highlight just as forcefully the main and indispensable aspects of our Christian identity. Moreover, it is essential to keep clearly in mind that our identity requires strength, clarity, and courage in light of the contradictions of the world in which we live. Thus, the text of the Letter continues:

"But you, beloved"—he is speaking to all of us—"build yourselves up on your most holy faith; pray in the Holy Spirit; keep yourselves in the love of God; wait for the mercy of our Lord Jesus Christ unto eternal life. And convince some, who doubt ... " (vv. 20–22). The Letter ends with these most beautiful words: "To him who is able to keep you from falling and to present you without blemish before the presence of his glory with rejoicing, to the only God, our Savior through Jesus Christ our Lord, be glory, majesty, dominion and authority, before all time and now and for ever. Amen" (vv. 24–25).

It is easy to see that the author of these lines lived to the full his own faith, to which realities as great as moral integrity and joy, trust, and lastly praise belong, since it is all motivated solely by the goodness of our one God and the mercy of our Lord Jesus Christ. Therefore, may both Simon the Cananaean and Jude Thaddeus help us to rediscover the beauty of the Christian faith ever anew and to live it without tiring, knowing how to bear a strong and at the same time peaceful witness to it.

(11 October 2006)

Saint Gaetano Errico

The ministry of Reconciliation ... is a ministry that is always relevant. The priest Gaetano Errico, Founder of the Congregation of the Missionaries of the Sacred Hearts of Jesus and Mary, devoted himself to it with diligence, perseverance, and patience, never refusing or sparing himself. He is thus enrolled among the extraordinary priestly figures who tirelessly made the confessional the place for dispensing God's mercy, helping people to find themselves, fight against sin, and progress on the path of the spiritual life. The street and the confessional were the privileged places of this new Saint's pastoral action. The street gave him the opportunity to meet people to whom he would address his customary invitation: *"God loves you, when will we see each other?"* And in the confessional he enabled them to encounter the mercy of the heavenly Father. How many wounded souls did he heal in this way! How many people did he reconcile with God through the Sacrament of forgiveness! Thus Saint Gaetano Errico became an expert in the "science" of forgiveness and was concerned to teach it to his missionaries, advising them: *"God, who does not desire the sinner's death, is always more merciful than his ministers; thus may you be as merciful as you can be, so that you will receive mercy from God."*

(12 October 2008)

All Saints' Day

Today we contemplate the mystery of the communion of saints in Heaven and on earth. We are not alone, but rather we are enfolded within a great cloud of witnesses: with them we form the Body of Christ; with them we are made holy in the Holy Spirit. Joy in Heaven, the earth exults! The glorious host of saints intercedes for us before the Lord; they accompany us on our journey toward the Kingdom; they urge us to keep our gaze fixed upon Jesus the Lord, who will come in glory together with his saints.

Our Eucharistic Celebration began with the exhortation: "Let us all rejoice in the Lord." The liturgy invites us to share in the heavenly jubilation of the saints, to taste their joy. The saints are not a small caste of chosen souls but an innumerable crowd to which the liturgy urges us to raise our eyes. This multitude includes not only the officially recognized saints, but the baptized of every epoch and nation who sought to carry out the divine will faithfully and lovingly. We are unacquainted with the faces and even the names of many of them, but with the eyes of faith we see them shine in God's firmament like glorious stars.

Today, the Church is celebrating her dignity as "Mother of the Saints, an image of the Eternal City" (A. Manzoni), and displays her beauty as the immaculate Bride of Christ,

Translated in part by Andrew Matt.

source and model of all holiness. She certainly does not lack contentious or even rebellious children, but it is in the saints that she recognizes her characteristic features and precisely in them savors her deepest joy. In the First Reading, the author of the Book of Revelation describes them as "a great multitude which no man could number, from every nation, from all tribes and peoples and tongues" (Rv 7:9). This people includes the saints of the Old Testament, starting with the righteous Abel and the faithful Patriarch, Abraham, those of the New Testament, the numerous early Christian martyrs and the blesseds and saints of later centuries, to the witnesses of Christ in this epoch of ours. They are all brought together by the common desire to incarnate the Gospel in their lives under the impulse of the Holy Spirit, the life-giving spirit of the People of God.

But "why should our praise and glorification, or even the celebration of this Solemnity, mean anything to the saints?" A famous homily of Saint Bernard for All Saints' Day begins with this question. It could equally well be asked today. And the response the Saint offers us is also timely: "The saints", he says, "have no need of honor from us; neither does our devotion add the slightest thing to what is theirs.... But I tell you, when I think of them, I feel myself inflamed by a tremendous yearning" (*Disc. 2, Opera Omnia Cisterc.* 5, 364ff.). This, then, is the meaning of today's Solemnity: looking at the shining example of the saints to reawaken within us the great longing to be like them; happy to live near God, in his light, in the great family of God's friends. Being a saint means living close to God, to live in his family. And this is the vocation of us all, vigorously reaffirmed by the Second Vatican Council and solemnly proposed today for our attention.

But how can we become holy, friends of God? We can first give a negative answer to this question: to be a saint requires neither extraordinary actions or works nor the possession of exceptional charisms. Then comes the positive reply: it is necessary first of all to listen to Jesus and then to follow him without losing heart when faced by difficulties. "If anyone serves me," he warns us, "he must follow me; and where I am, there shall my servant be also; if any one serves me, the Father will honor him" (Jn 12:26). Like the grain of wheat buried in the earth, those who trust him and love him sincerely accept dying to themselves. Indeed, he knows that whoever seeks to keep his life for himself loses it, and whoever gives himself loses himself and, in this very way, finds life (cf. Jn 12:24–25). The Church's experience shows that every form of holiness, even if it follows different paths, always passes through the Way of the Cross, the way of self-denial. The saints' biographies describe men and women who, docile to the divine plan, sometimes faced unspeakable trials and suffering, persecution and martyrdom. They persevered in their commitment: "they ... have come out of the great tribulation", one reads in Revelation, "they have washed their robes and made them white in the blood of the Lamb" (Rv 7:14). Their names are written in the book of life (cf. Rv 20:12), and Heaven is their eternal dwelling-place. The example of the saints encourages us to follow in their same footsteps and to experience the joy of those who trust in God, for the one true cause of sorrow and unhappiness for men and women is to live far from him.

Holiness demands a constant effort, but it is possible for everyone because, rather than a human effort, it is first and foremost a gift of God, thrice Holy (cf. Is 6:3). In the Second Reading, the Apostle John remarks: "See what love the Father has given us, that we should be called children of God; and so we are" (I Jn 3:1). It is God, therefore, who loved us first and made us his adoptive sons in Jesus. Everything in our lives is a gift of his love: how can we be indifferent before such a great mystery? How can we not respond to the Heavenly Father's love by living as grateful children? In Christ, he gave us the gift of his entire self and calls us to a personal and profound relationship with him. Consequently, the more we imitate Jesus and remain united to him, the more we enter into the mystery of his divine holiness. We discover that he loves us infinitely, and this prompts us in turn to love our brethren. Loving always entails an act of self-denial, "losing ourselves", and it is precisely this that makes us happy.

Thus, we have come to the Gospel of this feast, the proclamation of the Beatitudes which we have just heard resound in this Basilica. Jesus says: Blessed are the poor in spirit, blessed those who mourn, the meek; blessed those who hunger and thirst for justice, the merciful; blessed the pure in heart, the peacemakers, the persecuted for the sake of justice (cf. Mt 5:3–10). In truth, the blessed *par excellence* is only Jesus. He is, in fact, the true poor in spirit, the one afflicted, the meek one, the one hungering and thirsting for justice, the merciful, the pure of heart, the peacemaker. He is the one persecuted for the sake of justice. The Beatitudes show us the spiritual features of Jesus and thus express his mystery, the mystery of his death and Resurrection, of his Passion and of the joy of his Resurrection. This mystery, which is the mystery of true blessedness, invites us to follow Jesus and thus to walk toward it. To the extent that we accept his proposal and set out to follow him—each one in his own circumstances—we too can participate in his blessedness. With him, the impossible becomes possible and even a camel can pass through the eye of a needle (cf. Mk 10:25); with his help, only with his help, can we become perfect as the Heavenly Father is perfect (cf. Mt 5:48).

Dear brothers and sisters, we are now entering the heart of the Eucharistic Celebration that encourages and nourishes holiness. In a little while, Christ will make himself present in the most exalted way, Christ the true Vine to whom the faithful on earth and the saints in Heaven are united like branches. Thus, the communion of the pilgrim Church in the world with the Church triumphant in glory will increase. In the Preface we will proclaim that the saints are friends and models of life for us. Let us invoke them so that they may help us to imitate them and strive to respond generously, as they did, to the divine call. In particular, let us invoke Mary, Mother of the Lord and mirror of all holiness. May she, the All Holy, make us faithful disciples of her Son Jesus Christ! Amen.

(1 November 2006)

* * *

Today, we are celebrating the Solemnity of All Saints, allowing us to experience the joy of being part of the large family of God's friends or, as Saint Paul writes, to "share the lot of the saints in light" (Col 1:12). The liturgy reproposes the expression, full of wonder, of the Apostle John: "See what love the Father has bestowed on us in letting us be called children of God! Yet that is what we are" (I Jn 3:1). Yes, to become saints means to fulfill completely what we already are, raised to the dignity of God's adopted children, in Christ Jesus (cf. Eph 1:5; Rom 8:14–17). With the Incarnation of the Son and his death and Resurrection, God wanted to reconcile humanity to himself and open it up to sharing in his own life. Whoever believes in Christ, Son of God, is reborn "from above", regenerated through the work of the Holy Spirit (cf. Jn 3:1–8). This mystery is accomplished in the Sacrament of Baptism, through which Mother Church gives birth to "saints".

New life, received in Baptism, is not subject to corruption and the power of death. For those who live in Christ, death is the passage from the earthly pilgrimage to the Heavenly Homeland, where the Father welcomes all of his children "from every nation and race, people and tongue", as we read today in the Book of Revelation (7:9). For this reason, it is very significant and appropriate that after the Solemnity of All Saints, the liturgy tomorrow has us celebrate the Commemoration of all of the Faithful Departed. The "communion of saints", which we profess in the Creed, is a reality that is constructed here below but is fully made manifest when we will see God "as he is" (I Jn 3:2). It is the reality of a family bound together by deep bonds of spiritual solidarity that unites the faithful departed to those who are pilgrims in the world. It is a mysterious but real bond, nourished by prayer and participation in the Sacrament of the Eucharist. In the Mystical Body of Christ the souls of the faithful meet, overcoming the obstacle of death; they pray for one another, carrying out in charity an intimate exchange of gifts. In this dimension of faith one understands the practice of offering prayers of suffrage for the dead, especially in the Sacrament of the Eucharist, memorial of Christ's Pasch which opened to believers the passage to eternal life.

(1 November 2005)

All Souls' Day

This deeply felt liturgical celebration offers us a special opportunity to meditate upon eternal life. Is modern man still waiting for this eternal life, or does he consider it part of a mythology now obsolete? In our time more than in the past, people are so absorbed by earthly things that at times they find it difficult to think about God as the protagonist of history and of our own existence. By its nature, however, human life reaches out for something greater which transcends it; the human yearning for justice, truth, and full happiness is irrepressible. In the face of the enigma of death, the desire for and hope of meeting their loved ones again in Heaven is alive in many, just as there is a strong conviction that a Last Judgment will re-establish justice and the expectation of a definitive encounter in which each person will be given his reward.

For us as Christians, however, "eternal life" does not merely mean a life that lasts forever but rather a new quality of existence, fully immersed in God's love, which frees us from evil and death and places us in never-ending communion with all our brothers and sisters who share in the same Love. Thus, eternity can already be present at the heart of earthly and temporal life when the soul is united through grace with God; its ultimate foundation.

Translated in part by Andrew Matt.

Everything passes; God alone never changes. A Psalm says: "Though my flesh and my heart waste away, God is the rock of my heart and my portion for ever" (Ps 73[72]:26). All Christians, called to holiness, are men and women who live firmly anchored to this "Rock", their feet on the ground but their hearts already in Heaven, the final dwelling-place of friends of God.

Let us meditate on these realities with our souls turned toward our final and definitive destiny, which gives meaning to the circumstances of our daily lives. Let us enliven the joyous sentiment of the communion of saints and allow ourselves to be drawn by them toward the goal of our existence: the face-to-face encounter with God. Let us pray that this may be the inheritance of all the faithful departed, not only of our own loved ones, but also of all souls, especially those most forgotten and most in need of divine mercy. May the Virgin Mary, Queen of all the saints, guide us to choose the world of eternal life at every moment, "and life everlasting", as we say in the Creed; a world already inaugurated by the Resurrection of Christ, whose coming we can hasten with our sincere conversion and charitable acts.

(1 November 2006)

* * *

It is a fitting occasion to remember our loved ones in prayer and to meditate on the reality of death, which the so-called "affluent society" often seeks to remove from the consciousness of people, totally taken up by the concerns of daily life. In fact, death is part of life, and not only at its end but, upon a closer look, at every moment. Yet, despite all the distractions, the loss of a loved one enables us to rediscover the "problem" by making us sense death as a presence radically hostile and contrary to our natural vocation to life and happiness.

Jesus revolutionized the meaning of death. He did so with his teaching, but especially by facing death himself. "By dying he destroyed our death", the liturgy of the Easter Season says. "With the Spirit who could not die," a Father of the Church wrote, "Christ killed death that was killing man" (Melito of Sardis, *On Easter* 66). The Son of God thus desired to share our human condition to the very end, to reopen it to hope. After all, he was born to be able to die and thereby free us from the slavery of death. The Letter to the Hebrews says: "so that he might taste death for everyone" (Heb 2:9). Since then, death has not been the same: it was deprived, so to speak, of its "venom". Indeed, God's love working in Jesus gave new meaning to the whole of human existence and, thus, transformed death as well. If, in Christ, human life is a "[departure] from this world to the Father" (Jn 13:1), the hour of death is the moment when it is concretely brought about once and for all. Anyone who strives to live as he did is freed from the fear of death, which shows no longer the sarcastic sneer of an enemy but, as Saint Francis wrote in his Canticle of the Creature, the friendly face of a "sister" for whom one can also bless the Lord: "Praised be the Lord for our Sister, bodily Death." Faith reminds us that there is no need to be afraid of the death of the body because, whether we live or whether we die, we are the Lord's [Rm 14:8]. And with Saint Paul, we know that even if we are separated from our bodies we are with Christ, whose Risen Body, which we receive in the Eucharist, is our eternal and indestructible dwelling-place. True death, on the other hand, which is to be feared, is the death of the soul, which the Book of Revelation calls "the second death" (cf. Rv 20:14–15; 21:8). In fact, those who die in mortal sin without repentance, locked into their proud rejection of God's love, exclude themselves from the Kingdom of life.

Let us entreat the Lord, through the intercession of Mary Most Holy and of Saint Joseph, for the grace to prepare ourselves serenely to depart this world whenever he may desire to call us, in the hope of being able to dwell forever with him in the company of the saints and of our departed loved ones.

(5 November 2006)

4 NOVEMBER

Saint Charles Borromeo

[The] figure [of Charles Borromeo, Archbishop of Milan]
stands out in the sixteenth century as a model of an exemplary Pastor because of his charity, doctrine, apostolic zeal,
and, above all, his prayer. "Souls are won", he said, "on one's
knees." Charles Borromeo was consecrated a Bishop when
he was only twenty-five years old. He enforced the teaching of the Council of Trent that obliged Pastors to reside
in their respective dioceses and gave himself heart and soul
to the Ambrosian Church. He traveled up and down his
Diocese three times; he convoked six provincial and eleven
diocesan synods; he founded seminaries to train a new generation of priests; he built hospitals and earmarked his family riches for the service of the poor; he renewed religious
life and founded a new congregation of secular priests, the
Oblates. In 1576, when the plague was raging in Milan, he
visited, comforted, and spent all his money on the sick. His
motto consisted in one word: *"Humilitas"*. It was humility
that motivated him, like the Lord Jesus, to renounce himself
in order to make himself the servant of all.

(4 November 2007)

* * *

[Saint Charles Borromeo was] created a Cardinal at a very
young age [and] collaborated in the government of the

universal Church. It was immediately after the death of his elder brother that the Pontiff's young nephew began a process of spiritual development which led him to a profound conversion, marked by a decisive choice of evangelical life. Having become a Bishop, he devoted all his care to the Archdiocese of Milan. His biography clearly reveals the zeal with which he carried out his episcopal ministry, promoting the reform of the Church in accordance with the spirit of the Council of Trent, whose directives he employed in an exemplary manner, showing a constant closeness to the population, especially during the years of the plague, so that he became known as "the angel of the plague victims" precisely for his generous dedication. The human and spiritual experience of Saint Charles Borromeo shows how divine grace may transform the human heart and render it capable of love for the brethren, even to the point of sacrifice of self.

(13 December 2008)

Saint Willibrord

Saint Willibrord was born 1350 years ago and was consecrated Bishop by my Predecessor Saint Sergius I in 695. He was a zealous preacher of the Gospel who humbly administered the sacraments of God. A sincere friend to the poor and to princes alike, Saint Willibrord was a holy, just, and kind-hearted father. He never abandoned his pastoral duties even when beset by continual trials. With the help of Princess Irmina and Pepin II, he built a monastery in Echternach, in the duchy of Luxembourg, where he finally yielded his holy soul to the Lord in the year 739.

(2 April 2008)

Translated by Andrew Matt.

Saint Leo the Great

We encounter a Pope who in 1754 Benedict XIV proclaimed a Doctor of the Church: Saint Leo the Great. As the title soon attributed to him by tradition suggests, he was truly one of the greatest Pontiffs to have honored the Roman See and made a very important contribution to strengthening its authority and prestige. He was the first Bishop of Rome to have been called Leo, a name used subsequently by another twelve Supreme Pontiffs, and was also the first Pope whose preaching to the people who gathered around him during celebrations has come down to us. We spontaneously think of him also in the context of today's Wednesday General Audiences, events that in past decades have become a customary meeting of the Bishop of Rome with the faithful and the many visitors from every part of the world.

Leo was a Tuscan native. In about the year 430 A.D., he became a deacon of the Church of Rome, in which he acquired over time a very important position. In the year 440 his prominent role induced Galla Placidia, who then ruled the Empire of the West, to send him to Gaul to heal a difficult situation. But in the summer of that year, Pope Sixtus III, whose name is associated with the magnificent mosaics in Saint Mary Major's, died, and it was Leo who was elected to succeed him. Leo heard the news precisely while he was carrying out his peace mission in Gaul. Having returned to Rome, the new Pope was consecrated on

29 September 440. This is how his Pontificate began. It lasted more than twenty-one years and was undoubtedly one of the most important in the Church's history. Pope Leo died on 10 November 461 and was buried near the tomb of Saint Peter. Today, his relics are preserved in one of the altars in the Vatican Basilica.

The times in which Pope Leo lived were very difficult: constant barbarian invasions, the gradual weakening of imperial authority in the West, and the long, drawn-out social crisis forced the Bishop of Rome—as was to happen even more obviously a century and a half later during the Pontificate of Gregory the Great—to play an important role in civil and political events. This, naturally, could only add to the importance and prestige of the Roman See. The fame of one particular episode in Leo's life has endured. It dates back to 452, when the Pope, together with a Roman delegation, met Attila, chief of the Huns, in Mantua and dissuaded him from continuing the war of invasion by which he had already devastated the northeastern regions of Italy. Thus, he saved the rest of the Peninsula. This important event soon became memorable and lives on as an emblematic sign of the Pontiff's action for peace. Unfortunately, the outcome of another Papal initiative three years later was not as successful, yet it was a sign of courage that still amazes us: in the spring of 455 Leo did not manage to prevent Genseric's Vandals, who had reached the gates of Rome, from invading the undefended city that they plundered for two weeks. This gesture of the Pope—who, defenseless and surrounded by his clergy, went forth to meet the invader to implore him to desist—nevertheless prevented Rome from being burned and assured that the Basilicas of Saint Peter, Saint Paul, and Saint John, in which part of the terrified population sought refuge, were spared.

We are familiar with Pope Leo's action thanks to his most beautiful sermons—almost one hundred in a splendid and clear Latin have been preserved—and thanks to his approximately 150 letters. In these texts the Pontiff appears in all his greatness, devoted to the service of truth in charity through an assiduous exercise of the Word which shows him to us as both theologian and pastor. Leo the Great, constantly thoughtful of his faithful and of the people of Rome but also of communion between the different Churches and of their needs, was a tireless champion and upholder of the Roman Primacy, presenting himself as the Apostle Peter's authentic heir: the many Bishops who gathered at the Council of Chalcedon, the majority of whom came from the East, were well aware of this.

This Council, held in 451 and in which 350 Bishops took part, was the most important assembly ever to have been celebrated in the history of the Church. Chalcedon represents the actual Christological goal of the three previous Ecumenical Councils: Nicaea in 325, Constantinople in 381, and Ephesus in 431. By the sixth century these four Councils that sum up the faith of the ancient Church were already being compared to the four Gospels. This is what Gregory the Great affirms in a famous letter (I, 24): "I confess that I receive and revere, as the four books of the Gospel, so also the four Councils", because on them, Gregory explains further, "as on a four-square stone, rises the structure of the holy faith". The Council of Chalcedon, which rejected the heresy of Eutyches, who denied the true human nature of the Son of God, affirmed the union in his one Person, without confusion and without separation, of his two natures, human and divine.

The Pope asserted this faith in Jesus Christ, true God and true man, in an important doctrinal text addressed to the Bishop of Constantinople, the so-called *Tome to Flavian*, which, read at Chalcedon, was received by the Bishops present with an eloquent acclamation. Information on it has been preserved in the proceedings of the Council: "Peter has spoken through the mouth of Leo", the Council Fathers announced in unison. From this intervention in particular, but also from others made during the Christological controversy in those years, it is clear that the Pope felt with special urgency his responsibilities as Successor of Peter, whose role in the Church is unique, since "to one Apostle alone was entrusted what was communicated to all the Apostles", as Leo said in one of his sermons for the Feast of Saints Peter and Paul (83, 2). And the Pontiff was able to exercise these responsibilities, in the West as in the East, intervening in various circumstances with caution, firmness, and lucidity through his writings and legates. In this manner he showed how exercising the Roman Primacy was as necessary then as it is today to serve communion, a characteristic of Christ's one Church, effectively.

Aware of the historical period in which he lived and of the change that was taking place—from pagan Rome to Christian Rome—in a period of profound crisis, Leo the Great knew how to make himself close to the people and the faithful with his pastoral action and his preaching. He enlivened charity in a Rome tried by famines, an influx of refugees, injustice, and poverty. He opposed pagan superstitions and the actions of Manichaean groups. He associated the liturgy with the daily life of Christians: for example, by combining the practice of fasting with charity and almsgiving above all on the occasion of the *Quattro tempora*, which in the course of the year marked the change of seasons. In particular, Leo the Great taught his faithful—and his words still apply for us today—that the Christian liturgy is not the memory of past events, but the actualization of invisible realities which act in the lives of each one of us. This is what he stressed in a sermon (cf. 64, 1–2) on Easter, to be celebrated in every season of the year, "not so much as something of the past as rather an event of the present". All this fits into a precise project, the Holy Pontiff insisted: just as, in fact, the Creator enlivened with the breath of rational life man formed from the dust of the ground, after the original sin he sent his Son into the world to restore to man his lost dignity and to destroy the dominion of the devil through the new life of grace.

This is the Christological mystery to which Saint Leo the Great, with his Letter to the Council of Ephesus, made an effective and essential contribution, confirming for all time—through this Council—what Saint Peter said at Caesarea Philippi. With Peter and as Peter, he professed: "You are the Christ, the Son of the living God." And so it is that God and man together "are not foreign to the human race but alien to sin" (cf. *Serm.* 64). Through the force of this Christological faith, he was a great messenger of peace and love. He thus shows us the way: in faith we learn charity. Let us therefore learn with Saint Leo the Great to believe in Christ, true God and true man, and to implement this faith every day in action for peace and love of neighbor.

(5 March 2008)

17 November

Saint Elizabeth of Hungary

Elizabeth, a "European" Saint, was born into a social context of recent evangelization. Andrew and Gertrude, parents of this authentic pearl of the new Christian Hungary, were careful to instill in her an awareness of her own dignity as God's adoptive daughter. Elizabeth made her own the program of Jesus Christ, Son of God, who in becoming man "emptied himself, taking the form of a servant" (Phil 2:7). Thanks to the help of her excellent teachers, she trod in the footsteps of Saint Francis of Assisi and set Christ, the one Redeemer of humanity, as her personal and ultimate goal and model in life.

Called to be the wife of the Landgrave of Thuringia, she never ceased to devote herself to the care of the poor, in whom she recognized the likeness of the divine Master. She was able to combine her gifts as an exemplary wife and mother with the exercise of the Gospel virtues that she had learned at the school of the Saint of Assisi. She proved to be a true daughter of the Church, who bore a concrete, visible, and meaningful witness to Christ's love. Innumerable people down the ages followed her example, viewing her as a model who mirrored the Christian virtues, lived radically in marriage, in the family, and also in widowhood. Political figures have been inspired by her, drawing from her the incentive to work for reconciliation among nations.

(8 June 2007)

285

The Presentation of the Blessed Virgin Mary

On the occasion of the liturgical Memorial of the Presentation of Mary, we will be celebrating *Pro Orantibus* Day, dedicated to remembering cloistered religious communities. It is an especially appropriate opportunity to thank the Lord for the gift of the numerous people in monasteries and hermitages who are totally dedicated to God in prayer, silence, and concealment.

Some may wonder what meaning and value their presence could have in our time, when there are so many situations of poverty and neediness with which to cope. Why "enclose oneself" forever between the walls of a monastery and thereby deprive others of the contribution of one's own skills and experience? How effective can the prayer of these cloistered Religious be for the solution of all the practical problems that continue to afflict humanity?

Yet even today, often to the surprise of their friends and acquaintances, many people in fact frequently give up promising professional careers to embrace the austere rule of a cloistered monastery. What impels them to take such a demanding step other than the realization, as the Gospel teaches, that the Kingdom of Heaven is "a treasure" for which it is truly worth giving up everything (cf. Mt 13:44)? Indeed, these brothers and sisters of ours bear a silent witness to the fact that in the midst of the sometimes frenetic pace of daily events, the one support that never topples is God, the indestructible rock of faithfulness and love. "Everything passes, God never changes", the great spiritual master Teresa of Avila wrote in one of her famous texts. And in the face of the widespread need to get away from the daily routine of sprawling urban areas in search of places conducive to silence and meditation, monasteries of contemplative life offer themselves as "oases" in which human beings, pilgrims on earth, can draw more easily from the wellsprings of the Spirit and quench their thirst along the way. Thus, these apparently useless places are on the contrary indispensable, like the green "lungs" of a city: they do everyone good, even those who do not visit them and may not even know of their existence.

Dear brothers and sisters, let us thank the Lord, who in his Providence has desired male and female cloistered communities. May they have our spiritual and also our material support, so that they can carry out their mission to keep alive in the Church the ardent expectation of Christ's Second Coming. For this, let us invoke the intercession of Mary, whom we contemplate on the Memorial of her Presentation in the Temple as Mother and model of the Church, who welcomes in herself both vocations: to virginity and to marriage, to contemplative life and to active life.

(19 November 2006)

Saint Columban

The holy Abbot Columban [was] the best-known Irishman of the early Middle Ages. Since he worked as a monk, missionary, and writer in various countries of Western Europe, with good reason he can be called a "European" Saint. With the Irish of his time, he had a sense of Europe's cultural unity. The expression "*totius Europae*—of all Europe", with reference to the Church's presence on the Continent, is found for the first time in one of his letters, written around the year 600, addressed to Pope Gregory the Great (cf. *Epistula* I, 1).

Columban was born *ca.* 543 in the Province of Leinster in southeast Ireland. He was educated at home by excellent tutors who introduced him to the study of liberal arts. He was then entrusted to the guidance of Abbot Sinell of the community of Cleenish in Northern Ireland, where he was able to deepen his study of Sacred Scripture. At the age of about twenty, he entered the monastery of Bangor, in the northeast of the island, whose Abbot, Comgall, was a monk well known for his virtue and ascetic rigor. In full agreement with his Abbot, Columban zealously practiced the severe discipline of the monastery, leading a life of prayer, ascesis, and study. While there, he was also ordained a priest. His life at Bangor and the Abbot's example influenced the conception of monasticism that developed in Columban over time and that he subsequently spread in the course of his life.

When he was approximately fifty years old, following the characteristically Irish ascetic ideal of the *"peregrinatio pro Christo"*, namely, making oneself a pilgrim for the sake of Christ, Columban left his island with twelve companions to engage in missionary work on the European Continent. We should in fact bear in mind that the migration of people from the North and the East had caused whole areas, previously Christianized, to revert to paganism. Around the year 590, the small group of missionaries landed on the Breton coast. Welcomed kindly by the King of the Franks of Austrasia (present-day France), they asked only for a small piece of uncultivated land. They were given the ancient Roman fortress of Annegray, totally ruined and abandoned and covered by forest. Accustomed to a life of extreme hardship, in the span of a few months the monks managed to build the first hermitage on the ruins. Thus their re-evangelization began, in the first place, through the witness of their lives. With the new cultivation of the land, they also began a new cultivation of souls. The fame of those foreign religious who, living on prayer and in great austerity, built houses and worked the land spread rapidly, attracting pilgrims and penitents. In particular, many young men asked to be accepted by the monastic community in order to live, like them, this exemplary life which was renewing the cultivation of the land and of souls. It was not long before the foundation of a second monastery was required. It was built a few kilometers away on the ruins of an ancient spa, Luxeuil. This monastery was to become the center of the traditional Irish monastic and missionary outreach on the European Continent. A third monastery was erected at Fontaine, an hour's walk further north.

Columban lived at Luxeuil for almost twenty years. Here the Saint wrote for his followers the *Regula monachorum*—for a while more widespread in Europe than Benedict's

Rule—which portrayed the ideal image of the monk. It is the only ancient Irish monastic rule in our possession today. Columban integrated it with the *Regula coenobialis*, a sort of penal code for the offenses committed by monks, with punishments that are somewhat surprising to our modern sensibility and can only be explained by the mentality and environment of that time. With another famous work entitled: *De poenitentiarum misura taxanda*, also written at Luxeuil, Columban introduced Confession and private and frequent penance on the Continent. It was known as "tariffed" penance because of the proportion established between the gravity of the sin and the type of penance imposed by the confessor. These innovations roused the suspicion of local Bishops, a suspicion that became hostile when Columban had the courage to rebuke them openly for the practices of some of them. The controversy over the date of Easter was an opportunity to demonstrate their opposition: Ireland, in fact, followed the Eastern rather than the Roman tradition. The Irish monk was summoned in 603 to account to a Synod at Chalon-sur-Saône for his practices regarding penance and Easter. Instead of presenting himself before the Synod, he sent a letter in which he minimized the issue, inviting the Synod Fathers not only to discuss the problem of the date of Easter, in his opinion a negligible problem, "but also all the necessary canonical norms that—something more serious—are disregarded by many" (cf. *Epistula* II, I). At the same time he wrote to Pope Boniface IV—just as several years earlier he had turned to Pope Gregory the Great (cf. *Epistula* I)—asking him to defend the Irish tradition (cf. *Epistula* III).

Intransigent as he was in every moral matter, Columban then came into conflict with the royal house for having harshly reprimanded King Theuderic for his adulterous relations. This created a whole network of personal, religious,

and political intrigues and maneuvers which, in 610, culminated in a Decree of expulsion banishing Columban and
all the monks of Irish origin from Luxeuil and condemn-
ing them to definitive exile. They were escorted to the sea
and, at the expense of the court, boarded a ship bound for
Ireland. However, not far from shore the ship ran aground,
and the captain, who saw this as a sign from Heaven, abandoned the voyage and, for fear of being cursed by God,
brought the monks back to dry land. Instead of returning
to Luxeuil, they decided to begin a new work of evangelization. Thus, they embarked on a Rhine boat and traveled
up the river. After a first stop in Tuggen near Lake Zurich,
they went to the region of Bregenz, near Lake Constance,
to evangelize the Alemanni.

However, soon afterward, because of political events
unfavorable to his work, Columban decided to cross the
Alps with the majority of his disciples. Only one monk,
whose name was Gallus, stayed behind; it was from his hermitage that the famous Abbey of Saint Gall in Switzerland
subsequently developed. Having arrived in Italy, Columban
met with a warm welcome at the Lombard Royal Court
but was immediately faced with considerable difficulties:
the life of the Church was torn apart by the Arian heresy, still prevalent among the Lombards, and by a schism
which had detached most of the Church in Northern Italy
from communion with the Bishop of Rome. Columban
entered authoritatively into this context, writing a satiri-
cal pamphlet against Arianism and a letter to Boniface IV
to convince him to take some decisive steps with a view to
re-establishing unity (cf. *Epistula* V). When, in 612 or 613,
the King of the Lombards allocated to him a plot of land in
Bobbio, in the Trebbia Valley, Columban founded a new
monastery there which was later to become a cultural center on a par with the famous monastery of Monte Cassino.

Here he came to the end of his days: he died on 23 November 615 and to this day is commemorated on this date in the Roman rite.

Saint Columban's message is concentrated in a firm appeal to conversion and detachment from earthly goods, with a view to the eternal inheritance. With his ascetic life and conduct free from compromises when he faced the corruption of the powerful, he is reminiscent of the severe figure of Saint John the Baptist. His austerity, however, was never an end in itself but merely the means with which to open himself freely to God's love and to correspond with his whole being to the gifts received from him, thereby restoring in himself the image of God, while at the same time cultivating the earth and renewing human society. I quote from his *Instructiones*: "If man makes a correct use of those faculties that God has conceded to his soul, he will be likened to God. Let us remember that we must restore to him all those gifts which he deposited in us when we were in our original condition. He has taught us the way with his Commandments. The first of them tells us to love the Lord with all our heart, because he loved us first, from the beginning of time, even before we came into the light of this world" (cf. *Instructiones* XI). The Irish Saint truly incarnated these words in his own life. A man of great culture—he also wrote poetry in Latin and a grammar book—he proved rich in gifts of grace. He was a tireless builder of monasteries as well as an intransigent penitential preacher who spent every ounce of his energy on nurturing the Christian roots of Europe, which was coming into existence. With his spiritual energy, with his faith, with his love for God and neighbor, he truly became one of the Fathers of Europe. He shows us even today the roots from which our Europe can be reborn.

(11 June 2008)

Pope Saint Clement I

Saint Clement, Bishop of Rome in the last years of the first century, was the third Successor of Peter, after Linus and Anacletus. The most important testimony concerning his life comes from Saint Irenaeus, Bishop of Lyons until 202. He attests that Clement "had seen the blessed Apostles", "had been conversant with them", and "might be said to have the preaching of the Apostles still echoing [in his ears], and their traditions before his eyes" (*Adversus Haereses* 3, 3, 3). Later testimonies which date back to between the fourth and sixth centuries attribute to Clement the title of martyr.

The authority and prestige of this Bishop of Rome were such that various writings were attributed to him, but the only one that is certainly his is the *Letter to the Corinthians*. Eusebius of Caesarea, the great "archivist" of Christian beginnings, presents it in these terms: "There is extant an Epistle of this Clement which is acknowledged to be genuine and is of considerable length and of remarkable merit. He wrote it in the name of the Church of Rome to the Church of Corinth, when a sedition had arisen in the latter Church. We know that this Epistle also has been publicly used in a great many Churches both in former times and in our own" (*Hist. Eccl.* 3, 16). An almost canonical character was attributed to this Letter. At the beginning of this text—written in Greek—Clement expressed his regret that "the sudden and successive calamitous events which have happened to ourselves" (1, 1) had prevented him from intervening sooner. These "calamitous events" can be identified with Domitian's persecution: therefore, the Letter must have been written just after the Emperor's death and at the end of the persecution, that is, immediately after the year 96.

Clement's intervention—we are still in the first century—was prompted by the serious problems besetting the Church in Corinth: the elders of the community, in fact, had been deposed by some young contestants. The sorrowful event was recalled once again by Saint Irenaeus, who wrote: "In the time of this Clement, no small dissension having occurred among the brethren in Corinth, the Church in Rome dispatched a most powerful Letter to the Corinthians exhorting them to peace, renewing their faith, and declaring the tradition which it had lately received from the Apostles" (*Adversus Haereses* 3, 3, 3). Thus, we could say that this Letter was a first exercise of the Roman primacy after Saint Peter's death. Clement's Letter touches on topics that were dear to Saint Paul, who had written two important Letters to the Corinthians, in particular the theological dialectic, perennially current, between the *indicative* of salvation and the *imperative* of moral commitment. First of all came the joyful proclamation of saving grace. The Lord forewarns us and gives us his forgiveness, gives us his love and the grace to be Christians, his brothers and sisters. It is a proclamation that fills our life with joy and gives certainty to our action: the Lord always forewarns us with his goodness, and the Lord's goodness is always greater than all our sins. However, we must commit ourselves in a way that is consistent with the gift received and respond to the proclamation of salvation with a generous and courageous journey of conversion. In comparison with the Pauline model, the innovation added by Clement to the doctrinal and practical sections, which constituted all the Pauline Letters, is a "great prayer" that virtually concludes the Letter.

The Letter's immediate circumstances provided the Bishop of Rome with ample room for an intervention on the Church's identity and mission. If there were abuses in Corinth, Clement observed, the reason should be sought in the weakening of charity and of the other indispensable Christian virtues. He therefore calls the faithful to humility and fraternal love, two truly constitutive virtues of being in the Church: "Seeing, therefore, that we are the portion of the Holy One," he warned, "let us do all those things which pertain to holiness" (30, 1). In particular, the Bishop of Rome recalls that the Lord himself "has fixed by his own supreme will where and by whom he desires these things to be done, in order that all things, being piously done according to his good pleasure, may be acceptable unto him.... For his own peculiar services are assigned to the high priest, and their own proper place is prescribed to the priests, and their own special ministries devolve on the Levites. The layman is bound by the laws that pertain to laymen" (40, 1–5: it can be noted that here, in this early first-century Letter, the Greek word "*laikós*" appears for the first time in Christian literature, meaning "a member of the *laos*", that is, "of the People of God").

In this way, referring to the liturgy of ancient Israel, Clement revealed his ideal Church. She was assembled by "the one Spirit of grace poured out upon us", which breathes on the various members of the Body of Christ, where all, united without any divisions, are "members of one another" (46, 6–7). The clear distinction between the "lay person" and the hierarchy in no way signifies opposition, but only this organic connection of a body, an organism with its different functions. The Church, in fact, is not a place of confusion and anarchy where one can do what one likes all the time: each one in this organism, with an articulated structure, exercises his ministry in accordance with the vocation he has received. With regard to community leaders, Clement clearly explains the doctrine of Apostolic Succession. The norms that regulate it derive ultimately from God himself. The Father sent Jesus Christ, who in turn sent the Apostles. They then sent the first heads of communities and established that they would be succeeded by other worthy men. Everything, therefore, was made "in an orderly way, according to the will of God" (42). With these words, these sentences, Saint Clement underlined that the Church's structure was sacramental and not political. The action of God who comes to meet us in the liturgy precedes our decisions and our ideas. The Church is above all a gift of God and not something we ourselves created; consequently, this sacramental structure guarantees not only the common order but also this precedence of God's gift which we all need.

Finally, the "great prayer" confers a cosmic breath to the previous reasoning. Clement praises and thanks God for his marvelous providence of love that created the world and continues to save and sanctify it. The prayer for rulers and governors acquires special importance. Subsequent to the New Testament texts, it is the oldest prayer extant for political institutions. Thus, in the period following their persecution, Christians, well aware that the persecutions would continue, never ceased to pray for the very authorities who had unjustly condemned them. The reason is primarily Christological: it is necessary to pray for one's persecutors as Jesus did on the Cross. But this prayer also contains a teaching that guides the attitude of Christians toward politics and the State down the centuries. In praying for the authorities, Clement recognized the legitimacy of political institutions in the order established by God; at the same time, he expressed his concern that the authorities would be docile to God, "devoutly in peace and meekness exercising the power given them by [God]" (61, 2). Caesar is not everything. Another sovereignty emerges whose origins and essence are not of this world but of "the heavens above": it is that of Truth, which also claims a right to be heard by the State.

Thus, Clement's Letter addresses numerous themes of perennial timeliness. It is all the more meaningful since it represents, from the first century, the concern of the Church of Rome which presides in charity over all the other Churches. In this same Spirit, let us make our own the invocations of the "great prayer" in which the Bishop of Rome makes himself the voice of the entire world: "Yes, O Lord, make your face to shine upon us for good in peace, that we may be shielded by your mighty hand ... through the High Priest and Guardian of our souls, Jesus Christ, through whom be glory and majesty to you both now and from generation to generation, for evermore" (60–61).

(7 March 2007)

Saint Andrew, Apostle

The first striking characteristic of Andrew is his name: it is not Hebrew, as might have been expected, but Greek, indicative of a certain cultural openness in his family that cannot be ignored. We are in Galilee, where the Greek language and culture are quite present. Andrew comes second in the list of the Twelve, as in Matthew (10:1–4) and in Luke (6:13–16); or fourth, as in Mark (3:13–18) and in the Acts (1:13–14). In any case, he certainly enjoyed great prestige within the early Christian communities.

The kinship between Peter and Andrew, as well as the joint call that Jesus addressed to them, are explicitly mentioned in the Gospels. We read: "As he walked by the Sea of Galilee, he saw two brothers, Simon who is called Peter and Andrew his brother, casting a net into the sea; for they were fishermen. And he said to them, 'Follow me, and I will make you fishers of men'" (Mt 4:18–19; Mk 1:16–17). From the Fourth Gospel we know another important detail: Andrew had previously been a disciple of John the Baptist: and this shows us that he was a man who was searching, who shared in Israel's hope, who wanted to know better the word of the Lord, the presence of the Lord. He was truly a man of faith and hope; and one day he heard John the Baptist proclaiming Jesus as: "the Lamb of God" (Jn 1:36); so he was stirred and, with another unnamed disciple, followed Jesus, the one whom John had called "the Lamb of

God". The Evangelist says that "they saw where he was staying; and they stayed with him that day ... " (Jn 1:37–39).
Thus, Andrew enjoyed precious moments of intimacy with
Jesus. The account continues with one important annota-
tion: "One of the two who heard John speak, and followed
him, was Andrew, Simon Peter's brother. He first found his
brother Simon, and said to him, 'We have found the Messiah' (which means Christ). He brought him to Jesus" (Jn
1:40– 43), straightaway showing an unusual apostolic spirit.
Andrew, then, was the first of the Apostles to be called to
follow Jesus. Exactly for this reason the liturgy of the Byzantine Church honors him with the title: *Protokletos* [*proto-
clete*], which means, precisely, "the first called".

The Gospel traditions mention Andrew's name in particular on another three occasions that tell us something
more about this man. The first is that of the multiplication
of the loaves in Galilee. On that occasion, it was Andrew
who pointed out to Jesus the presence of a young boy who
had with him five barley loaves and two fish: not much, he
remarked, for the multitudes who had gathered in that place
(cf. Jn 6:8–9). In this case, it is worth highlighting Andrew's
realism. He noticed the boy, that is, he had already asked
the question: "but what good is that for so many?" (*ibid.*),
and recognized the insufficiency of his minimal resources.
Jesus, however, knew how to make them sufficient for the
multitude of people who had come to hear him. The second occasion was at Jerusalem. As he left the city, a disciple
drew Jesus' attention to the sight of the massive walls that
supported the Temple. The Teacher's response was surprising: he said that of those walls not one stone would be left
upon another. Then Andrew, together with Peter, James,
and John, questioned him: "Tell us, when will this be, and
what will be the sign when these things are all to be accomplished?" (Mk 13:1–4). In answer to this question Jesus gave

an important discourse on the destruction of Jerusalem and on the end of the world, in which he asked his disciples to be wise in interpreting the signs of the times and to be constantly on their guard. From this event we can deduce that we should not be afraid to ask Jesus questions but at the same time that we must be ready to accept even the surprising and difficult teachings that he offers us.

Lastly, a third initiative of Andrew is recorded in the Gospels: the scene is still Jerusalem, shortly before the Passion. For the Feast of the Passover, John recounts, some Greeks had come to the city, probably proselytes or God-fearing men who had come up to worship the God of Israel at the Passover Feast. Andrew and Philip, the two Apostles with Greek names, served as interpreters and mediators of this small group of Greeks with Jesus. The Lord's answer to their question—as so often in John's Gospel—appears enigmatic, but precisely in this way proves full of meaning. Jesus said to the two disciples and, through them, to the Greek world: "The hour has come for the Son of man to be glorified. I solemnly assure you, unless a grain of wheat falls to the earth and dies, it remains just a grain of wheat; but if it dies, it produces much fruit" (12:23–24). Jesus wants to say: Yes, my meeting with the Greeks will take place, but not as a simple, brief conversation between myself and a few others, motivated above all by curiosity. The hour of my glorification will come with my death, which can be compared with the falling into the earth of a grain of wheat. My death on the Cross will bring forth great fruitfulness: in the Resurrection the "dead grain of wheat"—a symbol of myself crucified—will become the bread of life for the world; it will be a light for the peoples and cultures. Yes, the encounter with the Greek soul, with the Greek world, will be achieved in that profundity to which the grain of wheat refers, which attracts to itself the forces of heaven and earth and becomes bread. In other words, Jesus was prophesying about the Church of the Greeks, the Church of the pagans, the Church of the world, as a fruit of his Pasch.

Some very ancient traditions not only see Andrew, who communicated these words to the Greeks, as the interpreter of some Greeks at the meeting with Jesus recalled here, but consider him the Apostle to the Greeks in the years subsequent to Pentecost. They enable us to know that for the rest of his life he was the preacher and interpreter of Jesus for the Greek world. Peter, his brother, traveled from Jerusalem through Antioch and reached Rome to exercise his universal mission; Andrew, instead, was the Apostle of the Greek world. So it is that in life and in death they appear as true brothers—a brotherhood that is symbolically expressed in the special reciprocal relations of the Sees of Rome and of Constantinople, which are truly Sister Churches. A later tradition, as has been mentioned, tells of Andrew's death at Patras, where he too suffered the torture of crucifixion. At that supreme moment, however, like his brother, Peter, he asked to be nailed to a cross different from the Cross of Jesus. In his case it was a diagonal or X-shaped cross, which has thus come to be known as "Saint Andrew's cross". This is what the Apostle is claimed to have said on that occasion, according to an ancient story (which dates back to the beginning of the sixth century), entitled *The Passion of Andrew*:

> Hail, O Cross, inaugurated by the Body of Christ and adorned with his limbs as though they were precious pearls. Before the Lord mounted you, you inspired an earthly fear. Now, instead, endowed with heavenly love, you are accepted as a gift.
>
> Believers know of the great joy that you possess, and of the multitude of gifts you have prepared. I come to you, therefore, confident and joyful, so that you too may receive

me exultant as a disciple of the One who was hung upon
you.... O blessed Cross, clothed in the majesty and beauty
of the Lord's limbs!... Take me, carry me far from men,
and restore me to my Teacher, so that, through you, the
one who redeemed me by you, may receive me. Hail, O
Cross; yes, hail indeed!

Here, as can be seen, is a very profound Christian spirituality. It does not view the Cross as an instrument of torture
but rather as the incomparable means for perfect configuration to the Redeemer, to the grain of wheat that fell into the
earth. Here we have a very important lesson to learn: our
own crosses acquire value if we consider them and accept
them as a part of the Cross of Christ, if a reflection of his
light illuminates them. It is by that Cross alone that our sufferings too are ennobled and acquire their true meaning.

The Apostle Andrew, therefore, teaches us to follow Jesus
with promptness (cf. Mt 4:20; Mk 1:18), to speak enthusiastically about him to those we meet, and, especially, to
cultivate a relationship of true familiarity with him, acutely
aware that in him alone can we find the ultimate meaning
of our life and death.

(14 June 2006)

Thanksgiving Day

In our Christian families, children are taught always to thank the Lord with a short prayer and the Sign of the Cross prior to eating. This custom should be preserved or rediscovered, for it teaches people not to take their "daily bread" for granted but to recognize it as a gift of Providence. We should become accustomed to blessing the Creator for all things: for air and water, precious elements on which life on our planet depends, as well as for the food that through the earth's fertility God offers to us for our sustenance. Jesus taught his disciples to pray by asking the Heavenly Father, not for "my", but for "our" daily bread. Thus, he desired every person to feel co-responsible for his brothers so that no one would want for what he needs in order to live. The earth's produce forms a gift which God has destined "for the entire human family".

And here we touch on a very sore point: the drama of hunger which, although it has recently been addressed at the most important institutions such as the United Nations and in particular at the Food and Agriculture Organization (FAO), continues to be very serious. The last annual report of the FAO has confirmed what the Church knows very well from her direct experience of the communities and missions: more than 800 million people are living in a condition of undernourishment and too many, especially children, die of hunger. How should we cope with this situation which, though repeatedly denounced, shows no sign of a solution and indeed, in some respects is worsening? It is certainly necessary to eliminate the structural causes linked to the system for regulating the world economy, which destines the majority of the planet's resources to a minority of the population. This injustice was stigmatized on various occasions by my venerable Predecessors, the Servants of God Paul VI and John Paul II. To be effective on a wide scale, it is necessary "to convert" the model of global development, required not only due to the scandal of hunger but also by environmental and energy emergencies. Yet, every person and every family can and must do something to alleviate hunger in the world by adopting a life-style and consumption compatible with the safeguarding of creation and with criteria of justice for those who cultivate the land in every country.

... Today's Thanksgiving Day invites us, on the one hand, to give thanks to God for the fruits of agricultural work; and on the other, it encourages us to commit ourselves concretely to defeat the scourge of hunger. May the Virgin Mary help us to be grateful for the benefits of Providence and to foster justice and solidarity in every part of the globe.

(12 November 2006)

2 December

Saint Chromatius of Aquileia

This Bishop exercised his ministry in the ancient Church of Aquileia, a fervent center of Christian life located in the Roman Empire's *Decima regione*, the *Venetia et Histria*. In 388 A.D., when Chromatius assumed the episcopal throne of the city, the local Christian communities had already developed a glorious history of Gospel fidelity. Between the middle of the third century and the early years of the fourth, the persecution of Decius, Valerian, and Diocletian had taken a heavy toll of martyrs. Furthermore, the Church of Aquileia, like so many other Churches of that time, had had to contend with the threat of the Arian heresy. Athanasius himself—a standard-bearer of Nicene orthodoxy whom the Arians had banished to exile—had for some time been in Aquileia, where he had taken refuge. Under the guidance of its Bishops, the Christian community withstood the snares of the heresy and reinforced their own attachment to the Catholic faith.

In September 381, Aquileia was the seat of a Synod that gathered about thirty-five Bishops from the coasts of Africa, the Rhone Valley, and the entire *Decima regione*. The Synod intended to eliminate the last remnants of Arianism in the West. Chromatius, a priest, also took part in the Council as *peritus* for Bishop Valerian of Aquileia (370 / 1 to 387 / 8). The years around the Synod of 381 were the "Golden Age" of the inhabitants of Aquileia. Saint Jerome, a native of Dalmatia, and Rufinus of Concordia spoke nostalgically of their sojourn in Aquileia (370–373), in that sort of theological cenacle which Jerome did not hesitate to define "*tamquam chorus beatorum*", "like a choir of blesseds" (*Cronaca: PL* 27, 697–698). It was in this Upper Room— some aspects of which are reminiscent of the community experiences directed by Eusebius of Vercelli and by Augustine—that the most outstanding figures of the Church of the Upper Adriatic were formed.

Chromatius, however, had already learned at home to know and love Christ. Jerome himself spoke of this in terms full of admiration and compared Chromatius' mother to the Prophetess Anna, his two sisters to the Wise Virgins of the Gospel Parable, and Chromatius himself and his brother Eusebius to the young Samuel (cf. *Ep.* 7: *PL* 22, 341). Jerome wrote further of Chromatius and Eusebius: "Blessed Chromatius and Saint Eusebius were brothers by blood, no less than by the identity of their ideals" (*Ep.* 8: *PL* 22, 342).

Chromatius was born in Aquileia in about 345 A.D. He was ordained a deacon, then a priest; finally, he was appointed Bishop of that Church (388). After receiving episcopal ordination from Bishop Ambrose, he dedicated himself courageously and energetically to an immense task because of the vast territory entrusted to his pastoral care: the ecclesiastical jurisdiction of Aquileia, in fact, stretched from the present-day territories of Switzerland, Bavaria, Austria, and Slovenia as far as Hungary. How well known and highly esteemed Chromatius was in the Church of his time we can deduce from an episode in the life of Saint John Chrysostom. When the Bishop of Constantinople was exiled from his See, he wrote three letters to those he considered the most important Bishops of the West seeking to obtain their support with the Emperors: he wrote one letter to the Bishop of Rome, the second to the Bishop of Milan,

and the third to the Bishop of Aquileia, precisely, Chromatius (*Ep.* 155: *PG* 52, 702). Those were difficult times also
for Chromatius because of the precarious political situation.
In all likelihood Chromatius died in exile, in Grado, while
he was attempting to escape the incursions of the barbarians
in 407, the same year when Chrysostom also died.

With regard to prestige and importance, Aquileia was
the fourth city of the Italian peninsula and the ninth of the
Roman Empire. This is another reason that explains why it
was a target that attracted both Goths and Huns. In addition to causing serious bereavements and destruction, the
invasions of these peoples gravely jeopardized the transmission of the works of the Fathers preserved in the episcopal
library, rich in codices. Saint Chromatius' writings were also
dispersed, ending up here and there, and were often attributed to other authors: to John Chrysostom (partly because
of the similar beginning of their two names, Chromatius
and Chrysostom); or to Ambrose or Augustine; or even to
Jerome, to whom Chromatius had given considerable help
in the revision of the text and in the Latin translation of the
Bible. The rediscovery of a large part of the work of Chromatius is due to fortunate events, which has made it possible
only in recent years to piece together a fairly consistent corpus of his writings: more than forty homilies, ten of which
are fragments, and more than sixty treatises of commentary
on Matthew's Gospel.

Chromatius was a wise *teacher* and a zealous *Pastor.* His first
and main commitment was to listen to the Word, to be able
subsequently to proclaim it: he always bases his teaching on
the Word of God and constantly returns to it. Certain subjects are particularly dear to him: first of all, the *Trinitarian
mystery*, which he contemplated in its revelation throughout
the history of salvation. Then, the theme of the *Holy Spirit*:
Chromatius constantly reminds the faithful of the presence

and action in the life of the Church of the Third Person of the Most Holy Trinity. But the holy Bishop returns with special insistence to the *mystery of Christ*. The incarnate Word is true God and true man: he took on humanity in its totality to endow it with his own divinity. These truths, which he also reaffirmed explicitly in order to counter Arianism, were to end up about fifty years later in the definition of the Council of Chalcedon. The heavy emphasis on Christ's human nature led Chromatius to speak of the *Virgin Mary*. His Mariological doctrine is clear and precise. To him we owe evocative descriptions of the Virgin Most Holy: Mary is the "evangelical Virgin capable of accepting God"; she is the "immaculate and inviolate ewe lamb" who conceived the "Lamb clad in purple" (cf. *Sermo* 23, 3: *Scrittori dell'area santambrosiana* 3 / 1, p. 134). The Bishop of Aquileia often compares the Virgin with the Church: both, in fact, are "virgins" and "mothers". Chromatius developed his *ecclesiology* above all in his commentary on Matthew. These are some of the recurring concepts: the Church is one, she is born from the Blood of Christ; she is a precious garment woven by the Holy Spirit; the Church is where the fact that Christ was born of a Virgin is proclaimed, where brotherhood and harmony flourish. One image of which Chromatius is especially fond is that of the ship in a storm—and his were stormy times, as we have heard: "There is no doubt", the holy Bishop says, "that this ship represents the Church" (cf. *Tractatus* 42, 5: *Scrittori dell'area santambrosiana* 3/2, p. 260).

As the zealous Pastor that he was, Chromatius was able to speak to his people with a fresh, colorful, and incisive language. Although he was not ignorant of the perfect Latin *cursus*, he preferred to use the vernacular, rich in images easy to understand. Thus, for example, drawing inspiration from the sea, he compared, on the one hand, the natural catching of fish, which, caught and landed, die; and on the other,

Gospel preaching, thanks to which men and women are saved from the murky waters of death and ushered into true life (cf. *Tractatus* 16, 3: *Scrittori dell'area santambrosiana* 3/2, p. 106). Again, in the perspective of a good Pastor, during a turbulent period such as his, ravaged by the incursions of barbarians, he was able to set himself beside the faithful to comfort them and open their minds to trust in God, who never abandons his children.

Lastly, as a conclusion to these reflections, let us include an exhortation of Chromatius which is still perfectly applicable today: "Let us pray to the Lord with all our heart and with all our faith", the Bishop of Aquileia recommends in one of his *Sermons*,

> let us pray to him to deliver us from all enemy incursions, from all fear of adversaries. Do not look at our merits but at his mercy, at him who also in the past deigned to set the Children of Israel free, not for their own merits but through his mercy. May he protect us with his customary merciful love and bring about for us what holy Moses said to the Children of Israel: *The Lord will fight to defend you, and you will be silent.* It is he who fights, it is he who wins the victory.... And so that he may condescend to do so, we must pray as much as possible. He himself said, in fact, through the mouth of the prophet: Call on me on the day of tribulation; *I will set you free and you will give me glory.* (*Sermo* 16, 4: *Scrittori dell'area santambrosiana* 3/2, pp. 100–102)

Thus, at the very beginning of the Advent Season, Saint Chromatius reminds us that Advent is a time of prayer in which it is essential to enter into contact with God. God knows us, he knows me, he knows each one of us, he loves me, he will not abandon me. Let us go forward with this trust in the liturgical season that has just begun.

(5 December 2007)

3 December

Saint Francis Xavier

This illustrious missionary, well-known above all in Spain, India, and Japan, speaks also to the men and women of our times of the salvific work of Our Lord Jesus Christ and of the universal character of the Gospel. This apostle, who tirelessly proclaimed Christ and converted many to the faith, is an extraordinary model of spiritual progress, an admirable servant of the Kingdom of God and a master of evangelization to the entire world.

(3 March 2006)

* * *

Saint Francis Xavier, whom my Predecessor Pius XI, of venerable memory, proclaimed the "Patron of Catholic Missions", saw as his own mission "opening new ways of access" to the Gospel "in the immense Continent of Asia". His apostolate in the Orient lasted barely ten years, but in the four and half centuries that the Society of Jesus has existed, it has proven wonderfully fruitful, for his example inspired a multitude of missionary vocations among young Jesuits, and he remains a reference point for the continuation of missionary activity in the great countries of the Asian Continent.

(22 April 2006)

Translated in part by Andrew Matt.

Saint Ambrose of Milan

Holy Bishop Ambrose ... died in Milan in the night between 3 and 4 April 397. It was dawn on Holy Saturday. The day before, at about five o'clock in the afternoon, he had settled down to pray, lying on his bed with his arms wide open in the form of a cross. Thus, he took part in the solemn Easter Triduum, in the death and Resurrection of the Lord. "We saw his lips moving," said Paulinus, the faithful deacon who wrote his *Life* at Saint Augustine's suggestion, "but we could not hear his voice." The situation suddenly became dramatic. Honoratus, Bishop of Vercelli, who was assisting Ambrose and was sleeping on the upper floor, was awoken by a voice saying again and again, "Get up quickly! Ambrose is dying...." "Honoratus hurried downstairs", Paulinus continues, "and offered the Saint the Body of the Lord. As soon as he had received and swallowed it, Ambrose gave up his spirit, taking the good Viaticum with him. His soul, thus refreshed by the virtue of that food, now enjoys the company of Angels" (*Life* 47). On that Holy Friday 397, the wide open arms of the dying Ambrose expressed his mystical participation in the death and Resurrection of the Lord. This was his last catechesis: in the silence of words, he continued to speak with the witness of his life.

Ambrose was not old when he died. He had not even reached the age of sixty, since he was born in about 340 A.D. in Treves, where his father was Prefect of the Gauls. His family was Christian. Upon his father's death while he was still a boy, his mother took him to Rome and educated him for a civil career, assuring him a sound instruction in rhetoric and jurisprudence. In about 370 he was sent to govern the Provinces of Emilia and Liguria, with headquarters in Milan. It was precisely there that the struggle between orthodox and Arians was raging and became particularly heated after the death of the Arian Bishop Auxentius. Ambrose intervened to pacify the members of the two opposing factions; his authority was such that although he was merely a catechumen, the people acclaimed him Bishop of Milan.

Until that moment, Ambrose had been the most senior magistrate of the Empire in Northern Italy. Culturally well-educated but at the same time ignorant of the Scriptures, the new Bishop briskly began to study them. From the works of Origen, the indisputable master of the "Alexandrian School", he learned to know and to comment on the Bible. Thus, Ambrose transferred to the Latin environment the meditation on the Scriptures which Origen had begun, introducing in the West the practice of *lectio divina*. The method of *lectio* served to guide all of Ambrose's preaching and writings, which stemmed precisely from *prayerful listening* to the Word of God. The famous introduction of an Ambrosian catechesis shows clearly how the holy Bishop applied the Old Testament to Christian life: "Every day, when we were reading about the lives of the Patriarchs and the maxims of the Proverbs, we addressed morality," the Bishop of Milan said to his catechumens and neophytes, "so that formed and instructed by them you may become accustomed to taking the path of the Fathers and to following the route of obedience to the divine precepts" (*On the Mysteries* 1, 1). In other words, the neophytes and catechumens, in accordance with the Bishop's decision, after having learned the art of a well-ordered life, could henceforth consider themselves prepared for Christ's great mysteries. Thus, Ambrose's preaching—which constitutes the structural nucleus of his immense literary opus—starts with the reading of the Sacred Books ("the Patriarchs" or the historical Books and "Proverbs", or in other words, the Wisdom Books) in order to live in conformity with divine Revelation.

It is obvious that the preacher's personal testimony and the level of exemplarity of the Christian community condition the effectiveness of the preaching. In this perspective, a passage from Saint Augustine's *Confessions* is relevant. He had come to Milan as a teacher of rhetoric; he was a sceptic and not Christian. He was seeking the Christian truth but was not capable of truly finding it. What moved the heart of the young African rhetorician, sceptic and downhearted, and what impelled him to definitive conversion was not above all Ambrose's splendid homilies (although he deeply appreciated them). It was rather the testimony of the Bishop and his Milanese Church that prayed and sang as one intact body. It was a Church that could resist the tyrannical ploys of the Emperor and his mother, who in early 386 again demanded a church building for the Arians' celebrations. In the building that was to be requisitioned, Augustine relates, "the devout people watched, ready to die with their Bishop." This testimony of the *Confessions* is precious because it points out that something was moving in Augustine, who continues: "We too, although spiritually tepid, shared in the excitement of the whole people" (*Confessions* 9, 7).

Augustine learned from the life and example of Bishop Ambrose to believe and to preach. We can refer to a famous sermon of the African, which centuries later merited citation in the conciliar Constitution on Divine Revelation, *Dei Verbum*: "Therefore, all clerics, particularly priests of Christ and others who, as deacons or catechists, are officially engaged in the ministry of the Word," *Dei Verbum* recommends, "should immerse themselves in the Scriptures by constant sacred reading and diligent study. For it must not happen that anyone becomes"—and this is Augustine's citation—"an empty preacher of the Word of God to others, not being a hearer of the Word in his own heart" (no. 25). Augustine had learned precisely from Ambrose how to "hear in his own heart" this perseverance in reading Sacred Scripture with a prayerful approach, so as truly to absorb and assimilate the Word of God in one's heart.

Dear brothers and sisters, I would like further to propose to you a sort of "patristic icon", which, interpreted in the light of what we have said, effectively represents "the heart" of Ambrosian doctrine. In the sixth book of the *Confessions*, Augustine tells of his meeting with Ambrose, an encounter that was indisputably of great importance in the history of the Church. He writes in his text that whenever he went to see the Bishop of Milan, he would regularly find him taken up with *catervae* of people full of problems for whose needs he did his utmost. There was always a long queue waiting to talk to Ambrose, seeking in him consolation and hope. When Ambrose was not with them, with the people (and this happened for the space of the briefest of moments), he was either restoring his body with the necessary food or nourishing his spirit with reading. Here Augustine marvels because Ambrose read the Scriptures with his mouth shut, only with his eyes (cf. *Confessions* 6, 3). Indeed, in the early Christian centuries reading was conceived of strictly for proclamation, and reading aloud also facilitated the reader's understanding. That Ambrose could scan the pages with his eyes alone suggested to the admiring Augustine a rare ability for reading and familiarity with the Scriptures. Well, in that "reading under one's breath", where the heart is committed to achieving knowledge of the Word of God—this is the "icon" to which we are referring—one can glimpse the method of Ambrosian catechesis; it is Scripture itself, intimately assimilated, which suggests the content to proclaim that will lead to the conversion of hearts.

Thus, with regard to the magisterium of Ambrose and of Augustine, catechesis is inseparable from witness of life. What I wrote on the theologian in the *Introduction to Christianity* might also be useful to the catechist. An educator in the faith cannot risk appearing like a sort of clown who recites a part "by profession". Rather—to use an image dear to Origen, a writer who was particularly appreciated by Ambrose—he must be like the beloved disciple who rested his head against his Master's heart and there learned the way to think, speak, and act. The true disciple is ultimately the one whose proclamation of the Gospel is the most credible and effective.

Like the Apostle John, Bishop Ambrose—who never tired of saying: "*Omnia Christus est nobis!* To us Christ is all!"—continues to be a genuine witness of the Lord. Let us thus conclude our Catechesis with his same words, full of love for Jesus: "*Omnia Christus est nobis!* If you have a wound to heal, he is the doctor; if you are parched by fever, he is the spring; if you are oppressed by injustice, he is justice; if you are in need of help, he is strength; if you fear death, he is life; if you desire Heaven, he is the way; if you are in the darkness, he is light.... Taste and see how good is the Lord: blessed is the man who hopes in him!" (*De Virginitate* 16, 99). Let us also hope in Christ. We shall thus be blessed and shall live in peace.

(24 October 2007)

The Immaculate Conception

Today, we are celebrating the Solemnity of the Immaculate Conception. It is a day of intense spiritual joy when we contemplate the Virgin Mary, "*high beyond all other, lowlier is none . . . the consummation planned by God's decree*", as is sung by the great poet Dante (*Par.* XXXIII, 3). In Mary shines forth the eternal goodness of the Creator, who chose her in his plan of salvation to be the mother of his Only-Begotten Son; God, foreseeing his death, preserved her from every stain of sin (cf. Concluding Prayer). In this way, in the Mother of Christ and our Mother the vocation of every human being is perfectly fulfilled. All men and women, according to Saint Paul, are called to be holy and blameless in God's sight, full of love (cf. Eph 1:4, 5). Looking at Mary, how can we, her children, fail to let the aspiration to beauty, goodness, and purity of heart be aroused in us? Her heavenly candor draws us to God, helping us to overcome the temptation to live a mediocre life composed of compromises with evil, and directs us decisively toward the authentic good that is the source of joy.

(8 December 2005)

Narcisa de Jesús Martillo Morán

Narcisa de Jesús Martillo Morán, a young Ecuadorian lay woman, offers us a perfect example of a prompt and generous response to the invitation that the Lord extends to us to share in his love.

Already at a very early age, in receiving the Sacrament of Confirmation, she felt clearly in her heart the call to live a life of holiness and devotion to God.

To sustain the Holy Spirit's action in her soul with docility, she always sought the counsel and guidance of good and expert priests, considering spiritual direction as one of the most effective means to arrive at holiness.

Saint Narcisa of Jesus shows us a path of Christian perfection obtainable for all the faithful. Despite the many and extraordinary graces that she received, she lived her life with great simplicity, dedicated to her work as a seamstress and to her apostolate as a catechist.

In her passionate love for Jesus, who led her on a path of intense prayer and torment and to identify herself increasingly with the mystery of the Cross, she offers us an attractive witness and a perfect example of a life totally dedicated to God and to her brothers and sisters.

(12 October 2008)

Saint Antônio de Sant'ana Galvão

The Franciscan charism, lived out in the spirit of the Gospel, has borne significant fruits through [the] witness [of Frei Galvão] as an ardent adorer of the Eucharist, as a prudent and wise guide of the souls who sought his counsel, and as a man with a great devotion to the Immaculate Conception of Mary, whose "son and perpetual servant" he considered himself to be....

The significance of Frei Galvão's example lies in his willingness to be of service to the people whenever he was asked. He was renowned as a counselor; he was a bringer of peace to souls and families and a dispenser of charity especially toward the poor and the sick. He was greatly sought out as a confessor, because he was zealous, wise, and prudent. It is characteristic of those who truly love that they do not want the Beloved to be offended; the conversion of sinners was therefore the great passion of our saint. Sister Helena Maria, the first religious sister destined to belong to the *Recolhimento de Nossa Senhora da Conceição*, witnessed to what Frei Galvão had said to her: "*Pray that the Lord our God will raise sinners with his mighty arm from the wretched depths of the sins in which they find themselves.*" May this insightful admonition serve as a stimulus to us to recognize in the Divine Mercy the path toward reconciliation with God and our neighbor, for the peace of our consciences.

United with the Lord in the supreme communion of the Eucharist and reconciled with him and our neighbor, we will thus become bearers of that peace which the world cannot give. Will the men and women of this world be able to find peace if they are not aware of the need to be reconciled with God, with their neighbor, and with themselves? Highly significant in this regard are the words written by the Assembly of the Senate of São Paulo to the Minister Provincial of the Franciscans at the end of the eighteenth century, describing Frei Galvão as a "man of peace and charity". What does the Lord ask of us? *"Love one another as I have loved you."* But immediately afterward he adds: *"Go out and bear fruit, fruit that will last"* (cf. Jn 15:12, 16). And what fruit does he ask of us if not that of knowing how to love, drawing inspiration from the example of the Saint of Guaratinguetá?

The renown of his immense charity knew no bounds. People from all over the country went to Frei Galvão, who offered a fatherly welcome to everyone. Among those who came to implore his help were the poor and the sick in body and spirit.

Jesus opens his heart and reveals to us the core of his entire saving message: *"No one has greater love than this: to lay down his life for his friends"* (Jn 15:13). He himself loved even to the extent of giving his life for us on the Cross. The action of the Church and of Christians in society must have this same inspiration. Pastoral initiatives for the building up of society, if directed toward the good of the poor and the sick, bear within themselves this divine seal. The Lord counts on us and calls us his friends, because it is only to those we love in this way that we are capable of giving the life offered by Jesus through his grace. . . .

In fact, the saint that we are celebrating gave himself irrevocably to the Mother of Jesus from his youth, desiring to belong to her forever, and he chose the Virgin Mary to be the Mother and Protector of his spiritual daughters.

My dearest friends, what a fine example Frei Galvão has left for us to follow! There is a phrase included in the formula of his consecration which sounds remarkably contemporary to us, who live in an age so full of hedonism: *"Take away my life before I offend your blessed Son, my Lord!"* They are strong words, the words of an impassioned soul, words that should be part of the normal life of every Christian, whether consecrated or not, and they enkindle a desire for fidelity to God in married couples as well as in the unmarried. The world needs transparent lives, clear souls, pure minds that refuse to be perceived as mere objects of pleasure. It is necessary to oppose those elements of the media that ridicule the sanctity of marriage and virginity before marriage.

(11 May 2007)

Saint Stephen

Yesterday, after solemnly celebrating Christ's Birth, today we are commemorating the birth in Heaven of Saint Stephen, the first martyr. A special bond links these two feasts, and it is summed up well in the Ambrosian liturgy by this affirmation: "Yesterday, the Lord was born on earth, that Stephen might be born in Heaven" (at the Breaking of the Bread). Just as Jesus on the Cross entrusted himself to the Father without reserve and pardoned those who killed him, at the moment of his death Saint Stephen prayed: "Lord Jesus, receive my spirit"; and further: "Lord, do not hold this sin against them" (cf. Acts 7:59–60). Stephen was a genuine disciple of Jesus and imitated him perfectly. With Stephen began that long series of martyrs who sealed their faith by offering their lives, proclaiming with their heroic witness that God became man to open the Kingdom of Heaven to mankind.

In the atmosphere of Christmas joy, the reference to the Martyr Saint Stephen does not seem out of place. Indeed, the shadow of the Cross was already extending over the manger in Bethlehem. It was foretold by the poverty of the stable in which the infant wailed, the prophecy of Simeon concerning the sign that would be opposed and the sword destined to pierce the heart of the Virgin, and Herod's persecution that would make necessary the flight to Egypt. It should not come as a surprise that this Child, having grown to adulthood, would one day ask his disciples to follow him with total trust and faithfulness on the Way of the Cross. Already at the dawn of the Church, many Christians, attracted by his example and sustained by his love, were to witness to their faith by pouring out their blood. The first martyrs would be followed by others down the centuries to our day. How can we not recognize that professing the Christian faith demands the heroism of the martyrs in our time too, in various parts of the world? Moreover, how can we not say that everywhere, even where there is no persecution, there is a high price to pay for consistently living the Gospel?

Contemplating the divine Child in Mary's arms and looking to the example of Saint Stephen, let us ask God for the grace to live our faith consistently, ever ready to answer those who ask us to account for the hope that is in us (cf. I Pt 3:15).

(26 December 2005)

* * *

Saint Stephen is the most representative of a group of seven companions. Tradition sees in this group the seed of the future ministry of "deacons", although it must be pointed out that this category is not present in the Book of Acts. In any case, Stephen's importance is due to the fact that Luke, in his important book, dedicates two whole chapters to him.

Luke's narrative starts with the observation of a widespread division in the primitive Church of Jerusalem: indeed, she consisted entirely of Christians of Jewish origin, but some came from the land of Israel and were called "Hebrews", while others, of the Old Testament Jewish faith, came from the Greek-speaking diaspora and were known as "Hellenists". This was the new problem: the most destitute of the Hellenists, especially widows deprived of any social support, ran the risk of being neglected in the daily distribution of their rations. To avoid this problem, the Apostles, continuing to devote themselves to prayer and the ministry of the Word, decided to appoint for this duty "seven men of good repute, full of the Spirit and of wisdom" to help them (Acts 6:2–4), that is, by carrying out a social and charitable service. To this end, as Luke wrote, at the Apostles' invitation the disciples chose seven men. We are even given their names. They were: "Stephen, a man full of faith and of the Holy Spirit, Philip, Prochorus, Nicanor, Timon, Parmenas and Nicolaus. These they set before the Apostles, and they prayed and laid their hands upon them" (cf. Acts 6:5–6).

The act of the laying on of hands can have various meanings. In the Old Testament, this gesture meant above all the transmission of an important office, just as Moses laid his hands on Joshua (cf. Nm 27:18–23), thereby designating his successor. Along the same lines, the Church of Antioch would also use this gesture in sending out Paul and Barnabas on their mission to the peoples of the world (cf. Acts 13:3). The two Pauline Letters addressed to Timothy (cf. 1 Tm 4:14; 2 Tm 1:6) refer to a similar imposition of hands on Timothy, to confer upon him an official responsibility. From what we read in the First Letter to Timothy, we can deduce that this was an important action to be carried out after discernment: "Do not be hasty in the laying on of hands, nor participate in another man's sins" (5:22). Thus, we see that the act of the laying on of hands developed along the lines of a sacramental sign. In the case of Stephen and his companions, it was certainly an official conferral of an office by the Apostles, but at the same time an entreaty for the grace to carry it out.

The most important thing to note is that in addition to charitable services, Stephen also carried out a task of evangelization among his compatriots, the so-called "Hellenists". Indeed, Luke insists on the fact that Stephen, "full of grace and power" (Acts 6:8), presented in Jesus' Name a new interpretation of Moses and of God's Law itself. He reread the Old Testament in the light of the proclamation of Christ's death and Resurrection. He gave the Old Testament a Christological reinterpretation and provoked reactions from the Jews, who took his words to be blasphemous (cf. Acts 6:11–14). For this reason he was condemned to stoning. And Saint Luke passes on to us the Saint's last discourse, a synthesis of his preaching. Just as Jesus had shown the disciples of Emmaus that the whole of the Old Testament speaks of him, of his Cross and his Resurrection, so Saint Stephen, following Jesus' teaching, interpreted the whole of the Old Testament in a Christological key. He shows that the mystery of the Cross stands at the center of the history of salvation as recounted in the Old Testament; it shows that Jesus, Crucified and Risen, is truly the goal of all this history. Saint Stephen also shows that the cult of the Temple was over and that Jesus, the Risen One, was the new, true "temple". It was precisely this "no" to the Temple and to its cult that led to the condemnation of Saint Stephen, who at this moment, Saint Luke tells us, gazed into Heaven and saw the glory of God, and Jesus standing at the right hand of God, and seeing Heaven, God, and Jesus, Saint Stephen said, "Behold, I see the heavens opened, and the Son of man standing at the right hand of God" (cf. Acts 7:56). This was followed by his martyrdom, modeled in fact on the Passion of Jesus himself, since he delivered his own spirit to the "Lord Jesus" and prayed that the sin of those who killed him would not be held against them (cf. Acts 7:59–60).

The place of Saint Stephen's martyrdom in Jerusalem has traditionally been located outside the Damascus Gate, to the north, where indeed the Church of Saint-Étienne

[Saint Stephen] stands beside the famous *École Biblique* of the Dominicans. The killing of Stephen, the first martyr of Christ, unleashed a local persecution of Christ's disciples (cf. Acts 8:1), the first one in the history of the Church. It was these circumstances that impelled the group of Judeo-Hellenist Christians to flee from Jerusalem and scatter. Hounded out of Jerusalem, they became itinerant missionaries: "Those who were scattered went about preaching the word" (Acts 8:4). Their persecution and consequent dispersion became a mission. Thus, the Gospel spread also to Samaria, Phoenicia, and Syria, as far as the great city of Antioch, where, according to Luke, it was proclaimed for the first time also to the pagans (cf. Acts 11:19–20) and where, for the first time, the name "Christians" was used (Acts 11:26).

In particular, Luke noted that those who stoned Stephen "laid down their garments at the feet of a young man named Saul" (Acts 7:58), the same man who from being a persecutor was to become an outstanding Apostle of the Gospel. This means that the young Saul must have heard Stephen's preaching and must therefore have been acquainted with its principal content. And Saint Paul was probably among those who, following and listening to this discourse, "were enraged and ... ground their teeth against him" (Acts 7:54). And at this point, we can see the marvels of divine Providence. After his encounter with the Risen Christ on the road to Damascus, Saul, a relentless enemy of Stephen's vision, took up the Christological interpretation of the Old Testament made by the First Martyr, deepening and completing it, and consequently became the "Apostle to the Gentiles". The Law is fulfilled, he taught, in the Cross of Christ. And faith in Christ, communion with Christ's love, is the true fulfillment of all the Law. This is the content of Paul's preaching. He showed in this way that the God of Abraham had become the God of all. And all believers in Jesus Christ, as children of Abraham, shared in the promises. Saint Stephen's vision was brought about in Saint Paul's mission.

Stephen's story tells us many things: for example, that charitable social commitment must never be separated from the courageous proclamation of the faith. He was one of the seven made responsible above all for charity. But it was impossible to separate charity and faith. Thus, with charity, he proclaimed the crucified Christ, to the point of accepting even martyrdom. This is the first lesson we can learn from the figure of Saint Stephen: charity and the proclamation of faith always go hand in hand. Above all, Saint Stephen speaks to us of Christ, of the Crucified and Risen Christ as the center of history and our life. We can understand that the Cross remains forever the center of the Church's life and also of our life. In the history of the Church, there will always be passion and persecution. And it is persecution itself which, according to Tertullian's famous words, becomes "the seed of Christians", the source of mission for Christians to come. I cite his words: "We multiply wherever we are mown down by you: the blood of Christians is seed ..." (*Apology*, 50, 13): *plures efficimur quoties metimur a vobis: semen est sanguis christianorum.* But in our life, too, the Cross that will never be absent becomes a blessing. And by accepting our cross, knowing that it becomes and is a blessing, we learn Christian joy even in moments of difficulty. The value of witness is irreplaceable, because the Gospel leads to it and the Church is nourished by it. Saint Stephen teaches us to treasure these lessons; he teaches us to love the Cross, because it is the path on which Christ comes among us ever anew.

(10 January 2007)

27 December

Saint John, Apostle and Evangelist

His typically Jewish name means: "the Lord has worked grace." He was mending his nets on the shore of Lake Tiberias when Jesus called him and his brother (cf. Mt 4:21; Mk 1:19). John was always among the small group that Jesus took with him on specific occasions. He was with Peter and James when Jesus entered Peter's house in Capernaum to cure his mother-in-law (cf. Mk 1:29); with the other two, he followed the Teacher into the house of Jairus, a ruler of the synagogue whose daughter he was to bring back to life (cf. Mk 5:37); he followed him when he climbed the mountain for his Transfiguration (cf. Mk 9:2). He was beside the Lord on the Mount of Olives when, before the impressive sight of the Temple of Jerusalem, he spoke of the end of the city and of the world (cf. Mk 13:3); and, lastly, he was close to him in the Garden of Gethsemane when he withdrew to pray to the Father before the Passion (cf. Mk 14:33). Shortly before the Passover, when Jesus chose two disciples to send them to prepare the room for the Supper, it was to him and to Peter that he entrusted this task (cf. Lk 22:8).

His prominent position in the group of the Twelve makes it somewhat easier to understand the initiative taken one day by his mother: she approached Jesus to ask him if her two sons—John and James—could sit next to him in the Kingdom, one on his right and one on his left (cf. Mt 20:20–21). As we know, Jesus answered by asking a question in turn:

he asked whether they were prepared to drink the cup that he was about to drink (cf. Mt 20:22). The intention behind those words was to open the two disciples' eyes, to introduce them to knowledge of the mystery of his person and to suggest their future calling to be his witnesses, even to the supreme trial of blood. A little later, in fact, Jesus explained that he had not come to be served, but to serve and to give his life as a ransom for many (cf. Mt 20:28). In the days after the Resurrection, we find "the sons of Zebedee" busy with Peter and some of the other disciples on a night when they caught nothing, but that was followed, after the intervention of the Risen One, by the miraculous catch: it was to be "the disciple Jesus loved" who first recognized "the Lord" and pointed him out to Peter (cf. Jn 21:1–13).

In the Church of Jerusalem, John occupied an important position in supervising the first group of Christians. Indeed, Paul lists him among those whom he calls the "pillars" of that community (cf. Gal 2:9). In fact, Luke in the Acts presents him together with Peter while they are going to pray in the Temple (cf. Acts 3:1–4, 11) or appear before the Sanhedrin to witness to their faith in Jesus Christ (cf. Acts 4:13, 19). Together with Peter, he is sent to the Church of Jerusalem to strengthen the people in Samaria who had accepted the Gospel, praying for them that they might receive the Holy Spirit (cf. Acts 8:14–15). In particular, we should remember what he affirmed with Peter to the Sanhedrin members who were accusing them: "We cannot but speak of what we have seen and heard" (Acts 4:20). It is precisely this frankness in confessing his faith that lives on as an example and a warning for all of us always to be ready to declare firmly our steadfast attachment to Christ, putting faith before any human calculation or concern.

According to tradition, John is the "disciple whom Jesus loved", who in the Fourth Gospel laid his head against the

Teacher's breast at the Last Supper (cf. Jn 13:23), stood at the foot of the Cross together with the Mother of Jesus (cf. Jn 19:25), and lastly, witnessed both the empty tomb and the presence of the Risen One himself (cf. Jn 20:2; 21:7). We know that this identification is disputed by scholars today, some of whom view him merely as the prototype of a disciple of Jesus. Leaving the exegetes to settle the matter, let us be content here with learning an important lesson for our lives: the Lord wishes to make each one of us a disciple who lives in personal friendship with him. To achieve this, it is not enough to follow him and to listen to him outwardly: it is also necessary to live with him and like him. This is only possible in the context of a relationship of deep familiarity, imbued with the warmth of total trust. This is what happens between friends; for this reason Jesus said one day: "Greater love has no man than this, that a man lay down his life for his friends.... No longer do I call you servants, for the servant does not know what his master is doing; but I have called you friends, for all that I have heard from my Father I have made known to you" (Jn 15:13, 15).

In the apocryphal *Acts of John*, the Apostle is not presented as the founder of Churches or as the guide of already established communities, but as a perpetual wayfarer, a communicator of the faith in the encounter with "souls capable of hoping and of being saved" (18:10; 23:8). All is motivated by the paradoxical intention to make visible the invisible. And indeed, the Oriental Church calls him quite simply "the Theologian", that is, the one who can speak in accessible terms of the divine, revealing an arcane access to God through attachment to Jesus.

Devotion to the Apostle John spread from the city of Ephesus where, according to an ancient tradition, he worked for many years and died in the end at an extraordinarily advanced age, during the reign of the Emperor Trajan. In

Ephesus in the sixth century, the Emperor Justinian had a great basilica built in his honor, whose impressive ruins are still standing today. Precisely in the East, he enjoyed and still enjoys great veneration. In Byzantine iconography he is often shown as very elderly—according to tradition, he died under the Emperor Trajan—in the process of intense contemplation, in the attitude, as it were, of those asking for silence.

Indeed, without sufficient recollection it is impossible to approach the supreme mystery of God and of his revelation. This explains why, years ago, Athenagoras, Ecumenical Patriarch of Constantinople, the man whom Pope Paul VI embraced at a memorable encounter, said: "John is the origin of our loftiest spirituality. Like him, 'the silent ones' experience that mysterious exchange of hearts, pray for John's presence, and their hearts are set on fire" (O. Clément, *Dialoghi con Atenagora*, Turin 1972, p. 159). May the Lord help us to study at John's school and learn the great lesson of love, so as to feel we are loved by Christ "to the end" (Jn 13:1), and spend our lives for him.

(5 July 2006)

Praise and Thanksgiving

At the end of a year which has been particularly eventful for the Church and for the world, mindful of the Apostle's order, "walk ... established in the faith ... abounding in thanksgiving" (cf. Col 2:6-7), we are gathered together this evening to raise a hymn of thanksgiving to God, Lord of time and of history....

Yes, it is our duty, as well as a need of our hearts, to praise and thank the Eternal One who accompanies us through time, never abandoning us, and who always watches over humanity with the fidelity of his merciful love.

We may well say that the Church lives to praise and thank God. She herself has been an "action of grace" down the ages, a faithful witness of a love that does not die, of a love that embraces people of every race and culture, fruitfully disseminating principles of true life. As the Second Vatican Council recalls, "the Church prays and likewise labors so that into the People of God, the Body of the Lord and the Temple of the Holy Spirit, may pass the fullness of the whole world and that in Christ, the head of all things, all honor and glory may be rendered to the Creator, the Father of the universe" (*Lumen Gentium*, no. 17). Sustained by the Holy Spirit, she "presses forward amid the persecutions of the world and the consolations of God" (Saint Augustine, *De Civitate Dei* XVIII, 51, 2), drawing strength from the Lord's help. Thus, in patience and in love, she overcomes "her sorrows and her difficulties, both those that are from within and those that are from without", and reveals "in the world, faithfully, however darkly, the mystery of her Lord until, in the consummation, it shall be manifested in full light" (*Lumen Gentium*, no. 8). The Church lives from Christ and with Christ. He offers her his spousal love, guiding her through the centuries; and she, with the abundance of her gifts, accompanies men and women on their journey so that those who accept Christ may have life and have it abundantly. . . .

Enlightened by the Word of God, we sang the "Te Deum" with faith. There are so many reasons that render our thanksgiving intense, making it a unanimous prayer. While we consider the many events that have marked the succession of months in this year that is coming to its end, I would like to remember especially those who are in difficulty: the poorest and the most abandoned people, those who have lost hope in a well-grounded sense of their own existence or who involuntarily become the victims of selfish interests without being asked for their support or their opinion. Making their sufferings our own, let us entrust them all to God, who knows how to bring everything to a good end; to him let us entrust our aspiration that every person's dignity as a child of God be respected. Let us ask the Lord of life to soothe with his grace the sufferings caused by evil and to continue to fortify our earthy existence by giving us the Bread and Wine of salvation to sustain us on our way toward the Heavenly Homeland.

While we take our leave of the year that is drawing to a close and set out for the new one, the liturgy of this First Vespers ushers us into the Feast of Mary, Mother of God, *Theotokos*. Eight days after the birth of Jesus, we will be celebrating the one whom God chose in advance to be the Mother of the Savior "when the fullness of time had come"

(Gal 4:4). The mother is the one who gives life but also who helps and teaches how to live. Mary is a Mother, the Mother of Jesus, to whom she gave her blood and her body. And it is she who presents to us the eternal Word of the Father, who came to dwell among us. Let us ask Mary to intercede for us. May her motherly protection accompany us today and forever, so that Christ will one day welcome us into his glory, into the assembly of the saints: *Aeterna fac cum sanctis tuis in gloria numerari.* Amen!

(31 December 2005)

Let us thank the Lord
for the gift of holiness
that is today resplendent in the Church with singular beauty.
Jesus invites each one of us to follow him,
like these saints,
on the way of the Cross,
so that we might then inherit the eternal life
that he, dying, gave to us.
May their examples
be an encouragement to us;
may their teachings
guide and comfort us;
may their intercession
sustain us in our daily efforts
so that we too may one day come to share with them and
    with all the saints
the joy of the eternal banquet
in the heavenly Jerusalem.
We obtain this grace especially through Mary
Queen of All Saints. . . .
Amen.

(BENEDICT XVI, *12 October 2008*)